D0909391

THEATER
AS
MUSIC

Michigan Monograph Series in Japanese Studies
Number 4

Center for Japanese Studies, The University of Michigan

THEATER AS MUSIC

The Bunraku Play "Mt. Imo and Mt. Se: An Exemplary Tale of Womanly Virtue"

C. Andrew Gerstle
Kiyoshi Inobe
William P. Malm

Ann Arbor, Center for Japanese Studies, The University of Michigan, 1990

Library of Congress Cataloging in Publication Data
Theater as music: the bunraku play "Mt. Imo and Mt. Se: an exem-
    plary tale of womanly virtue" / C. Andrew Gerstle, Kiyoshi Inobe,
    William P. Malm.
        p. cm. — (Michigan monograph series in Japanese studies; 4)
Bibliography: p. 275–.
Includes index.
ISBN 0-939512-38-6
        1. Imoseyama onna teikin. 2. Jōruri—History and criticism. 3.
Bunraku. I. Gerstle, C. Andrew, 1951- . II. Inobe, Kiyoshi, 1933- .
III. Malm, William P. IV. Imoseyama onna teikin. English. Selec-
tions. 1990. V. Series.
PL793.I43T48 1990
895.6′234—dc20   89-25139
                                                                      CIP

A NOTE ON THE TYPE
This book was set in Baskerville, a transitional typeface that bridged
the gap between Old Style and Modern typefaces. It was designed by
John Baskerville (1706-1775), an English printer and typographer who
was the printer to Cambridge University from 1758-1768, and has
been used as a standard book typeface.

Composed by Typographic Insight, Ltd., Ann Arbor, Michigan
Printed and bound by BookCrafters, Chelsea, Michigan
Book design by Lisa Jacobs
Printed in the United States of America

Contents

Preface

Bunraku is now recognized widely as a treasure of the world, in being a sophisticated adult, urban puppet theatrical tradition continuing for nearly 400 years. Though only one of many entertainments available in contemporary Japan, until the 1930s Bunraku was popular across the nation, with specialty magazines for fans and amateur performers; and women *gidayū* chanters were popular idols, much like singers on television. Bunraku still today becomes a passion for those touched by its power; *bunraku-kichigai* (Bunraku-crazy) is a term used for the dedicated Japanese (and occasional foreigner) who will travel from Tokyo to Osaka to sit through eight hours of performance and then rush back on the last train or late night bus after the final curtain. Fanatic devotion has for centuries been integral to the Bunraku experience. Recently traveling through Onomichi, a small city northeast of Hiroshima, we happened in a temple to see a "Bunraku" grave, a memorial stone erected in the early 19th century by patrons to their master chanter, Takemoto Yadayū. Though fewer in number today, one still encounters extreme devotees.

Spectators continue to be captivated by the puppeteers, chanters, and musicians who work together to produce fascinating drama. One cannot help but be surprised at how the wooden figures come to life and excite the sympathies of the audience, often drawing tears. One also cannot but be impressed by the histrionics of the chanter and shamisen player—in full view to the side of the stage—who speak for the puppets both with words and music. For most foreigners, however, the difficulty of the language makes it nearly impossible to appreciate the essence of the chanters' and musicians' art. There are pictorial studies of the puppets and scholarship on the plays as literature but, until recently, very little on the performance of the text and the role of shamisen accompaniment.

Bunraku is difficult to research because of its diverse elements: puppets, long and difficult texts, shamisen music, and chanters' techniques. Yet all of these contribute to the marvelous theatrical effects Bunraku achieves. Realizing the need for a collaborative effort to explore Bunraku as musical drama, we decided to focus on one piece in the vast repertoire and examine it in detail from our three perspectives. Our choice is not from the famous opus of Chikamatsu Monzaemon (1653–1725). Instead we have chosen a drama by Chikamatsu Hanji (1725–1783), the last major playwright in a century-long period during which several hundred full-length plays were composed. Though the plays of Hanji are not entirely satisfying as literature removed from the stage, many are theatrical gems and remain among the most frequently performed in Bunraku and Kabuki.

In choosing a representative piece, we wanted a work that was "musical" as well as "dramatic," and one that has been regularly performed to the present day. Our choice is the third scene of the third act of the play *Imoseyama onna teikin* (Mt. Imo and Mt. Se: An Exemplary Tale of Womanly Virtue, 1771). The *Yama no dan* ("The Mountains Scene," two hours in performance), as it is called, is a masterpiece of the repertoire and has proven to be an excellent specimen for our project. Written during the creative period and performed at least every three to four years since its initial run, we assumed it to be as close as we could get to 18th-century performance styles. Our task has been to discover how the play works, its formula for success. The piece has stood up well under our close scrutiny; in fact, we have found it to be increasingly fascinating as we delved into its intricacies and the history of its development over the last 200 years.

We have organized the material into two main parts: chapters one to seven cover the background and analysis of the play; the appendixes contain the Japanese text, including musical notation, with an English translation, and some further technical commentary. We wish to emphasize, however, that our "text" proper is the performance on the accompanying tapes, reproduced from King Record KHA49-50 *Imoseyama onna teikin* (1976) by permission of King Record Company, Ltd.

Further, in our approach we consider the written text an aid in understanding the performance, not, as is usually done, the other way around. The primary aim is to help readers understand this particular performance in depth, and thereby gain insight into the conventions of current Bunraku performance in general. To that end we have arranged for a tape of the record to be available with the book. The Japan Foundation has also made available, in connection with this study, a video tape of *Imoseyama onna teikin* ("The Mountains Scene" only) with English subtitles.

In the brief introduction Andrew Gerstle places the play *Mt. Imo and Mt. Se* into its historical context. In chapter two he outlines the entire five acts and shows how the "The Mountains Scene" fits as the core and climax of the day-long drama. Kiyoshi Inobe next discusses the musical conventions in Bunraku. In chapter four he analyzes "The Mountains Scene" text as music, giving a comprehensive explanation of the chanters' notation and the musical patterns at work in performance, using the idiom of traditional Japanese musicology. William Malm, in chapter five, gives a step-by-step analysis of "The Mountains Scene" in performance, using techniques familiar to Western musicologists. Chapter six, by Gerstle, covers the history of performance. Chapter seven, also by Gerstle, examines in some detail the history of the relationship of playwrights and performers in Bunraku, focusing on Chikamatsu Hanji, the shamisen player Tsuruzawa Bunzō, and the chanter Takemoto Sometayū, the creators of *Mt. Imo and Mt. Se*. The appendixes contain a Japanese text of "The Mountains Scene" with an English translation and Malm's detailed musical comments on the entire "Mountains Scene." This is followed by a glossary, bibliography, and index.

Most readers will want first to look at the introduction and chapter two, then to read the text in the appendix while listening to the tapes, and then to turn to the core "analysis" in chapters three, four, and five. Those interested in the history of the play will find chapters six and seven of interest. We have tried to make this book useful to students of music and drama. The subject is complex, and our treatment has necessarily included technical analysis. We hope, however, to have shown the complexity of Bunraku performance to be musically and theatrically rich and stimulating.

Acknowledgments

It is a pleasure to acknowledge some of the individuals and organizations that helped to make this book possible. Professors Takao Yoshinaga and Tadayoshi Ōhashi both gave their time and expertise generously. Dr. Chris Eade and Dr. Yoshinori Yasuda made valuable comments on the manuscript. The Bunraku performers Takemoto Sumitayū and Nozawa Kizaemon, in particular, gave their time most generously in order to help us analyze the record of "The Mountains Scene," each from his distinct perspective. We wish to thank King Record Company, Ltd., particularly Mr. Masaaki Seki and Mr. Sonken Chikatsu, for granting us permission to reproduce *Imoseyama onna teikin* on cassette tapes. We are further grateful to Mr. Seisuke Miyake for use of his photographs, and to both the National Bunraku Theater and the Bunraku Kyōkai for permission to reproduce them.

The East-West Center in Hawaii provided the three authors with the opportunity to meet and discuss each other's work and present public lectures. The Japan Foundation provided grants for Malm and Gerstle to spend time in Japan researching this project with Inobe. Since each author lives on a different continent, this project could not have been realized without such institutional assistance.

Chapter One   Introduction: The Golden Age, 1683–1783

C. Andrew Gerstle

Chikamatsu Hanji's death in 1783 closed a century of Bunraku[1] (Jōruri) playwriting that had begun with the performance of Chikamatsu Monzaemon's first play *Yotsugi Soga* (The Soga successor, 1683).[2] New plays continued to be written, but works composed during this time form the core of the repertoire we have today. These plays, mostly written in Osaka for the Takemoto or Toyotake theaters, had become during the 18th century, both in the study and on the stage, the dominant form of popular narrative. Their influence extended into Kabuki and fiction long after new plays ceased to be written, and they were widely read throughout the Edo and Meiji periods. The texts of popular dramas were reissued numerous times; in several cases new woodblocks were carved after having worn too thin with use, an unusual happening in Edo-period printing.[3]

Plays were appreciated in three distinct ways—in live performance, in amateur chanting, and as narrative literature. At first, they were read primarily in the Osaka-Kyoto, Edo, and in-between areas where theaters existed, such as Nagoya and Ise; gradually, however, the audience extended throughout the major cities of the entire country. One can still buy original texts today, though it is rare to find books in excellent condition; they are usually well-fingered and often marked up in red, having been used for practice by amateurs or professionals. Of course, many changes occurred during that crucial one hundred years of Jōruri puppet theater. After Chikamatsu Monzaemon, for instance, plays became increasingly more theatrical (rather than narrative) as puppet technology and musical accompaniment became more sophisticated.

Playwrights generally were not independent souls writing when their spirits so moved them. They were usually employed by a troupe initially as apprentices to senior, experienced writers; eventually they learned to write for particular performers, to meet regular deadlines, and to produce commercially successful works. The specific conditions within a theatrical organization naturally had an effect on the composition, and several major developments during the 18th century altered considerably the demands on the playwright's brush. From as early as Chikamatsu's time, the number of chanters in each troupe gradually increased, having the effect of encouraging playwrights to include more independent scenes in each act. A second factor, after Chikamatsu's death in 1725, was the practice of collaborative playwriting, in which a playwright would be responsible for one or two acts of a five-act play, further "fragmenting" the narrative. A third factor that pulled Jōruri further away from its roots in epic storytelling and toward the theatrical was the development of three-man puppets. Until a decade after Chikamatsu's death, the puppets were much smaller than today and were operated by one man. Obviously, the range of expression was more limited than with a puppet having movable eyes and mouth, worked by three men who could give movement to both the arms and legs.

The introduction of sophisticated puppets in 1734 marked a decisive stage in the theater's evolution; in fact, one could say that modern Bunraku drama began at that point, because few plays in the repertoire today predate this development. Most earlier plays were rewritten or gradually gave place to the dramas most famous today, namely *Sugawara denju tenarai kagami* (Sugawara and the secrets of calligraphy, 1746), *Yoshitsune senbon zakura* (Yoshitsune and the thousand cherry trees, 1747), *Kanadehon chūshingura* (The treasury of loyal retainers, 1748), and *Mt. Imo and Mt. Se: An Exemplary Tale of Womanly Virtue* (1771). With lifelike puppets, elaborate description by chanters became unnecessary if not impossible. Livelier puppets gave the audience more to enjoy on stage and, consequently, gave the puppeteers more authority in the troupe. Playwrights had to consider the talents and needs of puppeteers as well as those of master chanters. For best effect, puppets must be kept in motion, however slight, all the time. Too much explanatory narrative kills the effect of sophisticated puppets. Chikamatsu wrote plays for chanters; Takeda Izumo (d. 1747), Namiki Sōsuke (Senryū) (1695–1751), Takeda Izumo II (1691–1756), and Miyoshi Shōraku wrote for puppeteers as well as for chanters.

Evidence of the rising authority of puppeteers is the famous *Chūshingura* incident in 1748 when the puppeteer Yoshida Bunzaburō (d. 1760) had an argument with the chanter Takemoto Konotayū (Harima no shōjō's successor, later called Chikuzen no shōjō, 1700–1768) over the staging of a scene: Bunzaburō requested that Konotayū alter his chanting of act nine after the performance had been going on many days; the request was denied.[4] The chanter's authority, hitherto unquestioned, was delivered a severe blow when the troupe manager Takeda Izumo II agreed with the puppeteer. Konotayū was so angered he fled with his disciples (Shimatayū and Yuritayū) to the rival Toyotake theater. The Toyotake performer Takemoto Yamatonojō (1702–1766) was brought in to replace Konotayū, and the clear distinction between the styles of music in each theater ended. The puppeteer must have had the strong backing of patrons to breach tradition and question the senior chanter.

Though Jōruri was certainly a strong rival to Kabuki in the early 18th century, the mid-18th century saw an unprecedented rise in its popularity, even apparently to the eclipse of Osaka Kabuki. The situation has been described succinctly (though surely in an exaggerated phrase): "Jōruri is so popular (in the 1740s) that it is as if Kabuki had vanished."[5] Kabuki, however, soon retaliated in its typical eclectic fashion by taking into its repertoire all the popular Jōruri plays.

During the 1750s the playwrights Namiki Sōsuke and Takeda Izumo died, and then in the early 1760s famous performers also passed away, leaving the Jōruri theaters weakened in their creativity and vitality. Jōruri was no longer able to command large audiences, and in 1765 and 1767, respectively, the rival Toyotake and Takemoto theaters suffered financial collapse, ceasing to be solely puppet theaters.

In the late 1760s, nevertheless, the two theaters were restored and struggled along until 1771 when the immense success of *Mt. Imo and Mt. Se: An Exemplary Tale of Womanly Virtue* ushered in the final period of significant playwriting, primarily by Chikamatsu Hanji and Suga Sensuke (ca. 1767–1791). This last fountain too dried up by 1800, after which few new plays were written. Though nearly all the activity described above took place in Osaka, Edo was host to a brief period of Jōruri playwriting from the 1760s to 1790, during which about fifty plays were written by Edo writers such as Hiraga Gennai (1728–1779) and Utei Enba (1743–1822) for local theaters. This efflorescence was largely due to the support of Mitsui Jirōemon (1747–1799), the owner of the Mitsui business, who was an avid Jōruri fan.[6] He was no ordinary patron, being a playwright himself under the name Ki no Jōtarō. With his death, however, the brief period of Edo Jōruri ends.

While the development of three-man puppetry had fostered the golden age of popularity, the final era of great playwriting found new direction through the stimulus of increasingly sophisticated shamisen music. As literary texts these plays seem closer to Kabuki and more colloquial; in performance, however, they are musical masterpieces. From the last third of the 18th century, audiences began to enjoy Jōruri not only as theater but also as music, vocal and instrumental. This trend continued until recently, when selections of arialike *sawari* from several plays were produced on commercial records. The late 18th and 19th centuries, the most creative period of Bunraku shamisen music, saw a fundamental change in the attitude of the musicians. Shamisen players, who had during the early period been blind and the lowest members of the troupe, clearly under the thumb of chanters, began to articulate through music the essence of the text rather than just punctuate the expression of the chanter. Tsuruzawa Bunzō (active from the 1740s, d. 1807, and composer of the music for *Mt. Imo and Mt. Se*) was the pivotal figure in this development. This trend reaches full maturity in the work of Toyozawa Danpei (1827–1898), the legendary virtuoso who was the first shamisen player to achieve equal footing with the chanters and puppeteers as head of a troupe.[7] In Chikamatsu Hanji's time, musicians began to play an important role in both the composition and presentation of plays. Further, as the musicians' authority increased, each generation continued to transform the music of the repertoire until early in the 20th century.

A crucial step in this process was the creation of a system of notation for shamisen music, most likely initiated in the 1770s. Texts published from the 1680s onward had always contained extensive notation for performance, but this was inserted by chanters for the chanters' performance, though useful for the musicians as well. Several codes were tried but the system of Tsuruzawa Bunzō's disciple Matsuya (Tsuruzawa) Seishichi (1748–1826) eventually prevailed.[8] This notation was never published. It was a guarded tool of the trade, a memory device for musicians within the tradition who performed many plays over and over as well as created music for new works. Basic research in this area still remains to be done (and fortunately it is possible with the availability of manuscript collections in the Osaka City Library, Waseda Theater Museum Library, the Tokyo National Theater Library, the National Bunraku Theater Library, and the Osaka Music University Library) but, if I may venture an opinion after exploring only the manuscripts for "The Mountains Scene," 20th-century shamisen music in Bunraku performance is only partly an 18th-century product.

In a tradition where oral training from master to disciple is the norm, it is helpful to view the 18th century as a series of generations of performers and playwrights. We then see that transitional points between generations are crucial in the history of Jōruri. In fact, the three great periods of playwriting for the Takemoto theater—Chikamatsu's last ten years from 1715, the six or seven years from 1711, and Chikamatsu Hanji's career as senior playwright—all follow upon the passing of dominant chanters who had no one successor with absolute authority over the others. In each case eventually one chanter emerged to become senior chanter (*monshita*), but during the period when today's most famous plays were written and first staged, playwrights wrote for a group of chanters, each being responsible for the music of one act. With Takemoto Gidayū's death in 1714, Chikamatsu Monzaemon became the senior member of the troupe and commanded respect both within the theater and in the public eye, though until then he had been simply in the employ of Gidayū. Chikamatsu, who had written plays for Gidayū, now wrote for a group of chanters, and, furthermore, Takeda Izumo seems to have made suggestions about stage and puppet techniques. Playwriting became more of a cooperative endeavor among the writer, manager, and experienced chanters, the result for Chikamatsu being the creation of his most famous plays.

The second flourish of great Jōruri playwriting occurred under similar circumstances following the death, in 1744, of the *monshita* chanter Harima no shōjō.[9] Playwrights then wrote for a group of excellent younger *tayū* (chanters) rather than one figure with absolute authority. Takeda Izumo II, who had been writing for Harima no shōjō, was put in a position similar to Chikamatsu thirty years earlier in that he was (together with Namiki Senryū [Sōsuke] and Miyoshi Shōraku) writing for a group of chanters. However, each playwright tended to write an act for one chanter to set to music. Another major change after

Chikamatsu's time is the critical presence of the great puppeteer Yoshida Bunzaburō, who had obtained an equal, if not superior, position to the chanters in the troupe. The cooperative as well as competitive atmosphere worked well to foster the most famous plays in the Bunraku repertoire.

Chikamatsu Hanji, twenty years later, found himself too at a critical moment in the transition between generations. Hanji, however, did not have a group of star chanters who could turn the text into effective musical drama. The gap came to be filled by the shamisen player Tsuruzawa Bunzō, who had completed his apprenticeship under his mentor Tsuruzawa Tomojirō (d. 1749) and had matured under the great performers in the golden age of Jōruri. His turn came, then, to foster a new generation of chanters and shamisen players.

In histories of Bunraku the general impression given about this late phase, which witnessed the collapse of the Toyotake and Takemoto theaters, is that the puppet theater ceased to be popular entertainment and, further, that after 1800 it was no longer creative. To be sure, large theaters solely for puppet drama ceased to exist. In their stead was a proliferation of small theaters often set up on shrine or temple grounds. The actual number of performers, however, increased dramatically from the 1760s. Moreover, amateur activity, including professional women chanters (*onna gidayū*), which had been popular throughout the 18th century in Osaka, Kyoto, and Edo, spread to the smaller cities throughout Japan. After 1800 creativity flourished in performance rather than in the writing of new texts. Chanters and musicians again and again sought, and achieved, new ways and means of interpreting the many plays of the repertoire. Chanters' names came to be used for the distinctive styles or new melodies they created for passages and scenes.[10] This creativity ushered in a second "golden age" of performance in the 19th and early 20th centuries, particularly during the Meiji period when restrictions were lifted on theaters and women performers. This popularity, however, peaks in the late 1920s.[11] Therefore, the general image of Bunraku declining in popularity from the late 1700s is not entirely accurate. Significant decline does set in when modern entertainments, such as movies, radio, and phonographs, begin to compete for talent and audiences. With government support and a new National Bunraku Theater in Osaka, Bunraku will survive, and perhaps we may even see a revival after the relative gloom of postwar years.

Bunraku, nevertheless, is still the most fascinating puppet theater in the world, with one of the most sophisticated musical narrative traditions alive today. Chikamatsu Hanji's play *Mt. Imo and Mt. Se*, created during the fully mature period when the playwright had to write for (and therefore collaborate with) the talents of all three elements of Bunraku—voice, puppet, and music—is a masterpiece of theatricality. By focusing narrowly on this one work we hope to open a door to Bunraku as a performance tradition.

Chapter One   Notes

1 Bunraku is a 19th-century term for Jōruri puppet drama. I shall use the term 'Jōruri' when discussing 18th-century drama.

2 Though I shall speak of Chikamatsu Hanji as the playwright of a large body of dramas, he was usually writing (from the 1760s) as the senior member of a team. The other writers listed on the *Mt. Imo and Mt. Se* text are: Matsuda Baku, Chikamatsu Tōnan, Sakai Zenpei, and Miyoshi Shōraku as a "consultant."

3 Ōhashi Tadayoshi, after examining the woodblocks held in Tenri University Library, has pointed out to me that Jōruri blocks were carved deeper than those for other genre because of the expectation of numerous printings.

4 *Gidayū shusshin roku* (1819) in *Nihon shomin bunka shiryō shūsei* (hereafter *NSBSS*), vol. 7, pp. 56–59.

5 *Jōruri-fu* (1801) in *Chikamatsu sewa-jōruri shū* (1928), p. 707.

6 Jirōemon was also involved with Osaka Jōruri and helped in the publication of Hanji's posthumous *Hitori sabaki* (1787).

7 Even Danpei, however, was discriminated against by the puppeteer Yoshida Tamazō, who complained about a shamisen player becoming a *monshita* along with a chanter and puppeteer. See *Gidayū nenpyō—meiji-hen* (1956), pp. 21 and 97.

8 See Inobe, "Matsuya Seishichi no shushō," *Nihon ongaku to sono shūhen: Kikkawa Eiji sensei kanreki kinen ronbun shū* (1973), pp. 28–51.

9 Harima no shōjō at the peak of his career was performing the *kiri* (climaxes) of acts two, three, and four—a feat impossible today. Some examples from *Gidayū nenpyō—kinsei-hen*, vol. 1: p. 103 (1734), p. 107 (1736), p. 115 (1738), p. 123 (1740), p. 128 (1741), p. 132 (1741), p. 135 (1742), and p. 144 (1743).

10 *Jōruri hottan* (1825) in *NSBSS*, vol. 7, pp. 285–359 contains a catalog of these names.

11 One clear indication of popularity is the publication of practice texts for amateurs. These texts, in the traditional woodblock lettering style, were printed until the mid-1920s, more than two generations after other such Tokugawa-period woodblock publishing had ceased.

Chapter Two   The Play *Mt. Imo and Mt. Se:*
An Exemplary Tale of Womanly
Virtue

C. Andrew Gerstle

The five acts of *Mt. Imo and Mt. Se*, performed occasionally today almost in its entirety, weave together a vast array of historical and legendary characters into a marvelous day-long drama with comic, tragic, realistic, and fairy tale-like elements. The *sekai* (time setting) is the popular subject of the 7th-century struggle—between the "evil" Soga Iruka (and his father Emishi) and the "loyal" Fujiwara Kamatari—for control of the imperial household and the reins of government. Iruka tried to make himself emperor but failed due to Kamatari's intervention. Hanji makes use of ancient legends in the same general locality as the setting of the story, two of which are referred to in the subtitle (*Jūsan-gane, kinukake yanagi* or "Thirteen bells, Robe draped over a willow"). The first is central to act two and concerns the ancient punishment of burying alive under stones anyone caught killing a sacred deer in the Nara area. "Thirteen bells" refers to the ringing of the temple bell, signaling dawn when the sentence would be carried out. The latter legend, used in act one, concerns Emperor Tenchi's consort Uneme, who was said to have left her robe hanging on a tree before drowning herself in Sarusawa Pond in Nara. A third legend central to act four concerns the Miwa shrine in Yamato, the story of a princess who was visited each night by a lover (deity) whom she never saw in daylight. Curious to know his identity, she tied a string to his cloak and followed it to a cave. These various tales are woven masterfully into a tapestry, fascinating both for its detail and overall structure.

Although from a modern, literary perspective the play does not seem to hold together neatly as a story from beginning to end, the

audience of Hanji's time knew the general plot and characters sur-
rounding Iruka and Kamatari and enjoyed seeing how the playwright
could introduce new elements and weave diverse strands into the
drama. They expected to enjoy orchestrated contrasts of mood and
tenor over a day of performance. Enjoy it they did. *Mt. Imo and Mt. Se*
stands, in its immediate and enduring popularity, among *The Battles of
Coxinga, Yoshitsune and the Thousand Cherry Trees, Sugawara and the Secrets of Calligraphy*, and *Chūshingura* as a work that restored (or ushered
in) the fortunes of the Takemoto theater.

The overall structure of the five acts is similar in its design to these
past masterpieces. Each is full of musical contrasts and complements
among the many scenes and acts. Each is also basically circular in
form, in that the action returns in the end to the setting where it
began, usually the court of the time. *Mt. Imo and Mt. Se*, too, follows
this pattern: it begins at the palace, thrown into turmoil by the machinations of Lord Emishi; it ends with an auspicious restoration of order
after the overthrow of Emishi's son, Iruka. Acts two and four are com-
plementary in that both contain the most action and movement, and
that the main characters (Shibaroku in act two and Omiwa in act four)
are commoners with no direct connection to the court. In Bunraku,
act three is both the centerpiece of the play and usually the furthest
distance from the court. In this case the place is the Yoshino Mountains, the most remote point in the drama. Invariably, self-sacrifice is
the theme of this act; the deaths of Hinadori and Koganosuke are a
mixture of sacrifice both for one's lover and for one's sovereign, arche-
types within the tradition. In the earlier *Battles of Coxinga*, Chikamatsu
Monzaemon had clearly made the tragedies of act three the turning
point, after which a new "Coxinga" is born, who eventually overthrows
the Tartar enemies. In *Mt. Imo and Mt. Se*, the deaths of the young pair
are acts of defiance against Iruka's authority, and the final words of the
scene, "some day the corruption will end . . . . Their deaths will not be
wasted!" suggest that the "wheel of fortune" has turned against Iruka,
who will now be on the defensive. Shibaroku's loyalty to the court in act
two saves the emperor, and, by obtaining the black-hoofed deer, he
prepares the way for Iruka's eventual defeat; Hinadori and
Koganosuke's defiant self-sacrifices turn the tide against the enemy,
and Omiwa's death completes the strategy, begun in act two, of over-
throwing Iruka through supernatural means. By Hanji's time, act five
had become strictly ceremonial, since senior chanters would not perform

it. *Mt. Imo and Mt. Se* obviously lies within the conventions of the tradition.[1] One fundamental principle is the practice (common after Chikamatsu Monzaemon's time) of having the *kiri* (final scene) of acts two, three, and four contain tragedy, in order for the three senior playwrights to compose serious drama and the three star chanters to have good pieces to perform.

Since the play is long with many scenes, I have divided the summary into its component parts. The account is fairly detailed to show how the third act fits into the entire play.

Act I: *Scene one*, Court

The play begins in the formal setting of the imperial court where Soga no Emishi has brought charges of treason against Fujiwara Kamatari. Lord Kamatari is suspiciously absent, though his daughter Lady Uneme (Emperor Tenchi's consort) is present. The emperor is ill and has gone blind. During the discussions on Kamatari's fate, Lady Sadaka, the widow of Lord Dazai, arrives to present a request for her daughter Hinadori to take a husband, who will carry on the Dazai name. Genba, a retainer of Emishi, takes this opportunity to express that Lord Emishi wishes Hinadori to be his wife. The matter, however, is not settled, and a disturbed Lady Sadaka departs. Lady Uneme reports that the emperor has ordered Kamatari to report to the court today to answer the charges. Just then Kamatari arrives and is asked why he has secluded himself from court when the ill emperor needs his services. Before he can answer, however, Emishi has a box brought forward which has been offered to the Kasuga shrine. It contains a sickle (Kamatari's family treasure) and a request for "a male child to be born to rule throughout the land." Kamatari is accused of plotting to take control of the throne. He pleads ignorance but places himself under house arrest until the matter is settled.

Scene two, Kasuga shrine

Daihanji's handsome son Koganosuke, returning from a hunt, stops to rest near the shrine. A party of ladies in attendance on the pretty Hinadori is returning from the shrine. The young pair exchange glances and are entranced with each other. The maids intervene and get them to sit close together. They are, however, overseen

by Genba, who harbors a secret love for Hinadori. When he butts in
and speaks their names, both realize that they are children of feuding
parents. This scene is background for "The Mountains Scene" in act
three. Genba is made the fool in a comic scene and the women flee.

Koganosuke (Lady Uneme's guard) is told by Genba that Lady
Uneme has fled the palace. He finds her, and she explains about
Emishi's treachery against her father. He helps her escape.

Scene three, Emishi's residence

a. Lord Emishi is having a snow-viewing party in his garden when
two priests pass through unannounced on their way to visit Soga no
Iruka, Emishi's son. They are accosted by Emishi's henchmen and
humiliated in a comic scene before being evicted. Emishi is not happy
that his son is about to complete the 100-day Buddhist ritual that
ends in being buried alive—that is, entering Nirvana without phys-
ically dying.

b. Koganosuke arrives to answer questions about Lady Uneme's
whereabouts, since he is her bodyguard. Koganosuke reports that the
rumors of Uneme's drowning in Sarusawa Pond are indeed true.
Koganosuke then asks to join Emishi's service since he has been
disowned by his father Daihanji. Emishi replies that he wants
Koganosuke to convince Daihanji to join with him.

As Koganosuke takes his leave he is attacked by Emishi's retainers,
Genba and Yatōji, but manages to ward them off. During the scuffle
Koganosuke lifts a garden stone and an iron mesh falls from the
ceiling of the veranda. Emishi is impressed by Koganosuke's valor but
Koganosuke takes his leave quickly, trying to cover the awkwardness
of discovering Emishi's trap.

c. The climax of this act begins with the entrance of Iruka's wife
Lady Medo and Emishi's daughter Princess Tachibana. Both beg
Emishi to intervene and save Iruka. Princess Tachibana leaves to
present a request at court for Iruka's life to be spared.

d. Left behind, Lady Medo bares her woes at losing Iruka and
prays in the snow for his safety. She is the first virtuous lady to be
tested. Emishi interrogates Medo, trying to discover Iruka's real inten-
tions. She replies that her husband has taken the Buddhist vow as

penance for Emishi's machinations. If Emishi has a change of heart, Iruka will not go through with the ritual. Finally Lady Medo castigates Emishi for trying to overthrow the throne. She has a list of conspirators that Emishi tries to wrest from her. He slashes her in the shoulder but she manages to burn the list in the hibachi—a signal for the guards to attack Emishi. He kills her but is overtaken and commits ritual suicide at the command of Lord Yukinushi, the imperial messenger (also Lady Medo's father). But at the moment of Emishi's death, an arrow pierces Yukinushi's chest. Iruka emerges, with flowing long hair and Buddhist robes. He reveals his treacheries at having stolen the imperial sword and his plans to become emperor. Daihanji, though aghast at the turn of events, must submit and become Iruka's retainer. Emishi was a pleasant man compared with his son Iruka, who succeeds in destroying his wife, father in law, and father in one act of treachery.

Act II: *Scene one*, Sarusawa Pond

The scene opens with a dialogue of hunters talking about how much night hunting there has been lately. Their departure is followed by the entrance of the imperial carriage carrying a distraught (and blind) Emperor Tenchi, who is seeking Lady Uneme. He recites a poem at the pond where she drowned. Tankai (Lord Kamatari's son) approaches and asks to be forgiven for an earlier offense and to be taken back into the emperor's service. At that moment a messenger arrives who relates Iruka's treachery. Tankai makes a plan to fool the emperor into believing Iruka has been defeated. He has everyone around the blind emperor pretend a rustic hut is the palace.

Scene two, Mountain near Nara

Shibaroku (a hunter, but former retainer of Kamatari) with his son Sansaku (actually his wife's child from a former marriage) are stalking the rare, black-hoofed doe.

Scene three, Same

Shibaroku slays the deer.

Scene four, Shibaroku's humble home

a. The emperor and entourage have taken refuge in Shibaroku's hut. The blind emperor, however, thinks they have returned to the palace. The scene is at first comic with earthy language and joking. All the courtiers change into farmers' clothes. A bill-collector arrives but is tricked by Shibaroku into leaving unpaid, after he accosts Okiji, Shibaroku's wife. To entertain the emperor, Shibaroku and Sansaku perform a *manzai* comic dance and song.

b. Shibaroku tells Tankai that the black-hoofed doe (needed to overthrow Iruka) is in hand. Tankai then gives Shibaroku the good news that he will be reinstated in Kamatari's service soon.

c. Okiji mentions to Shibaroku that a sacred deer has been killed and that an investigation is under way. The punishment for such a crime is to be buried alive under stones.

Sansaku, worried about his father, writes a confessional note and has Sugimatsu (his half-brother) take it to the authorities.

Soldiers appear and accuse Shibaroku of harboring enemies of Iruka. Their threats against Sansaku make Shibaroku say he'll confess at the official's house. Tankai is suspicious of Shibaroku's motives.

Meanwhile, a party from Kōfukuji temple arrives to arrest Sansaku. Okiji tries to resist, but Sansaku confesses.

Shibaroku returns drunk and, after sleeping next to Sugimatsu for a moment, kills him to show his loyalty. The previous soldiers had been sent by Kamatari to test Shibaroku. Since he had shown weakness when his child was threatened, he acted to remove any doubts by killing his real child. When he learns that Sansaku is to die in a few minutes in his place, he rushes out to save him, but Kamatari stops him, saying that in the hole dug to bury Sansaku was found the imperial mirror. Kamatari has saved Sansaku. Sugimatsu is the sacrifice necessary to right Iruka's wrongs. The mirror also restores the emperor's sight.

Act III: *Scene one*, Comic scene, Dazai Residence

Preparations are being made for Lord Iruka's visit. His retainers, Aramaki and Yatōji, give honorary titles to servants and townsmen in order for them to wait on (Emperor) Iruka. The scene ends with jokes about contemporary Jōruri performers.

Scene two, Fragile blossoms

Daihanji arrives at the Dazai residence in answer to a summons by Iruka. Daihanji and Sadaka argue but are interrupted by Iruka, who accuses them both of conspiring against him because Hinadori and Koganosuke are betrothed. To prove their innocence and keep the children (flowered branches) from being destroyed, Iruka demands that Hinadori become his wife and Koganosuke enter his service.

Scene three, The mountains scene

The country residences of Daihanji and Sadaka face each other on either side of the Yoshino River. Hinadori and Koganosuke have come to their respective retreats because of the troubles. Hinadori seeks and eventually gets Koganosuke's attention, and expresses her wish to be with him forever. He shows his feelings but explains that, since he is under suspicion, he can do nothing at the moment. Just then the parents arrive, still defiant toward each other. They say they will try to get their children to submit to Iruka, though neither is in earnest. Both Koganosuke and Hinadori choose death rather than submission, though since each wishes the other to live, both sides drop a flowered branch (the agreed signal) into the river to indicate submission. The final part of the scene focuses on both parents' grief at killing their children. (Translated in appendix A.)

Act IV: *Scene one*, The cleaning of the village well

Comic in contrast to tragedy in previous act. Motome (Fujiwara Tankai in disguise) is taunted by neighbors for not helping in communal work.

Scene two, The Sugi saké shop

Omiwa, the maiden of the saké shop, has fallen in love with Motome. However, Motome has a secret lover (Princess Tachibana, sister of Iruka). Discovered by others, the princess is forced to flee and Motome goes after her. Motome ties a red ball of thread to the princess's kimono, and Omiwa likewise ties a white thread to Motome.

Scene three, Odamaki michiyuki (Balls of thread)

Journey of Princess Tachibana to Iruka's palace followed by Motome and then Omiwa. Dance scene.

Scene four, Iruka's palace

Fukashichi, a messenger from Kamatari, arrives and states that Kamatari wishes to submit to Iruka. Fukashichi is taken hostage. Tankai (Motome) realizes who the princess is and, since his identity has been uncovered, attempts to kill her. To prove her love and loyalty, she agrees to his request to steal back the imperial sword, which Iruka now has.

Omiwa arrives at the palace and is taunted by the ladies-in-waiting and made furiously jealous as they relate how Motome and the princess are enjoying each other. At this point, Fukashichi stabs her and explains that the blood of a jealous woman is needed to overthrow Iruka. After learning that her death will be for her lover Motome (Tankai), she dies contented.

Princess Tachibana manages to get the sword, though it is a fake. Iruka slashes her shoulder, but at that moment the notes of a flute are heard and Iruka collapses. The sword turns into a dragon, flying into the sky. Iruka is executed.

Act V: Shiga palace

Auspicious ending as the imperial line is restored in the new Shiga palace.

How does the "Mountains Scene" fit into the entire scheme of the five acts? The play begins and ends as most Bunraku—in the court. There is a crisis brought on by the Soga family, and sacrifices are exacted along the path to Iruka's overthrow at the end of act four.

Those sacrificed are women and children: Lady Medo in act one, Sugimatsu in act two, Hinadori and Koganosuke in act three, and Omiwa in act four. These scenes are the four climaxes of the play; their descending order of importance or intensity is: act three, act four, act two, and act one. Each death directly or indirectly contributes both to the overthrow of Emishi and Iruka and to the all-important return to order after civil strife. Lady Medo, Sugimatsu, Hinadori, Koganosuke, and Omiwa are all innocent paragons sacrificed for a higher cause— returning the world to order. These characters are modeled on "classi- cal" Jōruri, though Hanji puts the entire play in the realm of legend and the supernatural. Let us look now at "The Mountains Scene" in some detail.

"The Mountains Scene" is intricately parallel in its setting and mu- sic. The stage arrangement is grand: two mountains aglow with cherry blossoms, the Yoshino River flowing in between, and feuding houses on either side.[2] The contrast is further emphasized by having the chanters face each other as in competition. The yin-yang theory of male-female opposition is fundamental to the organization. Musically, the two traditional styles—*nishi* (west, meaning the Takemoto theater), of reserve, severity, intensity, minor scale; and *higashi* (east, meaning the rival Toyotake theater), of flamboyance, brightness, major scale— also form part of the dichotomy in performance.[3] Takemoto Some- tayū, who performed the male roles, had been trained under Masata- yū II in the *nishi* style, and Takemoto Harutayū (with his melodious voice) had been a disciple of Yamatonojō of the *higashi* line. What this means in musical terms is explained in the Inobe and Malm essays.

It is useful to see in outline the musical structure of the piece. The fundamental component of organization is the "primary unit." Simply put, this unit is the basic building block in the musical and narrative structure. It begins with a line slowly sung (*ji* or *ji-iro*) (see glossary for explanation of terms), followed by a variety of chanting styles (*iro - kotoba - ji - ji-iro - kotoba - ji*, etc.) in dialogue or monologue until reaching a musical cadence (*fushi*), after which a new unit begins again in *ji* or *ji-iro*. A complicated unit (as no. 4 below) will have incomplete or partial cadences (*fushi* followed by *kotoba*, or *suete* partial cadences) that mark subdivisions within the unit. Each unit is based on the *jo-ha- kyū* (introduction, intensification, quick conclusion) formula and reaches a peak, in both musical and dramatic intensity, before the cadence. The chanter, musician, and puppeteer follow this structure to pace their performance: they lead the audience into the psychology and action of the characters step by step, tightening and loosening the tension, each time bringing their audience closer to the peak of the entire scene, after which the grief of the surviving characters is portrayed. Playwrights, too, must have a clear understanding of conventions; they must structure the words and action to enable the chanter or shamisen player to set the work to music.

Though it may not exactly mirror a particular performance—in actual performance, a particular cadence may be swallowed up in a quick transition—the following outline shows the original structure upon which the artists create their show. The scene has been divided, according to the notation, into its component parts: the two major sections are marked by Roman numerals; the primary units (*ji* to *fushi* cadence) are designated by Arabic numerals; and the subsections of primary units are marked by small letters.[4] The Japanese terms are explained fully in the glossary. Briefly, the major terms used in this outline are: *ji* (song), *kotoba* (spoken), *naka* (low pitch, cadencelike), *kami* (high-pitch), *suete* (musical pattern used to express extreme emotion, usually leads to cadence), *fushigoto* (lyrical-musical section) and *dangiri* (finale, musical flourish).

Structure of "The Mountains Scene"

I. Hinadori and Koganosuke

Makura (preface) 1, 2

  1. (Koga) Setting (general)   (to line 8)
     Solemn, weighty beginning; use of *naka* to end phrases with cadencelike pattern on low note.
  2. (Koga) Description of Koganosuke's situation   (to line 15)
     (specific). Again use of *naka* cadence at end of nearly every line, creating a serious atmosphere. Image of Koganosuke as confined bird preparing to die. Chanting of sutras.
  3. (Hinadori and maids)
     a. Spring, Doll Festival (high pitch).   (to line 24)
        Contrast with Mt. Se; maids make for light comedy in joking atmosphere. Ends with agony of unfulfilled love.
     b. Decision to get Koga's attention;   (to line 57)
        Hina's love for Koga.
     c. View Koga deep in thought, low *naka*   (to line 97)
        note for Koga. Hina's love for Koganosuke.

d. Pitch missive tied to a rock, but   (to line 104)
   falls short into river.

e. *Kami* (high pitch) "Turn to stone   (to line 110)
   pining for love." First emotional peak in act; each subsection
   has a miniclimax.

4. (Koga and Hina)

   a. Long *kotoba* (spoken) section   (to line 136)
      when thinking of father. Greeting of pair at river. Puppets
      dance and pose; language is stretched in song for puppets'
      action.

   b. Hina expresses cruelty of being separated.   (to line 147)
      Second musical flourish: Hinadori dances to complicated mu-
      sic (*kami, gin, iru, suete*)

   c. Koga moved by Hina's love but explains   (to line 165)
      political situation (in spoken *kotoba*), then shifts to song (*ji*) as
      anguish at being a trapped bird is expressed; ends with *suete*.

   d. Dramatic: Hina cares not for world,   (to line 185)
      only wants Koga. Wants to swim across river. Narrative is
      quick paced in *ji* (song). Cool, rational words of Koga (spo-
      ken) stop Hina.

5. Transition   (to line 193)
   Return of parents, separation. Concludes with musical flourish
   expressing agony at parting (*kami, okuri, yuri*).

II. Sadaka and Daihanji

6. Daihanji, solemn beginning. Cool   (to line 204)
   greeting by Sadaka in *kotoba* (spoken).

7. Cool discussion (in *kotoba*) of   (to line 214)
   situation by Daihanji.

8. a. Cool discussion (in *kotoba*) by   (to line 243)
      Sadaka and Daihanji: public face.

   b. *Kotoba* until parting; shift   (to line 274)
      to song (*ji*) as their true feelings emerge; they will both force
      children to comply with Iruka's demands.

9. Sadaka and Hinadori

   a. Mother greets daughter.   (to line 279)

   b. Hinadori greets mother.   (to line 282)

10. Sadaka announces marriage proposal.

    a. Sadaka discussion in *kotoba*   (to line 297)
       (spoken) of Doll Festival.

b. Marriage proposal (in *kotoba*).   (to line 318)
   Song (*ji*) for Sadaka's worries (*sue, kakari*).
c. Husband to be is Iruka (*kotoba*).   (to line 329)
   Hinadori shocked (*ji u, suete*).
d. Persuasion by Sadaka (in *kotoba*).   (to line 341)
   Departure of maids.

11. Sadaka   (to line 386)
    Sadaka tries to persuade Hinadori to save Koga in *kotoba* (spoken). *Ji* (song) is used for tears. Koganosuke chanter completes (cadence) unit, as scene shifts to other mountain.

12. Daihanji
    a. Greetings in *kotoba* (spoken).   (to line 394)
       Koga is determined to die.
    b. Daihanji's explanation (in *kotoba*)   (to line 410)
       and pride in son (*ji* song).
    c. Daihanji's overt coolness (*kotoba*).   (to line 432)
       His feeling is expressed in *ji*. *Kami* (high pitch) is used for agony at thought of cutting son's head off (first peak of second part).

13. Sadaka and Hinadori
    a. Preparations to be princess (*kotoba*).   (to line 439)
    b. Decision to die. Hinadori speaks in *ji*   (to line 487)
       of her anger; after head falls off doll, Sadaka (in *kotoba*) expresses real plan to kill daughter because of duty. Then, when expressing love for daughter, voice is in *ji*. Cadence is swallowed as action shifts to Mt. Se.

14. Koganosuke and Daihanji   (to line 526)
    Quick-paced. Koga stabs himself. Expresses love for Hinadori and desire to save her. Daihanji sends flowered branch. His feelings are expressed in high-pitched song (*haru, kami, kami, gin*).

15. Death of Hinadori
    a. Hinadori ready to die; sends   (to line 544)
       flowered branch to save Koga.
    b. Both sides ready to kill children.   (to line 568)
       Dramatic moment. Cry of Sadaka as she kills daughter; realization that both must die. Climax.

16. Wedding and reconciliation   (to line 605)
    Sadaka asks Daihanji to accept daughter as Koga's wife. Reconciliation, but joy comes too late.

17. Song (*fushigoto*) with koto   (to line 615)
    Send Hinadori's wedding chests. Sadaka's love for daughter.
18. Song (*fushigoto*) with koto   (to line 622)
    Hinadori's head is sent across. Sadaka's love for daughter.
19. Daihanji and Sadaka
    a. Daihanji welcomes and praises Hinadori.   (to line 644)
       Daihanji in *kotoba*. Sadaka in song.
    b. Sadaka praises Koganosuke (*ji*).   (to line 667)
       Ō-otoshi (major cadence).
20. *Dangiri* finale, musical flourish
    Voice is quick and powerful (*ji*). Lovers will be together in next
    life. Agony of parents left behind.

The protagonists are caught in a tense structure of opposing forces. Public duty (in relation both to Iruka and to the feud) pushes the pair apart, and private feeling (of both parents and children) pulls them together. Koganosuke's introduction evokes an ominous mood, but this is followed immediately by the light-hearted miniscene of maidservants trying to cheer Hinadori during the Doll Festival, the most lively festival of the year for girls. The contrast is clear to the eye and ear. Koganosuke is motionless; the girls are bustling about. Koganosuke's voice is intense and the shamisen severe; the girls' voices are lively and the music melodious. Each chanter takes a turn giving an independent performance until their voices are joined in the first musical and dramatic peak when Hinadori and Koganosuke step down to the river bank to express their love and the anguish of separation (unit 4). This moment of intensity, however, is suppressed by the entrance of Daihanji and Sadaka. Daihanji's heart is leaden; both the chanter's voice and shamisen notes must express severe emotional restraint. The river alone no longer separates their houses, because forces outside their control now wield authority over their children.

Each side has a turn in the spotlight, first the women, and then the men. Initially the action is at one side or the other, but gradually the focus begins to shift back and forth more quickly until the death of Hinadori in unit 15, when the stage becomes one again as in unit 4. The scene begins poles apart, comes together in unit 4, stays together until after unit 8 when Daihanji and Sadaka part, and comes together again after the death of Hinadori in unit 15. Sadaka's song is a bridge across the water; the drama ceases for a moment as Sadaka's anguish is depicted in lyric-song. This is the *higashi*-style peak in the scene; music expresses what words cannot. In the final units (19, 20), Daihanji praises Hinadori, and Sadaka, Koganosuke; each takes off his public mask. Musically, this unit works splendidly. Daihanji speaks first in cool speech, and Sadaka in song, back and forth in dialogue until Daihanji's voice joins Sadaka in the crescendo of line 664, which is followed by the *ō-otoshi*, or major cadence, of the entire five-act play. The scene concludes with a *dangiri* (finale), a musical flourish sending the pair to reunion in the next world. As Tsubouchi Shōyō wrote many years ago, one must experience the play to understand its power and charm; we hope readers will use the tapes and the Japan Foundation video, and someday have the chance to see a live performance.

Chapter Two   Notes

1   See Gerstle, *Circles of Fantasy: Convention in the Plays of Chikamatsu* (1986), chapter 2 for more detail on the structure of period plays, particularly the concept of "orchestration" of contrasts so important in all performances.

2   Yokoyama Tadashi showed me the program of a Paris revue he happened to see a few years ago, which used "The Mountains Scene" stage arrangement.

3   Among the many conventions of Jōruri theater, the two held supreme by performers are the styles (*fū*) of both theater troupes and individual performers. During the 18th century the Takemoto-za and Toyotake-za were about 400 meters apart along the Dōtonbori River in Osaka's entertainment district. Since the Takemoto-za was to the west and Toyotake to the east, the former theater's style came to be called *nishi-fū* (western style), and the latter's, *higashi-fū* (eastern). These rival stages competed for more than sixty years for the hearts and minds of Osaka's "Naniwakko." Members of the Takemoto troupe took the surname Takemoto and consciously followed the traditions founded by Takemoto Gidayū in composition as well as performance, while those in the Toyotake troupe did likewise. The fierce competition between these theaters ushered in the golden age of Jōruri in the middle of the 18th century.

4   See Gerstle, *Circles of Fantasy: Convention in the Plays of Chikamatsu*, chapter 3 for more detail on primary units.

Chapter Three Musical Convention[1]

Kiyoshi Inobe

Musical Styles in "The Mountains Scene"

Gidayū music has various broad underlying conventions, listed below:

1. *Conventions current in a particular age*. Depending on the period of composition, a work will fall into certain distinctive patterns in the use and quantity of *kotoba* (spoken), *ji* (song), or *ji-iro* (rhythmical song), and in the shamisen patterns.

2. *Conventions of type:* jidaimono *(period play) and* sewamono *(contemporary-life play)*. Styles differ greatly between these two subgenre of Jōruri. There are plays, also, in which the two are consciously mixed, and in which parts of a play are performed in the opposing style.

3. *Conventions of* dan *(act) and* maki *(scene)*. The *jidaimono* has five *dan* while the *sewamono* has three *maki*. The music of each *dan* (or *maki*) will be different; in particular, the third and fourth *dan* (second and third *maki*) will contrast sharply.

4. *Conventions of* haba/kiri-ba *(introductory scene/climax scene) structure*. A *dan* (*maki*) is further divided into *haba* and *kiri-ba*, which have different musical styles.

5. *Lyrical scenes, songs, and* michiyuki. Lyrical parts of a play have fundamentally different musical characteristics.

6. *Conventions of a particular troupe or theater*. The Takemoto-za (*nishi-fū*) founded in 1684 by Takemoto Gidayū and the Toyotake-za (*higashi-fū*) founded by Toyotake Wakatayū in 1703 each have distinctive musical traditions.

7. *Styles of particular performers*. The style of a performer who either first performed or established a piece in the repertoire usually became part of the tradition.

8. *Musical styles for individual characters or character-types.* Variation in style depending on sex, age, occupation, social class, etc. was generally fixed, usually with reference to the particular type of puppet head used.

The above are of crucial importance for composers and performers and are still rigorously adhered to today. This strong resolve in preserving traditional distinctions of style reflects the high classical standard of contemporary Bunraku. Tradition does not allow individuals to disregard convention in composition or performance.

In 1771, when "The Mountains Scene" was composed, traditional "narrative" aspects had become less prominent in Jōruri, while "dramatic" elements had become more sophisticated; further, shamisen music had fully matured. "The Mountains Scene" is one of the most successful pieces from this epoch, when works were composed with both balance and tension among the three elements of narrative, theatricality, and music. As for category of genre, it is unmistakably a *jidaimono* and, as the *kiri-ba* of the third *dan*, is the most intense scene in the entire play. This is particularly pronounced for the male Mt. Se side, while the female Mt. Imo has some elements of the style of the fourth *dan*. Though the entire scene is dramatic (*jigoto*) rather than lyrical (*fushigoto*), the song that sends Hinadori and her belongings across to Mt. Se is an independent *fushigoto* section. As for the style of theater troupes, though the play was initially performed at the Takemoto-za, the performers consciously put the Mt. Se side in the Takemoto style (*nishi-fū*) and Mt. Imo in the Toyotake (*higashi-fū*), to create a structure of contrast. Performers today follow this tradition, as well as the styles of the original two chanters Takemoto Sometayū (Mt. Se) and Takemoto Harutayū (Mt. Imo). All of the four main and two minor roles clearly fall within the particular typecasts of a stern samurai, young girl, and so forth.

Since every work of Jōruri was created with the above in mind, both the composition of the music (originally and in alterations) and each particular performance rest upon the foundation of a relatively fixed set of styles and conventions. To look at it from another perspective, we can understand why a particular scene or character is performed in a certain way if we know the conventions of the tradition. Though this may seem constricting on first view, in fact composers and performers are able to (and, to a certain extent, must) break down the stereotype to seek and portray the essence and personality of an individual character. It is this tension, conflict, between tradition and individual expression that gives Jōruri its depth, power, and charm.

Until the mid-1740s when Takemoto Harima no shōjō (Gidayū's successor, d. 1744) and Toyotake Echizen no shōjō (Wakatayū, the founder of the Toyotake theater, retired 1745) left the stage, the styles of the Takemoto and Toyotake troupes were rigorously adhered to, but after their departure confusion arose because of movements between troupes. Finally, the *Chūshingura* incident in 1748 (see chapter one) ended the rigid distinction between *nishi-fū* and *higashi-fū*. For example, the influential Chikuzen no shōjō began to chant Toyotake pieces in Takemoto style. Or some pieces were played in *nishi-fū* during the first half and *higashi-fū* in the second. Furthermore, some pieces after this time seem to fit neither style. Following the collapse of the theaters, a new troupe was formed in 1769 with members from both groups, further eroding the distinction of styles.

Imoseyama was first performed, in 1771, during this period of flux. Among Bunraku members, it has been passed down by word of mouth that when "The Mountains Scene" was composed, the first shamisen Tsuruzawa Bunzō, along with the chanters Takemoto Sometayū and Takemoto Harutayū, and the second shamisen Tsuruzawa Matazō, decided to organize the piece into competing halves to display clearly the two styles: Mt. Se to represent *nishi-fū*, and Mt. Imo, *higashi-fū*. Regardless of the veracity of this anecdote, the result was a structure of contrast.

Higashi-fū and *nishi-fū* differ in several ways. The most striking difference is, as Professor Malm points out, the use of a whole step above pitch centers in *higashi-fū* and a half step pitch in *nishi-fū*. It is somewhat analogous to the difference heard in Western music between the use of a major third above tonic in major mode and a minor third in minor. This distinction is most obvious in comparing the *makura* (prelude) of Mt. Se (lines 1–15) and Mt. Imo (16–24). Further examples are lines 268, 271, and 664 to 665, where the chanters from both sides sing in unison, each maintaining his own scale. Second, melodic conventions contrast sharply, especially the relationship of the shamisen and chanting. For example, in *nishi-fū*, the chanter begins lower than the shamisen, eventually arriving at the same pitch. Conversely, in *higashi-fū*, the voice begins above the shamisen and gradually descends. A third distinction is in chanting styles, and a fourth is the difference in shamisen sound, quantity of notes, and accompanying technique. Further, there is variation in the performance of particular melodic patterns.

The *fū* of individual *tayū* comprise another category of style. Though we speak of the conventions of theaters or troupes, in fact these developed from individual performers. Essentially, the tradition of Takemoto Gidayū and his successor Takemoto Harima no shōjō is the basis of *nishi-fū*, and that of Toyotake Echizen no shōjō, the Toyotake-za's *higashi-fū*. Until the mid-18th century, chanters considered themselves to be in one or another of these lines. Chanters such as Harima no shōjō, Masatayū II, Sometayū, and Sumitayū are in the *nishi-fū*, while Echizen no shōjō, Yamatonojō, and Komatayū chanted in the *higashi-fū*. Therefore, it was only natural for Sometayū to take the Mt. Se role and chant it in *nishi-fū*.

According to sources published in the period 1761–1787, Sometayū's voice and style were characterized as follows: his voice, although not strong, was deep and elegant; he was talented in singing melodies, and popular among audiences.[2] He strongly maintained the traditional flavor of Harima no shōjō and had great skill in tightening and manipulating stage tension. He was known as a devoted student of the art, forever devising new techniques. A more recent text, *Jōruri shiroto kōshaku* (Amateur interpretations of Jōruri, 1926) by Sugiyama Sonohian (Shigemaru), which records material about the tradition handed down within the Bunraku troupe, says that Sometayū was able to chant mellifluously, as well as stretch out syllables in order to portray the emotion of a character.[3] The late Takemoto Tsunatayū VIII (1904–1969, National Treasure) contended that a particular characteristic of his style was to thrust his jaw back and forth (*ago o tsukau*) in chanting intense passages. The great Toyotake Yamashiro no shōjō (1878–1967, National Treasure), who was exacting on matters of *fū*, told Takechi Tetsuji that an aspect of *sometayū-fū* was to chant at the pitch of the low third string of the shamisen, regardless of the shamisen's playing, when stretching syllables out for histrionic effect.[4]

Listening to the Mt. Se chanting with these aspects of *sometayū-fū* in mind, we can discern much about this style. Initially, we find the technique of opening the scene at a lower pitch than the shamisen, which is representative of traditional *nishi-fū*, reflecting aspects of Harima no shōjō's method as described in sources. For example, the *shimoyakata* of line 10, *yamazumai* of line 12, *majiri* of line 114, and *kiri-gakure* of line 681 are chanted with a fierce intensity of emotion projected through a cadencelike, low-pitched delivery. The *Dai* of "Daihanji" in line 11 and the *kyō* of line 14, in which the pitch rises suddenly and the voice expands, is also a traditional technique. Further, lines 3, 9, and 524–525, in having a fast, rhythmical melody at the second-string pitch, also show the influence of Harima no shōjō.

We can see some elements particular to Sometayū's style in "The Mountains Scene." One is the characteristic, pointed out by Takechi Tetsuji, of sticking to the pitch of the low first string. The first string is expressed by the note G, and if we take the three open string notes to be B, E, B, nearly every phrase has a point where the pitch falls to the B to D range—this characteristic was unique to Sometayū. Having the end of a line drop to the B or E level is not unusual in *gidayū* music and is characteristic of *nishi-fū*. In "The Mountains Scene," when the voice falls to the lower note, usually it is independent of the pitch or melody of the shamisen.

As a rule the *tayū* chants independently of the shamisen, a technique that began about the time of Sometayū, before whom it was usual for the shamisen to set the pitch for the chanter and then to follow his melody. Sometayū's musical talent, in being able to chant independently, allowed this change to occur, but the change was influenced by the famous shamisen player Tsuruzawa Bunzō, Sometayū's more experienced partner (see chapter seven for the wider historical significance of Bunzō). Many of the pieces first performed by Bunzō have a style in which the shamisen plays independently of the chanter, neither designating the pitch nor following the melody. Therefore, we must acknowledge Bunzō's importance in developing a new chanter-shamisen relationship.

Today, when Bunraku performers speak of Sometayū, they regard, as Tsunatayū did, the moving of the jaw sideways as his most distinctive characteristic. Indeed, "The Mountains Scene" has many such examples: *mesa* in line 183, *mesa* in 213, *ibara* in 214, and *yama* at the beginning of 269, all stand out clearly in the performances of Oritayū and Tsudayū on the tape. Some chanters use the technique on several other words, and in all cases the effect is of masculine severity, samurai forcefulness.

This technique is fundamental to *gidayū* music. It is not unique to Sometayū and does not appear in all Sometayū pieces. Nevertheless, it seems to have become associated with Sometayū because of his frequent and extremely effective use of it in "The Mountains Scene."

A distinctive technique used by the famous Yamashiro no shōjō, a meticulous and avid researcher of *fū*, in performing Mt. Se was to chant the initial two syllables of phrases at the same pitch, as in lines 1 to 7:

(1) *Ini*shie no
(2) *Kami*yo no mukashi   *yama*ato no
(4) *Imo*se no hajime   *yama*   *yama* no
(5) *Naka* o   *naga*ruru   *Yoshi*nogawa
(6) *Chiri* mo   *aku*ta mo   *hana* no yama
(7) *Ge ni* yo ni   *aso*bu utab:to no.

Yet Yamashiro no shōjō's disciples have not followed his example, and thus the transmission of this characteristic of *sometayū-fū* has been broken. Invariably the second syllable is on a higher note.

The style of Takemoto Harutayū was almost the opposite to Sometayū. While Sometayū had been greatly influenced by the old master Harima no shōjō, Harutayū seemed to have been under the sway of Takemoto Yamatonojō and Toyotake Komatayū. Sources published in the period 1747 to 1806 portray Harutayū as having a beautiful, elegant, high-pitched, subtle, and gentle voice.[5] A criticism was that he lacked pathos. In the *Jōruri shiroto kōshaku* his voice is described as being rhythmical, high-pitched, bright, and lively.[6]

In contemporary performance, these characteristics are more pronounced in the role of Hinadori than Sadaka. In fact, it is standard for Hinadori to be performed by a middle-level *tayū* with a beautiful voice, explaining why the pitch tends to be high. The opening Mt. Imo *makura* is the best example of this style though it is prevalent throughout. Further, whereas *sometayū-fū* often has great variation in pitch levels, *harutayū* is more regular in pitch, with strong rhythm. Melodies are sung more smoothly.

Before the "*Chūshingura* Incident" of 1748, Harutayū was at the Toyotake-za, but he moved with Yamatonojō to the Takemoto-za, changing his name from Toyotake Harutayū to Takemoto Harutayū. Since he had experience in both theaters, he was trained in both *higashi-fū* and *nishi-fū*. He was, therefore, a perfect choice for the *higashi-fū* Mt. Imo roles. The characteristics of his style were standard *higashi-fū*: his voice began on a higher note than the shamisen and then descended, and his use of *gin* was most effective. His style had all the elements of traditional *higashi-fū*. However, the role of Sadaka is more complex, containing elements of *nishi-fū*. In her opening lines (198–204), the impression is strongly *nishi-fū*; for example, the *iji* of line 199 is in the Takemoto-za style of Harima no shōjō.

Though Sadaka is a woman, she is the head of the Dazai family, and the more somber *nishi-fū* is employed to give her a greater sense of presence, stature. Since Harutayū was conversant with both traditions, perhaps he intentionally mixed styles to distinguish between the roles of mother and daughter. Or perhaps this change occurred after the 1820s when four chanters performed instead of two. In any case, "The Mountains Scene," performed by four chanters, as today, or by two, as long ago, with its contrasting styles in competition between Sometayū's Mt. Se and Harutayū's Mt. Imo, is a masterpiece in the repertoire both as music and as theater.

The Structure of *kiri-ba* (Climax Scenes)

Preface (makura)

Plays with settings before the Tokugawa period (before 1603) are termed *jidaimono*, and works about contemporary life are *sewamono*. *Imoseyama* is a representative *jidaimono*. *Jidaimono* usually have five acts, the first four of which further divide into *kuchi* (introduction), *naka* (middle), and *kiri* (climax) scenes. The most important and intensely dramatic scenes are the *kiri*, which are preceded by a *haba* (*kuchi* or *naka*) scene. The various types of scenes are as follows:

```
[O michiyuki (journey)]
1. kuchi       —     introductory haba
2. naka        —                  haba
   kiri        —                  kiri-ba
[3. ato (extra scene)]
```

Occasionally, an extra scene (*ato*) will follow the *kiri*, and act four often will begin with a lyrical *michiyuki* before the *kuchi*. Though this is the general pattern, exceptions are common, particularly the omission of the *naka* scene.

Let us look at the structure of the crucial *kiri* of *jidaimono*, using "The Mountains Scene" as a reference point. Every *kuchi* scene in a play begins with a shamisen prelude (*sonae*), while *naka* or *kiri* commence with the shamisen playing a *sanjū, odori, shika-odori,* or *hiki-dashi* melody. The *sanjū, okuri,* and *shika-odori* prelude melodies lead into *ji,* while *hiki-dashi* is followed by a song. This first musical section is termed a *makura* (pillow or prelude).

In general throughout classical Japanese music, before entering the body of a piece, a short *makura* is played: for example, the *netori* in Gagaku, Nō's *shidai,* the *oki-uta* of Nagauta, Bungo-jōruri's *oki-jōruri,* and *rakugo's makura* all have similar functions. *Gidayū,* too, always commences with a *makura,* which introduces the theme and atmosphere. It may vary in length from thirty seconds to one minute, to several minutes. The content places the scene in the larger context, introducing characters and the setting. During the *makura* the puppets usually remain still; if they do move, it is unrelated to the content, and in some scenes the stage is left empty. "The Mountains Scene" opens with a red and white hanging curtain hiding the stage. Midway through the *makura* (end of line 12), it is lowered, though the audience sees no puppets. During line 20 of the Mt. Imo *makura* the *shōji* doors open, finally revealing Hinadori and the two maids. Nearly eight minutes elapse before the audience sees any puppets; the chanters and musicians command full attention.

The *makura* of a *gidayū* piece is considered of utmost importance. Chanters and shamisen players emphasize the extreme difficulty of its performance. First of all, performers are conscious of the tradition: they must follow in the particular style of the performer who first put his stamp on the piece. The *makura* is thought to contain the essence of the tradition. In "The Mountains Scene" the first fifteen lines, the Mt. Se *makura,* are in *sometayū-fū,* whereas lines 16 to 24, Mt. Imo's *makura,* are in *harutayū-fū.* "The Mountains Scene," due to its peculiar parallel structure, is unique in having two *makura.*

During the *makura,* performers, with the particularities of the tradition in mind, must express the essence of the piece, as well as evoke the atmosphere for the audience, leading them into the world of the drama. A performer is thought to be able to handle the entire piece if he has mastered the *makura.*

Themes

As the *makura* concludes with a musical cadence (*fushi-ochi*), the puppets come to life and the drama commences. The chanter then guides his audience through the scene with constant voice variations (*ji* or *ji-iro - iro - kotoba - ji*, etc.) punctuated by cadences (*fushi-ochi, suete, okuri*). When the *tayū* speaks the words of the puppets, his voice (as *kotoba*) is extremely realistic when compared with all other Japanese traditional performing arts, because it must put life into the inanimate puppet. The *tayū* will vary his delivery, to contrast with this realistic style, through the use of the many stock melodies of the tradition.

Plays are built upon a relatively fixed number of themes or theme-types: *mi-gawari* (sacrifice for loyalty); *aisō-zukashi, enkiri* (severing ties to lover); *renbo* (love); *seppuku* (suicide for loyalty or duty); *kaishin* (change of heart from bad to good); *koroshi* (murder); *miarawashi* (revealing of true identity after time in disguise); *chūshin* (returning from battle and relating events); *kandō* (disinheritance), *iken* (advice); *kyōran* (madness); *seme* (torture); *sengi* (investigation); *kudoki* (expression of love); *monogatari* (long monologue); *chari* (comedy); *shura* (battle action); *jikken* (verification of authenticity); and *fushigoto* (independent song). The music for each theme-type is similar from piece to piece.

In "The Mountains Scene," we encounter the themes: *renbo* (love), *seppuku* (suicide), *fushigoto* (song), and *kudoki* (expression of love). Since the love affair of Hinadori and Koganosuke is central to the first part, we would expect the theme of *renbo*. In Jōruri or Kabuki, it is conventional for the woman to plead to her lover, and in this scene Hinadori expresses her love openly to Koganosuke three times: lines 40–57; 107–110; and 129–132. In all cases, the voice is high-pitched, melodious, and seductive—full of emotion.

Though Koganosuke's *seppuku*, from the time of inserting the sword until his death, takes a very long time, the fact that it is presented less painfully than other such scenes is because the focus is on the main roles Daihanji and Sadaka; Koganosuke, at this point, is in the background.

The miniscene (lines 606–620), when Hinadori and her wedding gifts are sent across the Yoshino River, which flows down through mountains arrayed with cherry blossoms, is a *fushigoto* (song); a koto accompanies the voice for these lines only. *Fushigoto* appear most often as beautiful, lyrical scenes in the fourth act. The *tayū* sings rather than chants, and the shamisen plays complicated melodies, often changing pitch in order to distinguish the section from the body of the scene. Though "The Mountains Scene" is in the third act, the setting, amid the blossoming cherry trees, lends itself well to this lyrical song, which expresses elegantly the anguish of parents who have killed, or must yet kill, their beloved children. Though *gidayū* music inevitably expresses pathos, it is always done through spectacular musical flourishes. In the song the pitch is raised a whole step to express the emotion of four shattered souls through elegant, brilliant melodies, producing a tragic catharsis for the audience.

No serious *gidayū* piece is without a *kudoki* (expression of love). Of course, the love of a woman for a man is included, as well as love for children, parents, or siblings; in each case the emotions expressed are intensely sad. The pattern is to begin in *kotoba* (spoken; or *kakari*), shift to *ji* or *ji-iro* (song), and revert to *kotoba* occasionally; in the latter half the rhythm and tempo quicken as the emotion becomes more intense. The voice will sometimes break down into sobs; at other times it will rise into song (*sawari* or *kudoki* melodic patterns), and the shamisen will play particular patterns (*yotsuma, kami-mori, shimo-mori*, etc.) conventional to the theme. When the *kudoki* is as long as about ten minutes, it will fall into the traditional Japanese musical form of *jo* (introduction), *ha* (intensification), and *kyū* (quick conclusion).

"The Mountains Scene" contains two *kudoki*, neither of large scale. In the first, lines 140–147, Hinadori's beautiful, though frustrated, love of Koganosuke is expressed in a high-pitched voice through a complicated melody (*kami, iru, suete, gin, sawari*). The passage concludes with the words *to kudokigoto*. The second example, lines 576–583, expresses the love and anguish of Sadaka, who has just killed her daughter. Though the words are not conventional *kudoki*, the music is. Specifically, the voice twice rises to *kami* (high-pitch), and the shamisen, at the end of lines 578, 579, and 580, plays, respectively, the variant *shimo-mori, yotsuma,* and *shimo-mori*, conventional to the *kudoki* pattern.

From ō-otoshi (Grand Finale) to dangiri (End)

The action moves along through the various minithemes and melodic patterns that comprise the scene. With the *ō-otoshi* pattern, toward the end, the piece achieves its musical climax, though this may or may not coincide with the dramatic climax. In "The Mountains Scene" the dramatic peak comes in lines 564–568 with the shocking realization that both children have been killed. The *ō-otoshi*, however, does not come until lines 666–667. In general, when the *ō-otoshi* is reached, the audience knows that the drama is complete; the remaining part is simply the conclusion to the story. Particularly in fourth-act pieces, at this point, or a little further along, the pitch is raised two full tones, and the shamisen clearly takes over the lead role, as the pressure is lifted from the *tayū*. Though "The Mountains Scene" is not in act four and the pitch does not change, the same effect occurs as the tense atmosphere is relaxed a bit.

One peculiar characteristic of "The Mountains Scene" is that the pitch of the voices is lowered with the entrance of Daihanji in line 194. It is conventional for the pitch to be lowered at the change of chanters during the transition from a *haba* (introductory) scene to a *kiri*, but it is exceptional for the pitch to be lowered in the middle of a *kiri* scene. This seems to have occurred after the change, in the 1820s, from two to four chanters. The effect is to distinguish the second two "master" *tayū* from the younger performers who take the roles of Hinadori and Koganosuke. Therefore, the love scene between the youngsters in the first part is played to give the impression of a *haba* (introductory) scene. Since the piece has been performed by four chanters now for more than 150 years, this arrangement has become standard.

Directly after the *ō-otoshi* (or a few lines later) the conclusive *dangiri* commences. In "The Mountains Scene" it begins with line 668. Though *dangiri* may vary among plays in scale, between *jidaimono* and *sewamono*, or between major and minor works, the musical structure is similar. At this point, song and shamisen music dominate content; with a lively, quick rhythm (one note to one syllable), the piece ends in a musical flourish. Therefore, even if *kotoba* is found, it is chanted rhythmically like *kotoba-nori* to shamisen accompaniment, almost indistinguishable from the *ji* parts. Many melodies are used, such as: *yobidashi, gin, kami, kuriage, yotsu-ori, chikara, kujira, kodama*; and, in martial-like *jidaimono, roppō* is used, while in extremely sad pieces *ura-roppō* is found; for intense pathos, *tataki* is used. The *dangiri* is a complex musical composition through which the emotional catharsis is softened and concluded majestically, a fitting finale for this sophisticated performing art comprised of dramatic, narrative, and musical aspects.

(translated by C. Andrew Gerstle)

Chapter Three   Notes

1 Japanese terms are defined in more detail in the glossary.
2 *Take no haru* (1761), *Hyōban tori awase* (1765), *Hyōban sangokushi* (1766), and *Yami no tsubete* (1781) in *NSBSS*, vol. 7.
3 Sugiyama Sonohian, *Jōruri shiroto kōshaku* (1926), p. 9.
4 Bandō Mitsugorō and Takechi Tetsuji, *Geijūya* (Ten nights of art, 1972) and Takechi Tetsuji, *Fū no rinri* (The ethics of style, 1955).
5 *Sōkyoku Naniwa no ashi* (1751), *Ayatsuri awase kendai* (1757), *Take no haru* (1761), and *Yami no tsubute* (1781) in *NSBSS*, vol. 7.
6 Sugiyama, pp. 7, 257–65.

Chapter Four Reading "The Mountains
Scene" as Music:
The Chanter's Notation[1]

Kiyoshi Inobe

Musical Structure and the Form of the Text

Gidayū music exists both as part of the Bunraku puppet theater and
as one example in the long and varied Japanese storytelling tradition.
The language of the text is divided into spoken and narrative parts.
Spoken parts are called *kotoba,* and as a rule they are the words of the
puppet (character) on the stage. In modern drama, films, or television
these would be the lines of the actors or actresses. Since Bunraku
puppets—fashioned of wood and covered with robes—cannot, of
course, speak, the chanter (*tayū*) must be the voice of each puppet.
This peculiar situation is a special characteristic of *gidayū* music. In
contrast to *kotoba* is the explanatory *ji,* in which the happenings on
stage as well as the feelings and thoughts of characters are described.
In some ways *gidayū* resembles a novel with its contrast of dialogue and
narration. It is in the *ji* parts that we find the link between *gidayū* and
earlier narrative tradition.

How do we explain *gidayū* as music? In simplest terms, the fundamental pattern is that *ji* (narrative) passages are sung to a melody
(lyrical), while *kotoba* (dialogue) is declaimed without melody; in between (often transitional) is the style of delivery *iro,* which is close to
kotoba but is accompanied by the shamisen. Unfortunately, the same
terms (*kotoba* and *ji*) are used not only to distinguish between the "first
person" (dialogue) and "third person" (narrative) divisions but also to
describe performance styles within both of them. The former usage
refers to the distinction in the text between the words delivered by the
chanter as narrator and those delivered as the voice of a character. In
the latter usage *kotoba* and *ji* refer to the chanter's musical style, no
matter whether the lines are in first or third person.

When a text is performed as *gidayū*, generally the *ji* (narrative) parts are sung (*ji*) to a melody, the "spoken" parts are declaimed without melody in the *kotoba* style. However, if the chanting were always thus it would be simplistic as music and lack flavor. Therefore, "spoken" parts are sometimes in the *ji* or *iro* style, and, vice versa, "narrative" is occasionally in *kotoba* or *iro* style. The text, therefore, is read best not as a work of literature but as musical narrative. (From this point I shall use *ji* [song/lyrical] and *kotoba* [spoken] only as musical terms.)

The usual pattern of chanting "spoken" lines is for the first part to be in *kotoba* and the latter in *ji*. There are, of course, many variations. For example, let us examine lines 189–191 from "The Mountains Scene" (the Japanese is followed by literal English translations; quotation marks enclose "spoken" lines):

ji (kotoba)	iro (ji)	kotoba (kotoba)
"Kore nō matte"	*no koebakari.*	*"Kōshitsusama onide"* to.
"Please wait!"	voice	"Madame Sadaka has returned!"

ji (ji)
Tsuguru shimobe ni senkata mo.
at announcement—nothing to do

Although *Kore nō matte* is a "spoken" line, it is chanted in *ji* style. *Koebakari* is narrative but is in *iro*. *Kōshitsusama onide* is a "spoken" line and delivered in *kotoba*. *To tsuguru shimobe ni senkata mo* is narrative and chanted in *ji*. Another example is (lines 86–91):

iro (kotoba)	kotoba (kotoba)
"Nō areare.	*Tsukue ni motarete Kogasama no.*
"Oh, look, look.	Leaning on his desk,

ji (kotoba)
Mono omowashi okaomochi. Oshaku gana
his distraught face.   He must be

iro (kotoba)	kotoba (kotoba)	
okoritsuran.	*Ee osoba e yukitai.*	*Kore koko ni"*
sick.	I must go to him.	Look, over here!"

The whole passage is "spoken" though chanted in various styles. In only two places is the chanting without musical accompaniment. The pattern is: *iro - kotoba - ji - iro - kotoba.*

Since in *gidayū* the text is not delivered in a style that makes clear the division between "first-person" dialogue and "third-person" narrative, the uninitiated listener may find the music confusing or difficult. After gaining an acquaintance with the conventions, however, one realizes that the diversity of expression is the beauty of the musical form, and that it is a highly sophisticated technique. Furthermore, one gradually begins to hear in these constant variations and quick changes a form of music endlessly fascinating.

An Outline of Musical Structure

A closer look at the structure of *gidayū* music reveals that the three styles of *kotoba*, *iro*, and *ji* can be further divided as in the following chart:

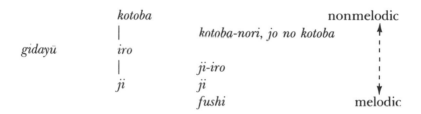

Let us begin with *kotoba*. As remarked earlier, this style of chanting is without melody or shamisen accompaniment and normally is used for the speech of characters in dialogue or monologue. Among the traditional genres of Japanese music, the *kotoba* of *gidayū* is the closest to actual speech. The performer attempts, as much as possible, to imitate the manner of speech of a particular character or type. Through *kotoba*, chanters express with great skill all aspects of the character's age, vocation, social status, sex, situation, thoughts, feelings, personality, and whether or not he is honest or dishonest, upright or villain. Of course, the actions of weeping, laughing, coughing, choking, sneezing, exclamation, and so forth are all expressed realistically through *kotoba*. In "The Mountains Scene," one can tell much about each of the four main characters and two maids by carefully listening to the *kotoba* for each role. Chanters use various techniques to distinguish characters. It is not true, however, to say that *kotoba* is 100 percent realistic; it is of course a "theatrical" style of delivery. In *jidai-mono* (period) pieces, especially, a particular cadence is used to create stereotype voices for historical personages.

Let us next look at *iro*, which is somewhat more melodic than *kotoba* but far from the melodic style of *ji*. It falls between the two and is sometimes hard to distinguish from *kotoba*. Most often it functions as a transition from *ji* to *kotoba*. Since an abrupt change from song to speech is harsh for the ear, *iro* is used to smooth the transition. In this case the shamisen often plays a particular cadencelike pattern (*iro-dome*), which brings the *iro* to a close before the chanter shifts voices:

Example 1

iro-dome

In "The Mountains Scene" the following lines contain examples: 32, 60, 111, 123, 150, 159, 201, 205, 215, 283, 318, 343, 388, 515, 519, 527, 569, 633.

In between *iro* and *kotoba* is *kotoba-nori* and *jo no kotoba*. Though *kotoba-nori* is considered a variety of *kotoba*, it is not as "realistic" as *kotoba*; rather, the chanter recites in a strongly rhythmical manner. *Kotoba* is generally unaccompanied except for passages that use shamisen background music (*meriyasu*). A special characteristic of *kotoba-nori*, however, is that the shamisen accompanies as in *ji-iro* passages. *Kotoba-nori* usually is found late in a piece, and lines 669–670 from "The Mountains Scene" are a good example. *Jo no kotoba* is used as the preface to a five-act *jidaimono*, and since "The Mountains Scene" is in act three, we find no example.

Ji, which is chanted to a melody, can further be divided into *ji* and *fushi*, a distinction difficult to define. *Ji* is the *gidayū* style of singing, while *fushi* are melodies originally from non-*gidayū* songs.

In terms of content, *ji* is used to express feelings, dramatic situation, explanation, description of characters' actions, thoughts, and psychology. Further, dialogue or monologue passages are often partly, and occasionally fully, chanted in *ji*. The following is a catalog of major *ji* melody types:

1. Melodies used at openings, endings, transitions: *sonae, okuri, sanjū, dōgu-gaeshi, fushi-ochi (fushi-otoshi), kari, oroshi, tsunagi, otoshi, dangiri*

2. Basic melodies: *haru fushi, honbushi, nagaji, suete, harima, kei, yobidashi, yotsuma, kami-mori, shimo-mori*

3. Melodies related to pitch and voice delivery: *haru, u, naka, kami (kan), shimo, haru u, naka gin, ya, kowari, u gin, haru gin, kami u*

4. Melodies related to voice technique and rhythm: *iru, kuru, hiroi, noru, hatsumi, yuri, kuriage*

5. Melodies developed by famous chanters: *kawachi-ji, yamato-ji, harima-ji, nishiki*

6. Background music: various kinds of *meriyasu*

As a general rule, *fushi* is more melodic than *ji*. The performer "sings" rather than "chants," and the shamisen plays a beautiful melody that, in comparison to the style accompanying *ji*, is independent of the voice. Furthermore, the various kinds of *fushi* are often used to create a particular flavor or mood: for example, *reizen* for elegance; *sekkyō, bun'ya,* and *kakutayū* for pathos; *edo* or *geki* for martial flavor; *utai* or *shibagaki* for solemnity; *tataki* for the agony at parting. Besides these uses, *fushi* are used as independent songs to give a scene a particular atmosphere. The third kind of *fushi* is the *sawari*, a non-*gidayū* tune borrowed or alluded to.

Some of the major kinds of *fushi* melody types are listed below:

1. Melodies from earlier performing arts: *heike, utai, mai, sekkyō*

2. 'Old' Joruri: *amido, reizen, kakutayū, bun'ya, geiki, tosa, hyōgu, dōguya, edo*

3. Melodies from Jōruri other than *gidayū*: *hanchū, miyazono, shōden, shigetayū, handayū*

4. Popular songs or dances: *ai no yama, saimon, tataki, utazaimon, shika odori, jizōkyō, rinsei*

5. Folk songs: *funa-uta, komurobushi, itoayatsuri-uta, komori-uta, okazaki, mago-uta, yari ondo*

6. Miscellaneous: *junrei-uta, ji-uta, shibagaki, hayari-uta*

"The Mountains Scene" contains examples of *mai* (line 13), *ai no yama* (18), *sawari* (146, 533), *tataki* (104, 609, 616), *utai* (625), and *bun'ya* (539).

Finally, there is *ji-iro*, which is between *ji* and *iro*. It is more rhythmic and less melodic than *ji* but is more melodic than *iro*, and it can be considered a type of *ji*. As a rule, each syllable has one note and is chanted at a relatively fast tempo; the shamisen usually leads the voice with a particular rhythm. The most frequent notes are the open second string "E," the open third string "B," and the third string fifth position, "F." A sliding left-hand movement along the neck (*suri-age, suri-sage*) is frequently used, as well as an improvisational style of accompaniment, which does not sound "melodic"; the voice and shamisen follow separate lines. Though not as melodic as *ji*, it does have the variations of pitch and voice technique of *haru, u, naka, kami,* and *naka u*. In "The Mountains Scene" the following lines are in *ji-iro*: 31–32, 371, 408–409, 415, 422, 424–426, 527, 553–556, 625–629, 631–633, 639–642, 668. For both the chanter and shamisen, *ji-iro* is difficult to master, and those able to chant or play *ji-iro* skillfully are considered mature performers.

A *gidayū* piece, then, is a mixture of these melodies and chanting styles, which are not always easy to distinguish during performance. Unless one's ear is conversant with the medium and unless one is accustomed to listening analytically, it is difficult to distinguish between *kotoba* and *iro, kotoba-nori* and *ji-iro, ji* and *fushi,* and *iro* and *ji naka* (*ji* line ending with cadencelike falling pitch). The differences are often subtle. In other words, *gidayū* is an extremely complex musical form that requires a high level of skill to perform. "The Mountains Scene" contains several complex examples. Line 164 is *ji*; however, even though the shamisen does accompany the chanter, if one listens only to the chanting, it sounds like *kotoba*. Line 472 is *kotoba*, but the shamisen plays and the voice sounds like *ji*.

Conventions of Form

These various elements, melodies, and styles are, of course, not randomly arranged. Each follows conventions and must suit the language of each particular text. Let us look at the rules:

Beginnings and Endings (sanjū, okuri, dangiri)

Each of the five acts commences with a variation of the *sonae* shamisen prelude. It is traditional to repeat the final two low notes as a solemn opening for the first act. Some performers still follow this tradition, but most play it only once. After these notes, a preface (*jo no kotoba*) is usually chanted, which may be in *ji* or *uta* (song). This *sonae* pattern may also be used in the middle of a scene, a good example being at the end of line 197 in "The Mountains Scene" where the shamisen plays a variation to express succinctly that the mood has changed. The final scenes of each act are opened with the *okuri*, *sanjū*, or *shika-odori* accompanied by the shamisen.

In each of these openings, the phrase is split into two, with the first part being the ending of the previous scene and the second being the beginning of the new scene. Basically the same melody is repeated and is thus termed the *kaeshi* (repeat). The lines:

(a) *shutjin no koma o hayamete*　　　(b) *kakeriyuku*
　　hurrying his horse to battle,　　　　　he gallops off

are sung by one chanter to finish the previous scene, "Fragile Blossoms," while the next chanter begins "The Mountains Scene" with the same phrase (b). On first encounter with Bunraku, this may seem strange, but the repetition links two scenes when there has been a break due to a change in performers.

Okuri is used for the exit of a major character. When the scenery changes, *sanjū* or *dōgu-gaeshi* (literally "scenery changing") is performed by the new chanter. Due, therefore, to a change of scenery,

"The Mountains Scene" begins with a *sanjū* melody. Of course, there are exceptions to this rule. For example, in line 622 of "The Mountains Scene" *dōgu-gaeshi* is played though the scenery does not change. One of the various *sanjū*—*kami sanjū, shimo sanjū,* or *urei sanjū*—is normally used to begin scenes, while either *saguri sanjū, kioi sanjū, urei sanjū, ōsanjū, shikoro sanjū, hikitori sanjū,* or *nenbutsu sanjū* is used as the cadence (both voice and shamisen) to a scene. *Sanjū* may also be used within a scene. In "The Mountains Scene," *kami sanjū* (meaning a *sanjū* at a high pitch) is used for the word *kakeriyuku* (gallops off), which begins the scene. The chanter and shamisen must, through music, give a suggestion of galloping horses.

In contrast, *okuri* is used as a transition between scenes when there is no change of setting, but as one might expect, there are many variations of melody and exceptions to the rule. For opening scenes, we have the several broad categories of *okuri* styles: *higashi-fū* (east style)— *nishi-fū* (west), *jidaimono* (period play)—*sewamono* (contemporary-life play), act three—act four, *haba* (introductory scene)—*kiri-ba* (climax scene). There are specific *okuri* melodies (*komatayū okuri* and *miyato okuri*), and *okuri* may be used in the middle of a scene: *u okuri, iro okuri, ko okuri, gin okuri, fushi okuri, musha okuri, rinsei okuri, hina okuri, tennō okuri, amido okuri, ai no yama okuri.*

Okuri are used at five crucial points in "The Mountains Scene." The *u okuri* of line 23 is a special case where the *okuri* melody is used for its musical flavor rather than as a cadence or prelude. However, the *iro okuri* of line 192 is used at the transitional point when the senior chanters enter to take the main roles of Daihanji and Sadaka, marking the end of the first part. The *okuri* of line 274 concludes the intensely antagonistic dialogue of Daihanji and Sadaka, signaling the entrance into the tragic core of the scene. The *okuri* of line 573 brings the entire scene to a climax as both houses come to realize the tragedy of the other; this transition leads to the end of the feud and to the marriage of the children. The last (*fushi*) *okuri* (line 620) is used during the song when the koto accompanies the shamisen. As a cadence, it brings the song to a close. *Fushi okuri* is usually used in *michiyuki* as a melody in the song. Among all the various *okuri*, it is the longest and most elegant melody. "In The Mountains Scene," however, it has been greatly abridged.

Though exceptions such as *u okuri* do exist, basically *okuri* is used as a transition between scenes, as a musical cadence or prelude. When a scene ends an act, however, the *dangiri* melody is used, as in line 695 where, after the words are finished, the chanter often adds meaningless sounds (*o* or *n*) to complete the musical phrase.

Musical Cadences of Voice and Shamisen *(fushi-ochi, otoshi, naka, iro)*

It takes from one half to nearly two hours for one chanter to perform a scene in Bunraku. "The Mountains Scene" is one of the longer pieces in the repertoire and, as any piece, is composed of many musical units. Various cadence melodies such as *fushi-otoshi, ō-otoshi,* and nine different *yuri* bring these units to a close.

In "The Mountains Scene" we find twenty-seven examples of these musical cadences. Most are *fushi-ochi,* but line 15 is a *yuri nagashi;* 81 is a *nanatsu-yuri fushi;* 243 and 282 are *hinagata-bushi* (or *yanagi*); 297, 487, and 544 are *mitsu yuri;* 386 is *u fushi;* 394 is *naka fushi;* 410 and 615 are *hitotsu yuri;* 644 is *gyōgi* (or *kioi*); and 667 is an *ō-otoshi,* the longest and most compelling cadence in *gidayū.* There are other examples of several now forgotten melodic patterns, two of which are in "The Mountains Scene": line 110 is *kuruma bushi,* and line 203 is *kasane bushi.* "The Mountains Scene" is, therefore, best understood as a structure based upon musical units marked by the various cadences such as *sanjū, okuri,* and *fushi-ochi.* These various melodies usually give a full sense of musical cadence. There are, however, other "lighter" cadences such as *naka* and *iro. Naka* appears within a *ji* or *ji-iro* line and gives a light sense of cadence through the dropping of pitch. One variant of *naka* keeps the pitch at the level of the open second string, giving a relaxed feeling. Some examples are as follows (lines 9–12):

ji naka   u   **haru**
Imoyama wa Dazai no Shōni Ku'nindo no ryōchi nite.
Mt. Imo is the land of Dazai no Shōni Ku'nindo.

                    naka
Kawa e mikoshi no shimoyakata.
Across the river Daihanji Kiyozumi

u   u
Seyama no kata wa Daihanji Kiyozumi no ryōnai.
has a retreat on Mt. Se where

haru u **naka**
Shisoku Kiyofune itsuzoya yori koko ni kanki no yamazumai.
his son Koganosuke, disgraced, is confined.

In this passage *naka* is used three times. Listening to a tape or performance, one immediately hears the cadencelike falling pattern used for *shimoyakata* and *yamazumai*, and the low note used to begin the line *Imoyama*.

Iro, also, is used frequently as a light cadence, most often as a transition from *ji* to *kotoba*. The function of *iro* is to "close" the melody to let the chanter shift to the *kotoba* delivery style, allowing for a smoother transition. In "The Mountains Scene," *iro* is used forty times, twenty-seven in the pattern of *ji* (*ji-iro*)—*iro*—*kotoba*. The second most frequent use (eleven times) is to give variety to the music: *ji* (*ji-iro*)—*iro*—*ji* (*ji-iro*); one time it is used to flavor a *kotoba* line: *kotoba*—*iro*—*kotoba*. In nearly all cases it is one short line of text, transitional between chanting styles. It is not, however, necessary to use *iro* when changing delivery styles. In fact, "The Mountains Scene" has fifteen examples where the chanter switches from *ji* straight to *kotoba*, most in the intensely dramatic last half of the scene, when *iro* would tend to disrupt the quick tempo.

When the *tayū* chants in *iro*, the shamisen usually plays the conclusive two notes (*iro-dome*) as in example 1. This is used in lines 32, 60, 111, 123, 150, 159, 201, 205, 215, 283, 318, 343, 388, 515, 519, 527, 569, and 633. Though *iro-dome* may vary depending on the type of character or act, the effect is similar. The exact way the shamisen plays these notes depends on the musician's interpretation of the action or words. He may vary the strength and time (*ma*) between notes—he is free to improvise and give the pattern his personal stamp.

Iro-dome, as for all musical patterns in *gidayū* (and Japanese music in general), may vary slightly from scene to scene and from performer to performer. Though based on a model, a pattern will vary considerably with each particular context and each individual artist's interpretation. It is difficult, if not impossible in some cases, to tell which is the variant, which the original model. We must, therefore, be aware of this practice when analyzing patterns or aspects of Japanese music.

When *iro-dome* is played, we know the preceding line is in *iro*. Unfortunately, without *iro-dome* it is sometimes difficult to distinguish between *iro* and *naka*. In general, one can say that *naka* is slightly more

melodic than *iro*, but unless one is accustomed to analyzing performance tapes, it is difficult to distinguish the two. Moreover, there are few
tayū today who can chant them distinctly.

Melodic Patterns Used to Express Intense Emotion (suete, sue, sue kakari)

Among the various emotions expressed in *gidayū* the most important is pathos. Since *gidayū* is dramatic music, often extreme emotions
such as anguish are expressed with great force. One pattern used to
bring these moments of anguish to the highest intensity is *suete*. Further, there are the abbreviated patterns *sue* and *sue kakari*. The following are examples from "The Mountains Scene."

suete   **naka**
hashi wa nai ka to kudokigoto   (147)
is there no bridge, she pleads

suete   **naka**
Mamanaranu yo o uraminaki   (165)
Bitter tears, cruel world.

suete   **naka**
kotoba wa namida. Gumubakari   (328–329)
words drowned in tears

iru   **sue naka**
watto hirefusu oyako no makoto   (432)
collapse, truly father and son

kami u   **suete**   **naka**
Kuyamu mo naku mo ittoki ni akirete kotoba mo. Nakarishiga
                                                              (567–568)
Thunderstruck by the turn of events, no tears of regret or
grief, no words flow forth.

As we can see, each example is a moment of intense emotion when
characters collapse in tears. Line 147 is considered an especially difficult *suete* to chant. Line 165, in *nishi-fū*, is a fine example of a "third-
act" *suete*; chanters must take particular care with it. Other examples
are:

suete　　　　　**naka**
Mamorasetamae to shinchū ni　　　　　　　　　　　　(83)
praying in his heart that his father is safe

sue kakari　**naka**
Mune wa　*shinku no*　　　　　　　　　　　　　　　(317)
heart inflamed with worry

In these lines strong emotions are expressed with full force. A final example is not as common:

suete　　　　　**naka**
Kamiyo no mukashi yamaato no　　　　　　　　　　　(2)
in the mythical age, the land of Yamato

Here *suete* is used in the prelude to create an atmosphere of solemn serenity. These patterns, *suete, sue,* and *sue kakari,* express extreme passion and anguish, with great power, giving a strong impression to the listener. The latter half of *suete* often have the notation *naka,* meaning that the pitch gradually falls, bringing the passage to a musical cadence after the emotional climax.

Other Melodic Patterns

Sometimes when a happening or miniscene has ended, *haru fushi* serves as a transition to the next section. The following are two examples:

haru fushi　　　　　**u**　　　　**naka**
Koro wa　　　　　*yayoi no*　　*hajimetsukata*　　(16)
The time is early spring

haru fushi　　**naka**
Mirai　　　*e okuru*　　　　　　　　　　　　　(606)
send to the next world

Line 16, the beginning of the Mt. Imo chanting, follows the solemn *makura* (prelude) sung by the Mt. Se chanter. A sudden change brings a bright, lively atmosphere enveloping the three young women. In line 606, *haru fushi* is again transitional to the *fushigoto* song that accompanies Hinadori and her belongings across the river. In either case, *haru fushi* radically alters the mood. Sometimes *haru fushi* is used simply for its melody, but no such examples are found in "The Mountains Scene."

Another of these elegant melodies is *nagaji*, normally found in pairs (or triplets) of alternating seven to five syllable lines. It is a high-pitched, slow melody that repeats:

nagaji
Musuboretokenu   waga omoi   koishi yukashii
clinging to an ephemeral string of hope. "Dearest

Kiyofunesama   (44)
Koganosuke,"

nagaji
Iso iso tachi wa tachi nagara musume no
Sadaka slowly stands up, in sympathy with

kokoro omoiyari. Wakare no kushi no hakanasa mo   (383–384)
the pain that racks her daughter's heart. The comb,

The first example repeats twice and the second three times; each expresses the gentle feelings of the women characters Hinadori (44) and Sadaka (333–384).

A similar, short shamisen pattern called *kei* is used to portray the emotions of elegant characters, usually beautiful women and gentle young men, and often introduces such characters. It is common in fourth-act pieces or *michiyuki*, and consequently, no example exists in the third-act "Mountains Scene."

In contrast to these elegant, gentle melodies, *harima* expresses gravity or solemnity. *Harima* was developed by Inoue Harimanojō (d. 1685), Takemoto Gidayū's mentor, and is commonly found in *nishi-fū* pieces. In "The Mountains Scene" it is used seven times, though the word *harima* does not appear in the published texts:

haru
Shisoku Kiyofune itsuzoya yori (12)
his son Koganosuke, disgraced

u
Anjiittaru kaokatachi (85)
face deep in thought

haru
Kiku Kiyofune mo kaji araba (148)
Were there an oar to row,

haya wataritaki yukashisa o (148)
he'd rush across the stream.

naka
kokoro no mama ni uguisu no (162)
like a trapped bush warbler

ji haru kami   **naka**
hayamari   *mesarena to* (183)
you mustn't do anything rash

u
Rippa ni ii wa hanashitemo (275)
Though she spoke so assuredly,

Among the above, only line 275 is not from the Mt. Se side in the *nishi-fū*. Usually a man's emotions are expressed, but in the last example Lady Sadaka's emotions are expressed in *higashi-fū*. Accordingly, this passage portrays her strong will and determined attitude, giving her character a masculine touch. Musically the effect is imposing and weighty.

Among these seven examples, the repetition of the melody in line 148 gives a particularly strong impression to the listener. Further, for line 183 on the *ha* of *haya* and the *na* of *mesarena* the chanter moves his jaw back and forth to give an extremely severe tone to the line. This passage is one of the most difficult for chanters, but if done well, the tragic emotions underlying the drama dance before the audience's eyes and ears.

Another old melodic pattern, *honbushi*, gives the formal and solemn atmosphere of a *jidaimono*; line 8 is a fine example:

honbushi
Koto no hagusa no sutedokoro
to cast verse among the grasses

A pattern (not notated in printed texts) that depicts powerfully the pent-up emotions of women is *kudoki*. *Kudoki*, as a popular term, refers to the miniscene of arialike passages when a woman voices her feelings for a husband or lover. The *kudoki* to which I refer, however, is a specific melodic pattern whose content is usually a woman's love. The pattern is normally found in *kudoki* miniscenes, but it is not uncommon for it to be used at other points:

ji kami
gojūnenrai shirazarishi to.   (426)
never dreamed in all my fifty years

haru u   fushi
Hitotsu ni otsuru mitsusegawa.   (487)
flow together into the Three Rivers of Hell.

u   kami
Sennen mo mannen mo   (531)
for a thousand, myriad years

Of these three examples from "The Mountains Scene" only line 531, though short, has the flavor of a *kudoki* miniscene. Line 426, though of the samurai Daihanji, sings the love, grief, and agony of a father at the approaching death of his son. The latter two examples, in contrast, portray a woman's feelings. In *kudoki* miniscenes, aside from the voice pattern *kudoki*, many shamisen patterns are used, such as *yotsuma*, *kami-mori*, *shimo-mori*.

Voice Technique and Pitch

The four categories thus far explained contain melodies that I have described as "patterns" (*senritsukei*). In *gidayū*, these melodic patterns are used, following long-standing conventions, to suit the content of a particular line. The melodic parts of *gidayū*, however, do not consist simply of a continuous flow of these melodic patterns. In between such relatively fixed melodies are melodies that cannot be categorized as a pattern. These, in fact, form the bulk of melodic (*ji*) passages, filling the space between the more isolated, though important, melodic patterns. *Gidayū* is a mixture of melodies: some (fixed patterns) used because they suit a crucial passage (by implication the playwright may have such patterns in mind when writing the scene), and others (unfixed) composed to suit the particular phrase or sentence. Let us look at some of these "unfixed" *ji* or *ji-iro* elements of the music.

In this category, the primary elements are techniques of voice delivery and pitch level, namely, *haru, u, kami, naka, shita, gin, ya, kowari*, and the mixtures of these, such as *haru u, naka u, gin, kami u*, and *shita kowari*. Basically, *haru* means to chant with the voice "taut"; *u* comes from the idea of having the voice float (*uku*). *Kami, naka*, and *shita* refer basically to high, middle, and low pitch, respectively. The terms *gin, ya*, and *kowari* refer to pitch levels of both the shamisen and voice.

These various terms come from the earlier Nō drama into Jōruri puppet theater. In Nō, the basic scale of *yowagin* is shown in example 2.

Example 2

Here the three pitch centers *shita* (*ge*), *naka* (*chū*), and *kami* (*jō*) are a fourth apart; above the *naka* and *kami* notes are the basic pitches, *uki*, which in *gidayū* is notated as *u*.

What does the *gidayū* scale look like? Example 3 shows how much more complicated the basic *gidayū* scale is compared to Nō.

Example 3

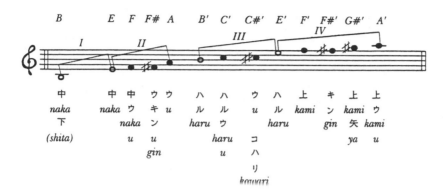

In Nō the low note B is called *shita* (*ge*); in *gidayū* it was originally termed *shita* but later was called *naka*. The *nishi-fū* pieces performed initially by Harima no shōjō, Masatayū (II), and some chanters who cherished this early tradition occasionally contain the notation *shita*. The fourth above this *naka* (B) is *naka* (E). Then, the fourth above the E (*naka*) is *haru* (B') and again the fourth above is *haru* (E'). These four notes are the pitch centers in *gidayū*.

U (A) is also an important pitch, though its role in the scale is difficult to explain. It is the leading note between tetrachords II and III. An octave above *u* (A) is *kami u* (A'); these two notes are the highest in tetrachords II and IV, respectively. (*U* C#' is perhaps better explained as being in the group of three notes a whole step above the pitch centers, as explained below.)

We turn now to the important notes *naka u* and *haru u* in tetrachords II and III and their relationship to their respective tone centers. The convention is different from that in Nō: *naku u* and *haru u* (and *kami* in tetrachord IV) are each a half step higher than *naka* (E) and *haru* (B') (and *haru* E'), as shown in example 4.

Example 4

Example 5 shows the scale when A(*u*) and A' (*kami u*) are added:

Example 5

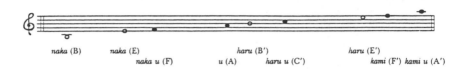

naka (B)   naka (E)   haru (B')   haru (E')
                naka u (F)   u (A)   haru u (C')   kami (F') kami u (A')

In Nō, on the other hand, the notes above the pitch centers, *naka uki* and *kami uki*, are both a whole step higher. In *gidayū* the notes a whole step higher are: *u gin* (F#) (for *naka* E), *kowari* (*u* C#') (for *haru* B'), and *gin* (F#') (for *haru* E'). The major sonic difference, therefore, between Nō music theory and that of *gidayū* is the concentration on basic pitches above the tone centers as being a whole step in Nō and a half step in *gidayū*. (A further complication resides in tetrachord IV where there is a second *kami* (*ya* G#'); its function is to form a bridge to the highest note, *kami u* A'.) Both systems are logical but different, and both reflect a firm sense of music tonal theory behind a highly developed performance practice based on oral training.

In *gidayū* music, elements can be explained with the kind of logic noted above, but there are exceptions. Furthermore, using two different terms for the same note and using the same term for different notes causes confusion. Yet these various notations, as pitch centers and in the frequency of use, have an intimate connection with all the musical elements discussed thus far.

The most important question is, What relation do these notations have to the content of the drama, and on what kind of phrases are they pertinent? For example, *haru* is meant to project a feeling of high-strung emotion, while in *u* the voice is more melodious, giving an elegant and gently wavering feeling to the words sung. *Naka* is the voice for composure or a secure presence of mind. *Gin* expresses gay, flowery elegance; *ya*, strength; *kowari*, a martial spirit; and the fifth lower *shita kowari*, an eerie atmosphere. Each has a specific function, a specific mood, and each must suit the particular character: his sex, age, and role. In general, we can say that *haru* and *u* are more often used for women or youths, rather than men or the aged.

With the function or characteristics of these notations in mind, reading a Jōruri book can almost be as exciting an experience as listening to a performance. One can imagine the kind of voice each role will have and the changes of feeling and action of the characters, and the drama can come alive vividly in the mind of the reader. Thus, one can experience a Jōruri text in a different way from a novel or poem, and enjoy the peculiar flavor of Bunraku drama.

Transitions from kotoba to ji (or ji-iro)

As we have seen, *iro* is often used to smooth the transition from *ji* to *kotoba*. Going the opposite direction, occasionally *kakari* is employed (*kotoba - kakari - ji*), though the term is not usually printed in the published text. In "The Mountains Scene," lines 51, 261, 379, 414, 503, and 571 are examples. *Kakari* begins with the shamisen playing the note *urei* (F) or *gin* (F#). *Urei* is played in lines 51, 379, and 503, while *gin* is used in 261, 414, and 571. The former depicts the feeling of agony or pathos, and the latter, serenity or solemnity. After this one (or two) note(s), the *tayū* chants slowly and carefully but the shamisen does not play. Then the chanting moves into the *ji*, though, in general, one can consider *kakari* as a subcategory of *ji*. The form *kakaru* is distinguished from *kakari* by the fact that the *tayū* begins without the shamisen note. In either case, the pattern softens the transition from *kotoba* to *ji*.

It is not necessary to have this *kakari* or *kakaru* when changing from *kotoba* to *ji*; in fact, it is the norm to switch directly from *kotoba* to *ji*. *Kakari* is not found at moments of intense drama or when the action needs to advance quickly. It highlights a particular emotion (pathos or serenity) to give the line added significance. The short line leads the audience, through slow, careful singing, into the emotions of the character.

Many *kakari* that do not function as a transition or introduction are so termed because of the melodic pattern. For example, *fushi kakari* (line 279) and *sue kakari* (lines 317–318) use *kakari* because the pattern is similar to, or a variation of, the *fushi* cadence or *suete* melody.

Notation: Conventions and Uses

Notation Found in Printed Texts

Each of the various Jōruri texts—*maruhon* (also called *inbon* or *shōhon*), *yukahon* (performance texts), *keiko-bon* (practice texts)—contain both the words and the notation that indicate how the line is delivered. The conventions of inserting notation varies slightly according to the type of text. The notation in the *maruhon*, which contains the original complete play, reflects the initial performance, but there are certain conventions used that readers must be made aware of.

In contrast to the *maruhon*, the large hand-written *yukahon* contains only the particular scene from a *maruhon* performed by one chanter, and the printed *keiko-bon*, used by *tayū* and shamisen players when practicing, also contains only one scene in large print. These single-scene texts are likely to be closer to actual performance than *maruhon*; they may reflect the changes in performance that evolved after the initial run. Though there are minor differences the fundamental method of inserting notation is the same. I shall discuss "The Mountains Scene" *yukahon* or *keiko-bon*, but the principles apply to *maruhon* as well.

The notation found above the body of the text (in Japanese, along the right side of the words) is not like a Western score, which denotes exactly the pitches or length of notes; it is more like a musical tablature explaining performance techniques. It also denotes different aspects of performance such as:

1. Musical structure;
2. Voice technique, pitch, and rhythm;
3. Melodic patterns;
4. *Gomashō* marks, which signal voice changes;
5. Other.

Among these, only *gomashō* marks are not indicated by letters (*kana* or *kanji*).

The first category of notation contains the basic terms, *kotoba*, *ji*, and *ji-iro*, which indicate how the particular line is delivered. Let me explain through an analysis of lines 452–462.

kotoba
Musume judaisasu to yūtta wa . . .
sending you to court's a lie . . .

ji haru iru

Arigatai to.	*Fushiogamu te o totte.*
thank you.	Bends and takes her hand.

kami u

Nō judai sezu ni shinuruno o sorehodo ni

"Could I possibly not know that my daughter would be happier

	u	**iro**

ureshigaru. Musume no kokoro shiraide narōka

to die rather than go to court?

kotoba

Atto uketemo jigaishite . . .

While I knew you'd be ready to sacrifice . . ."

The voice begins in *kotoba*, shifts to *ji*, and continues through a series of pitch and voice changes: (*ji*) *haru, iru, kami, u* and *u*, all variations within *ji* (though *ji* is only written once at the beginning). The voice, then, alters to *iro* and finally returns to *kotoba*.

Texts are not always consistent in marking when the voice changes from *ji-iro* to *ji*, sometimes omitting the *ji*. In our text, however, we have noted such changes in the delivery styles as they occur in the performance. On the other hand, after a *fushi-ochi* cadence when the voice continues in the *ji* style, it is a practice to insert the term *ji* for the new passage. For example, in lines 15–16

fushi	**ji haru fushi**	**u**
Kokorobosoku mo awarenari. Koro wa		*yayoi no*
Pity the fate of this young man. The time is early spring,		

the notation *ji* is, in a way, redundant since the previous line also is in *ji*, but the *ji* signals the beginning of a new musical paragraph after the cadence. In "The Mountains Scene," sometimes *ji* is inserted when the action shifts from one side of the stage to the other, and a different chanter takes over the voice. In cases when the shifting is frequent (as in lines 135–136 or 268–274), *ji* is not inserted. Though *gidayū* has its rules of notation, it also has consistent exceptions, perhaps because of the oral training within the tradition.

Category II includes *haru, u, kami, naka, haru u, kami u, kowari, gin,* and other terms referring to pitch and voice technique, and *toru, kuru,* and *hiroi,* which refer to the shamisen rhythms. These are all varieties within the *ji* or *ji-iro* styles. *Kotoba noru* and *kotoba nori* also have shamisen accompaniment whose rhythm they follow.

Category III contains the fixed melodic patterns such as *okuri, sanjū, suete, nagaji, fushi,* and *haru fushi,* which all have further subdivisions. Though numerous varieties of cadence melodies (*fushi-ochi, okuri*) may be used, a text gives only the general term.

How far do the melodies (indicated by the notation) continue? As a general rule, until the next notation appears (excluding those for pitch). As for *fushi* (cadence), it continues over the following lines 192–193 (12 syllables):

fushi   haru
sora ni. Shirarenu hanagumori.
a flower clouded in darkness

and line 544 (12 syllables):

fushi   naka
Onajiku kawa ni ukaburebanna.
in the same way a branch is floated in the river

Two examples of *haru fushi* are:

haru fushi   u   naka
Koro wa   yayoi no hajimetsukata
The time is early spring,   line 16 (13 syllables)

haru fushi   naka
Mirai e   okuru.
send to the next world   line 606 (7 syllables)

The pattern *nagaji,* as its name implies, is long and continues over two full lines as in lines 44–45 (32 syllables) and 383–384 (36 syllables). The *suete* melody, however, does not continue for as long. It is one line or less than one line long in lines 2 (12 syllables), 83 (14 syllables), 147 (12 syllables), and 155 (12 syllables) or covers two short lines as in 328–329 (12 syllables) and 567–568 (13 syllables). All the above *suete* finish with a *naka*, cadencelike falling pitch. Lines 317–318 (13 syllables) and 432 (7 syllables) are variations (*sue kakari* and *sue naka*, respectively) without the same cadence ending. Other *fushi* notations such as *utai* and *tataki* function the same as *ji* melodies, and in many cases one must listen to a performance to determine exactly how far the melody continues.

Category IV: we have not included the *gomashō* marks contained in Jōruri texts. They indicate the rising and falling of pitch and variations in melodies. The term *goma* (sesame seeds) is used because the marks resemble sesame seeds scattered on a page. These marks originated in the early classical music *shōmyō* (Buddhist chanting), were used in *sōga* ("fast" songs) and Heike recitation, and were perfected in Nō drama texts as one kind of musical notation. In *gidayū*, however, they are not used in as much detail or to such an extent as in Nō, and they cannot be used to re-create completely a melody lost to the oral tradition. Since we have not included the *gomashō*, I shall forego a detailed explanation.[2]

Category V: aside from the above notations, there are several others found in Jōruri texts. Some, like *ni agari* and *san sagari*, refer to the tuning of the shamisen. The No. 1 string is the thickest of the three with the lowest pitch. The middle (No. 2) string is tuned to a perfect fourth higher, while the thinnest string (No. 3) is tuned one octave higher. This arrangement is termed *hon-chōshi* and is the standard tuning for *gidayū* shamisen. However, occasionally in the middle of a piece, one section will be played to a different tuning; these will be marked by *ni agari* (the second string is raised a whole tone) or *san sagari* (the third string is lowered a whole tone) (see example 6).

Example 6

Naosu indicates that the voice and shamisen return to the *hon-chōshi*, or it follows non-*gidayū* music and signals a return to *ji*. The *naosu* used in lines 614 and 621 indicate that the shamisen is returning to the *hon-chōshi* tuning from the *ni agari* tuning used during the song. *Naosu* tells the reader that the song (including the koto accompaniment) has concluded. Therefore, *naosu* indicates a return of the performance to "normal" *gidayū* music after a variation.

In pieces like "The Mountains Scene" or a *michiyuki*, which are chanted by more than one performer, the names of the original performers (Sometayū and Harutayū in "The Mountains Scene") are included in published or manuscript texts. We have not, however, included these names.

Musical Patterns Not Noted in Texts

It is conventional not to note in published texts certain specific melodic patterns. This is the third peculiar characteristic of *gidayū* notation. However, since it is difficult, if not impossible, to discover these "secret" patterns, we have noted them in appendix A and put a single line under the passage. The listener, then, can follow the melody with our text.

The following is a list of some patterns not notated: *harima, ō-otoshi, sonae, hinagata-bushi, gyōgi, dangiri, sawari, yamato-ji, kawachi-ji, nishiki.*

A few may or may not be inserted; *kakari* is one example. Since *kakari* appears in song (*fushi*) sections referring to a specific melody, it is not noted when it is used as a transition from *kotoba* to *ji*, as discussed earlier. Another rule is that patterns developed or inserted after initial performances and publication of the Jōruri text are not notated: examples are line 13, *mai*; line 18, *ai no yama*; line 104, *fushi tataki*; and line 539, *bun'ya*.

Many of the names for these hidden or "secret" patterns are no longer even known by performers today. One work from the first half of the 19th century, *Jōruri hottan* (Introduction to Jōruri, 1825), based mainly on the Edo Takemoto Miyatodayū line, lists a great range of terms with examples from plays.[3] Some examples from "The Mountains Scene" noted in this work are: *orinobashi* (6), *kuruma bushi* (110), *kasumi* (129), *narabi* (128, 540), *haneru* (199), *kasane bushi* (203), *yanagi* (243, 282), *kioi* (644), *chikuzen* (158), *sometayū* (187, 393–394), *kudoki* (426, 487, 531), *shirimochi* (144, 693–694). Since *yanagi* is better known as *hinagata-bushi*, and *kioi*, as *gyōgi*, and since Takemoto Sumitayū said that he had heard of *narabi*, it appears that some of these terms still survive among certain experienced performers in the Bunraku troupe.

As is evident from the above discussion, the method of notating a Jōruri text follows complicated rules and conventions. Since these notations delineate the structure of the text, it is necessary to have a familiarity with them when reading a play. Though the insertion of the notation may "muddy" the presentation, the reader is better able to follow and enjoy the intricacies of the text as performance.[4]

(translated by C. Andrew Gerstle)

Chapter Four   Notes

1   Japanese terms are described in more detail in the glossary.
2   See Hirano Kenji, "Gidayū-bushi keiko tebikisho to gomashō," *Dōkyō daigaku kyōshogaku kenkyū 5* (1971), pp. 67–84 for more information on *gomashō*.
3   *Jōruri hottan* in *NSBSS* (1975), vol. 7.
4   An unusual aspect of our text in the appendix is that we have notated it exactly as in the performance that appears on our tapes from the King Record *Imoseyama onna teikin—yama no dan* (1976). Since Jōruri texts are never matched to an actual performance, the text here is unique and consequently an invaluable source for research into *gidayū* music. We wish to acknowledge the cooperation of Takemoto Sumitayū VII in its preparation. The performers on the tapes are: Mt. Se—Takemoto Oritayū (Koganosuke), Takemoto Tsudayū (Daihanji), Tsuruzawa Kanji (shamisen); Mt. Imo—Takemoto Nambudayū (Hinadori and maids), Takemoto Tsunatayū (Sadaka), Takezawa Yashichi (shamisen), Takezawa Danroku (koto).

Chapter Five   A Musical Analysis of "The Mountains Scene"

William P. Malm

Through a study of the previous chapters by Gerstle and Inobe, the reader can acquire a good overview of the structure of a *gidayū*-accompanied play and an introduction to the myriad technical terms that are found in *gidayū* nomenclature. In review, let us recall that both scholars emphasized the importance of musical conventions linked together in a mosaic manner and in the cyclicity of the overall form of a scene or an entire play. The function of this chapter is to enrich our awareness of the artistry of this play and of the *gidayū* tradition in general by a study of specific music examples from "The Mountains Scene."

Theoretical Tone Systems

Our first musical task is to understand the *gidayū* tone system (see p. 55) in the context of general Japanese music theory. The traditional versions of the *yō* and *in* scales are shown in example 1. In both one sees a five-tone (pentatonic) core plus exchange tones. However, to appreciate tonal functions in *gidayū* it is more effective to think in terms of pitch centers, often a fourth or a fifth apart, and what can be called their upper and lower leading tones. The standard movements around the pitches E and B are shown in example 1. The note E surrounded by D and F or F sharp and the pitch B surrounded by A and C or C sharp are our basic sonic building blocks.[1]

The Music/Drama Tradition

Our next need is to remember that this is a narrative tradition. The story is the *raison d'être* of the music. Gerstle has emphasized this in addition to the interrelation of the grammar of the text and the musical structure. One result of this story/text orientation is that both the

Example 1

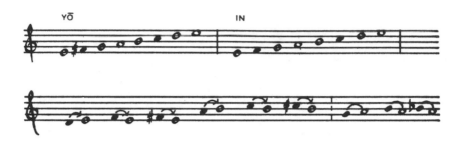

singers and the shamisen players may alter the pitches used in a given passage to enhance their personal interpretation. This is an important point to make early in our presentation because any *gidayū* example heard or notated has to be considered as *one* version of the moment, not *the* version.

Let us now turn to this one performance of "The Mountains Scene." With the translation we are able to follow the story easily and see those symbols concerning performance that appeared in the original text (cf. appendix A). Inobe reveals many of the historical and musical meanings of these notations in the original texts as well as their interpretations in contemporary performances. He enhances his explanation with references to specific locations where such conventions appear in this scene. To help the reader follow our musical discussion in the context of the entire *dan*, the excerpts are discussed in the order of their appearance, and the numbers and letters of Gerstle's literary divisions (see appendix A) will be used as guideposts. Line numbers and technical *gidayū* musical terms will also be derived from his translation.

The function of this study is to analyze musically excerpts from "The Mountains Scene" in order to demonstrate specific ways in which some of the general principles described in this book are applied in actual performance. Most of the examples come from the first half of the drama in order to give them a sense of continuity, but in the spirit of Inobe's study, reference may be made to similar passages found later in the play. Musical comments on the entire *dan* are found in appendix B so one can locate explanations of particular musical activities as one listens to the tape or studies the text. The analyses are written by someone who is familiar with the idiom but who listens to the music with a Western ear. The Gerstle and Inobe chapters may be referred to, but the analytic interpretations are mine. The contents of this chapter plus that of the appendix B combine, in musical terms, both the microcosm and macrocosm of one of the world's best musical narratives.

Applied Tone Systems

The opening *makura* of the *dan* is discussed in chapter three (see p. 33) and appendix B. Our first task here is to illustrate the tonal system that has been described in chapter four (see pp. 54–56). Example 2 is an outline transcription of the opening two lines of the play. The B and E pitch center tones dominate.[2] With the addition of the F sharp fifth of B and the lower leading tones A and D, a basic pentatonic vocabulary (E, F sharp, A, B, D) has been established.

The only music notations in the original text of the first two lines are *sanjū kami, ji u gin, haru suete*, and *naka*. The first term leads us upward (*kami*) out of the *sanjū*, and the second follows a conventional movement from E to A to B. The third is the strongest moment (*suete*) in the unit with its emphasis on higher pitches and its intense vocal style. The last unit (*naka*) leads the music downward to a cadence (cf. chapter four, pp. 47–48). In sum, the first lines are a microcosm of the tone system and the conventional patterns that are characteristic of the whole *gidayū* tradition.

Lines 7 and 8 (in example 3) add the half-step upper leading tones (F and C) to our tonal vocabulary. *Gidayū* notation marks the last words with the term *honbushi*, thus indicating a full cadence ending of a major unit. After some four minutes of such mood and tone setting, we are ready for the story to begin.

As seen in the last line of example 3, the opening of the action of "The Mountains Scene" (lines 9–23) is performed with further emphasis on the upper and lower leading tones or fifths common to *gidayū* music. Note that C sharp appears, thus completing the basic sonic vocabulary of the piece. Line 9 begins with clear repetitions of the pitch center E. The shamisen then produces sonic tension by playing an A that waits for resolution as the lower leading tone of B, while the singer uses the upper leading tone and fifth. This simple example demonstrates the fundamental means of melodic tension in

Example 2

Example 3

(continued on next page)

(Example 3 continued)

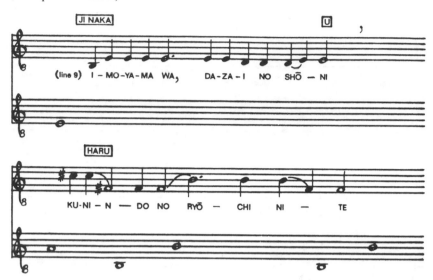

gidayū and many other Japanese musics: the pausing on a pitch above or below a pitch center. Such a convention is not uniquely Japanese, but its function in Japanese music is especially important because such music is almost totally linear, that is, it has no vertical harmonic sounds or a bass line to drive it forward. Rhythm is not emphasized in this particular example, though the long vowels and the divisions between five- and seven-syllable units are rendered very carefully. In such a context, the small sonic messages of pitch centers and their leading tones are very powerful.

Text Setting

An example of deliberate dramatization of text is heard in line 10. The *tayū* declaims the word *shimoyakata* to emphasize the importance of another residence across the river. He also uses much time and intensity in pronouncing the name Daihanji Kiyozumi (line 11) and the mountain confinement (*yamazumai*) of Koganosuke. Both are marked in the original text with the term *naka*, which calls for a downward motion of the melody (as it did in example 2; cf. chapter four, pp. 47–48). Inobe has pointed out (p. 31) that the interpretation of this line also reflects the *nishi-fū* style necessary for material from the Mt. Se side of the drama.

The shamisen responses to the text can be seen in example 4, an outline of the music for lines 13–16. As the text makes references to young birds' cries and *sūtra* chanting, the shamisen "flies" an octave higher than the voice and makes pizzicato "chirping" sounds. In an actual play production one may also hear an off-stage bird call when the warbler is mentioned. Other literal shamisen word paintings are obvious when, for example, the window is flung open (line 80), the stream current has waves (line 92), a rock falls into the water (line 102), or a head is cut off (line 561). However, most of the shamisen reactions to the text are more subtle. The pitiful mood of line 15 is supported by a drooping set of slides from B through A to the half-step upper leading tone F that leads to E. Note the fresh sound of F sharp that appears just before the final cadence. Its function may be to prepare us for a move across the river to a different scene and narrator. An emphasis on F sharp is certainly evident in line 16 when such a move occurs.

Similar tonal preparations and contrast occur often in the play when the drama moves across the river and the *tayū* is changed (cf. line 82). They are examples of the so-called *nishi* and *higashi* styles of performance (see pp. 28–33). It was noted earlier in the book that, musically, these styles are sometimes characterized as being the difference between a *higashi-fū* emphasis of whole-step and *nishi-fū* preference for half-step upper leading tones. In our transcriptions this would be a contrast between an emphasis on F and C up to the middle of line 15 and on F sharp and C sharp in line 16. This *dan* is ideally suited for such musical contrasts, not only because it uses two *tayū* (or two sets in the recording) but also because one side of the stage is entirely feminine and the other masculine. The settings of lines 15–16 show both the transition and the contrast of this musical convention.

Our first short excerpts have been rich in data toward an understanding of how *gidayū* musicians respond to text and to the need for tension and release in time. We turn now to the large challenges of form.

Music Styles and Form

Let us first recall that the art of *gidayū* music is found in part in its constant flow between styles. The three basic styles were noted by Inobe as being speech (literally "words," *kotoba*), parlando (*iro*), and lyrical (*ji*). The flow in, out, and between such styles is fundamental to the art

Example 4

(continued on next page)

(Example 4 continued)

(continued on next page)

(Example 4 continued)

of *gidayū*. Inobe has stated that the general order of textures of the music is as follows: A—*ji* or *ji iro*; B—*kotoba* to *ji/ji iro*; C—*fushi-otoshi*. In general Western terms this would be: A—lyric or parlando; B—speech to lyric/parlando; C—full cadence. To see how these styles operate let us turn to the first major lyrical moment of the play, lines 40–57. The analysis and transcription will best be followed by using them in conjunction with the cassette.

The preparatory lines are spoken with a quick tempo appropriate to the class and personality of the maid. The more romantic lines (31 and 38) are supported by a parlando style, but the peasant tempo and pentatonic tendency remain. Line 39 is performed as speech, though it is marked as an *iro* because it provides a proper contrast before the parlando opening of Hinadori's lament.

If we use only the guide terms in the text of this section as guides and abstract them to the general English version of Inobe's model given above, the formal conventions of this passage are clear.

Line   40   41   42   43
Term *ji haru u:u ,naka: u, u: u, u:*
Form [A] parlando/lyric

Line 44   45   46
Term *nagaji haru,u : u,kami:iro:*
Form lyric

Line 47–50   51
Term *kotoba:*   *kakari:*
Form [B] speech   parlando

Line 52   53   54   55 56
Term *ji haru,u,naka: u,u:kami: u: u,naka:*
Form lyric

Line 57
Term *haru fushi, naka haru*
Form [C] cadence

At first one is struck by the similarity in the sequence of terms for lines 40–41 with 52. One also can make comparisons between the terms on lines 44–46 and 52–56. The latter two contain the musical high points (*kami*) in the music. The second has a longer build-up in a manner well known to anyone familiar with Western opera aria patterns, that is, a lyrical climax is hinted at part way into an aria, but it actually occurs shortly before the final cadence. The downward cadential motion of *naka* patterns mark off the first musical phrase (41), the phrase before the climax (52) and the moment before the final cadence (56). The transitions into (46) and out of (51) speech are marked with traditional performance guides. The opening of each phrase calls for an emotionally strong voice (*haru*), while a major part of the piece is less taut (*u*) so that contrast can be made. The very first phrase is interpreted less dramatically (40, the *u* of *ji haru u*), while the preparation for the first high moment gives the performer an option for a longer vocal solo (44, the *naga* of *nagaji haru*).

Let us remember that all these terms are notated basically to help the singer perform the piece in the manner desired by the author or by an earlier interpreter, and thus they might better be called guide words. As seen in the model given above and discussed in abstraction, the guide words also help one see the form of *gidayū*. However, they are not themes or stereotyped patterns in the Western sense. Recall also (chapter four, example 3, p. 55) that many of the guide words seen here may imply pitches as much as style or pattern. Thus, we must go one step further and combine a transcription of lines 40–57 in example 5 with the above model (and ideally with a listening to the cassette). In this way we may learn to appreciate the relation of *gidayū* notation and form to the actual performance. Let us look at each type of guide word separately.

Ji Haru—*40, 44, 52*

Tonally all three melodic lines (*ji*) concentrate in the same areas (E-B). The pathos of line 40 is enhanced by the shamisen starting on the upper leading tone of B (C), a pitch sometimes designated as *haru u*. The shamisen plays B for line 44 as the singer's first major solo phrase begins. The singer includes personal style in his handling of the word love (*koi*, cf. with line 42 or later line 101). Note that the solo is enhanced with a new sound, C sharp, a pitch sometimes called *u*. The *ji haru* of line 52 is actually prepared for by the transitional *kakari* phrase (51), which opens with the pathos of an F natural (upper leading tone to E) before cadencing on B. The line drives down to a low E, perhaps to enhance the drama of the movement back up toward the highest pitch in line 54. The *haru fushi* of the final cadence conforms with the tradition of bringing some shamisen melodic unit into the ending. We next survey the terms most frequently appearing in the lyrical sections.

Example 5

(continued on next page)

(Example 5 continued)

(continued on next page)

(Example 5 continued)

(continued on next page)

(Example 5 continued)

(continued on next page)

(Example 5 continued)

U–41, 42, 43, 44, 45, 52, 53, 55, 56

The term *u* sometimes implies that a less tense voice quality is used and that the text moves more quickly. It is also applied to various pitches (see chapter four, example 3, p. 55), particularly A and C sharp. A survey of all the *u* in this section shows that the pitch areas vary greatly, but, in general, the texture is denser and faster in the *u* sections. The *u* of line 55 is higher than the rest, as it is coming out of the climax in line 54. One could argue that it refers to the high pitch A (*kami u*), but the quicker style of the interpretation seems the more logical explanation of what it implies for the performance of this phrase.

Naka–41, 52, 56, 57

The descending contour of *naka* patterns is evident in all four cases, three of them (lines 41, 56, and 57) taking the phrase to the low pitch *naka*. To understand the middle range of the cadence for line 52 one must follow the contour of the entire period from lines 52–56. It is beautifully designed to create the climax and end of a lyric section.

Kami–45, 54

The climaxes have in common the entrance of the highest pitch in the example and their choice of dramatic words for the pitch (high B). The first (45) is on the word "you" (*anata*), while the second (54) deals with the hindering of the lover's meeting (*isso hedatete koiwabiru*). The tonal contour of the exit from both climaxes is likewise similar. However, note how much more dramatic is the preparation for the leap in line 54 with its disjunct vocal line and the emphasis on F natural rather than F sharp (cf. line 45). Note also the repeated B in the shamisen in 54. This is a conventional preparation for most "big" moments in *gidayū* lyric sections.

There is still more that can be learned from a study of this first romantic moment, but its function here is to provide one example of certain basic principles that can be found throughout this piece and in most of the *gidayū* tradition. While Inobe (p. 53) has limited the term *kudoki* to only two moments in the play, the musical conventions noted here are characteristic of *kudoki* as well. We have seen how the Gerstle and Inobe formal schemes appear in performance, and we also see how the varied meanings of *gidayū* technical terms can still be used as guides toward reading or performing a composition.

Fluid Style Changes

Lines 57–61 have been added to example 5 to illustrate both the fluidity of movement from one dramatic/musical section to another and the importance of interpretation in the understanding of *gidayū* dramas. A full low cadence of the *naka* has occurred on "*tomo ni.*" However, there is still one word left in the text, "maid" (*koshimotodomo*), and it is marked *haru*. The *tayū* declaims this word loudly in the style of a maid in preparation for the maid's line that follows. The shamisen jumps to a B to give a sense of modulation or half cadence. This also may be a response to the guide term *iro* that appears for line 58 (cf. line 60). Other interpretations of the vocal and instrumental guide terms are possible, but the ones chosen best push the listener toward a new unit by changes in style.

Line 58 continues in the peasant style of speech adumbrated by the last word of the previous line. However, line 59 is marked with the terms *haru u u naka*, so the speech style is quickly replaced with an intense "surely strange" (*hon ni hyonna*) and fast-paced (*u*) squabbling. All this is done in the "folk" (*inaka*) pentatonic scale because the speaker is lower class. The line contours down (*naka*), ending on the pitch center B. The *tayū* renders the word *goryōbun* ("both parents") intensely (*haru*) by beginning on the lower leading tone (A), a seventh above that B, and ending on the upper leading tone (C sharp). This is followed by speech declamation for the last words of the line, accompanied by a conventional shamisen *iro* (*iro-dome*) pattern (cf. chapter four, example 1, p. 42). Other hints of *iro* patterns in the play create a smoother transition to words by ending the shamisen conventional pattern on an unresolved tone (listen to line 583 or 601).

Our study of this one transfer point has shown us much about the manner in which such basic conventions as *haru*, *naka*, and *iro* can be interpreted, and we have seen *fushi* (line 57) used to imply a shamisen melody. The dialogue (*kotoba*) that follows has its own interpretive challenges. These are best understood by listening to the cassettes while reading the text. The high strung, rapid talk of the maids not only supports the characters but also increases the density of the sound. Example 6 shows the very busy music that accompanies the end of the action on the feminine side of the river. It may also serve as a contrast to the very slow and thinner sounds heard as we enter Koganosuke's retreat. The smoothness of this transition across the river and to new musicians can be seen by comparing the final passage of line 81 with the start of line 82. The pitches are the same except for a one octave displacement of the F sharp and slide to A.

Listening to the performance of the opening of line 85, one hears a gravity Inobe noted (p. 51) as characteristic of passages done in the *harima* style. Example 6 cannot render this impressive style in notation. However, it does illustrate another manner of conveying the move across the river. For a musician, the striking aspect of the setting of the word "face" (*kao*) is the use of the pitch B flat for the first time in the piece. In other shamisen genres, the use of B flat and its implied modulation to an "exotic" A centered *in* scale usually occurs when something unusual is mentioned in the text.[3] In line 85, the topic is a face full of concern. The sudden brief modulation to A after a long period of E and B centered music may also be used to alert us to the change that will occur in the next line. The *tayū* from the "feminine" side of the stage completes the thought with a totally new tonality in the *higashi* style. Note as well that the vocal and shamisen lines need not be the same. A review of the previous examples will reveal many cases where they differ greatly (cf. line 54, example 5).

The excerpts discussed so far have illustrated the power and creative conventionality of the musical structure of *gidayū*. It was an analogous set of conventionalities that made it possible for Western composers such as Bach, Handel, Haydn, and Mozart to create a stream of "original" compositions. In Japan, the musical idiom is radically different, but the principle is the same. With the confidence that listeners are at least subliminally aware of the conventional signals, composers, East or West, are able to direct their energies to fresh communications rather than totally new idioms. However, the traditional roles of the performer/interpreter in *gidayū* and Western vocal music is radically different. In *gidayū* both the original performer/composer and the present day *tayū* are interpreting the text, not the music. Only a few terms guide a *tayū* to the actual sounds he is going to produce. Thus, the *tayū* has a more flexible and challenging view of interpretation than, say, a Western opera singer. The Western singer certainly responds to the meaning of a libretto, but the sonic guide for such responses is basically pitch notation. Indeed, the most frequent Western measure of interpretation is its supposed "authenticity," its correct rendering of notated music, not guide terms. Both *gidayū* and Western vocal music produce many fine moments. The Western singer interprets in terms of tone, dynamics, and rhythm. To this *tayū* adds the

Example 6

(continued on next page)

(Example 6 continued)

(continued on next page)

(Example 6 continued)

dimension of pitch. Since we have already seen tone, dynamics, and pitch in operation in *gidayū*, let us turn to the matter of rhythm.

Time and Rhythm

All our musical transcriptions have been devoid of time signatures or bar lines because such Western restrictions are contrary to the *gidayū* approach to time. In the transcriptions of this study I have placed the shamisen pitches at a different physical position than that of a vocal pitch in an attempt to show the deliberate displacement of the parts. This so-called neutrality (*fusoku furi*) between vocal lines and their accompaniment is characteristic of shamisen music and might be called a form of heterophony.[4] The constant use of rubato, or changes in tempo, further frustrates efforts to render this music in Western notation. Perhaps the deeper meaning of the rhythmic orientation of *gidayū* text is found in the speech (*kotoba*) sections. Listen, for example, to the virtuoso rhythmic renditions of lines 176–182 or the deliberate pacing of every spoken monologue (see figure 2 below). Unaccompanied sections are filled with timing and spaces (*ma*).[5] Of course there are metric moments, particularly when there is dance or other action on stage. However, the heavy word orientation of *gidayū* has created a special concern in the use of rhythm and time: the relation of the shamisen accompaniment to the poetry structure.

Accompanied words (*kotoba-nori*) often use the shamisen as a text unit marker in a manner that reminds one of the drum accompaniments of Nō drama text.[6] Example 7 illustrates this technique, used in this performance when Hinadori decides to break the ban and ford the river, and when Koganosuke reacts.

Example 7

Lines 173–174

```
1  23    4   56  7, 1 2 3 4  5     1 2   3  4 5 6 7,   1 2 3 4    5
Watashi wa soko e yukimasu to. / Sude ni tobikomu  kawagishi ni.
      B        B       C#    E D        E    D          E        D
(1 2 3   1   2 3   1 2 31 2  3 [4] 1 2   3  1 2 3 1    2 3 1 2    3)
```

Lines 175–176

```
12 3  45 6  7, 1 2 3 4   5 6  7 8      12 34  5 6 7     8
Awate odoroki todomuru  koshimoto.    Iyaiya hanasha  to
   E      D     E E                 E F    F F   A    A     B
12 3  12 3   1 2 3  1 2 3    4  5  6 7    12 12[1]2 1 2   1 2
```

Lines 173–176 are shown with the syllable count (above) and the accompaniment (below). Note that the first two lines fall into the conventional Japanese poetic count of seven plus five. Note in addition that the shamisen tends to mark off every third syllable. In lines 175 and 176 the length is different, so the shamisen makes the necessary adjustment, 175 still being marked off in basically 3 beat units. Line 176 differs because the exclamation "*iya*" calls for a second beat accent. Once a listener is aware of this system, the "off-beat" text punctuations of the shamisen become very evident in those passages in which the words literally ride (*nori*) the shamisen accompaniment. In this context look at and listen to line 53 or example 5 again. Such a literally driving force in the music occurs more often as the drama progresses. For example, listen to Daihanji's reply to Sadaka after the death of Hinadori (lines 623–644).

Overall Structure—Timing and Density

We have discussed the basic *gidayū* musical conventions in action in the first half of the play. With that as a background one can observe their use throughout the drama as well as in other plays. Our next task is to view the music in the context of the entire *dan*. With the Gerstle plot outline as a base (pp. 20–23), table 1 provides us with the data for this study. Recall that Gerstle separated units of the scene on the basis of full cadences (*fushi*) and breaks in the text or plot. I have further divided some sections for musical reasons. The basic person or action of each unit is listed to help one recall where one is in the play. The reader is already aware of the constant change of styles in *gidayū* and thus will appreciate that the basic style column of table 1 is highly abstracted. We discussed earlier some of the many Japanese terms that may appear to represent a musical style. For the sake of comparison I have limited the vocabulary to one of four English terms: l (lyric), p (parlando), s (speech), and rs (rhythmic speech). The choice of terms is primarily musical rather than a strict application of Japanese terms as they may appear in the original text. Our earlier analyses have concentrated on the lyrical and parlando sections. They were found to be most flexible in tempo changes. Speech is naturally varied in speed. However, to show the overall growth of drama in the *dan*, the general metronome tempo of major speech or lyric sections has been shown in parentheses. The line numbers are listed for text orientation. The length of lines is quite varied. Thus, the mere number of lines in a unit is not meaningful by itself. However, there is still much to be learned if we look at the number of lines in each unit, the timing of each, and the simplified time totals of dramatic units. The time length of each section varies with performers. The approximations listed here come from the King recording. A tabulation of the length of each unit in minutes and seconds would of course not reflect all performance practice, particularly if different *tayū* are involved. Still, the ratio between events will be the same. The function of table 1 is to provide comparative data that will enable us to envision the overall musical design of "The Mountains Scene."

TABLE 1

A Musical Outline of "The Mountains Scene"

Section	Persons	basic styles & tempo	lines	number of lines	length	overall time (rounded)
		PART I				
1-2	Prelude, Koga	1(88)	1-15	**15**	4'46"	5
3a	maids	1(106)	16-24	9	2'06"	
3b		s(184)	25-39	15	58"	
	Hinadori	1,s(84),1	40-57	18	4'40"	
3c	maid	s(184),1	58-81	24	3'15"	
	Koga	p(88)	82-86	5	1'35"	
	Hinadori/maid	p(92,144)	87-97	11	1'38"	
3d	Hinadori (rock)	p,1(126)	98-104	7	1'25"	
3e		1(96)	105-110	6	1'30"	
subtotal				**95**		17
4a	Koganosuke	s(88)	111-117	7	1'	
		p,1(69)	118-122	5	1'40"	
	maid, Hina	s(106),p,1(92)	123-132	10	2'10"	
	Duet	p,1(72)	133-136	4	1'50"	
4b	Hina, Koga	s,p,l(76)	137-147	11	2'35"	
4c	Koga	p,s(100)	148-157	10	1'25"	
		p,s,1	158-165	18	2'15"	
4d	Hina	s(104),p,rs(132)	166-176	11	1'10"	
	Koga	s(152),1	177-185	20	1'20"	
5	transition	p,1(100)	186-193	8	1'55"	
subtotal				**83**		17

(continued on next page)

TABLE 1 *(continued)*

Section	Persons	basic styles & tempo	lines	number of lines	length	overall time (rounded)
		PART II				
6	parents	p(69)	194-204	**11**	2'35"	3
7	Daihanji	s(84),p	205-214	10	3'	
8a	Sada, Dai	S(92,84)	215-243	29	3'15"	
8b	parents (duet)	S(92,88),p	244-274	31	5'50"	
subtotal				**70**		12
9a	Sada, Hina	p	275-279	5	2'	
9b	Hina	s(84),p	280-282	3	30"	
10a	Sadaka, maid	s(84),p	283-297	15	3'45"	
10b	Sadaka, Hina, maid	s(96),p	298-318	21	1'40"	
10c	Sadaka, Hina	s(96-100),p	319-329	11	1'30"	
10d	Sadaka	s(108),p	330-341	12	50"	
subtotal				**67**		10
11	Sada/Hina	p,s(106)	342-369	28	2'45"	
		1,s(72),p	370-386	17	3'	
subtotal				**45**		6
12a	Koga	p,s(100),p	387-394	8	1'10"	
12b	Daihanji	s(129),p	395-410	16	1'55"	
12c	Dai/Koga	s(120),p,1,rs(136)	411-432	22	3'35"	
subtotal				**46**		7
13a	Sada	s(104),p	433-439	7	35"	
13b	Hina	rs(88),p(112)	440-451	12	1'10"	
	Sada/Hina	s(144),p,s	452-458	7	30"	
	Sada	1,s(138),p,s,1	459-487	29	2'15"	
subtotal				**55**		5
14	Dai	rs(160)	488-498	11	55"	
	Koga	s(148),1,s,p	499-514	16	1'13"	
	Dai	p,s(92),1	515-526	12	1'01"	
subtotal				**39**		3

(continued on next page)

TABLE 1 *(continued)*

Section	Persons	basic styles & tempo	lines	number of lines	length	overall time (rounded)
		PART II *(continued)*				
15a	Hina/Sada	s(96),1,rs(160)	527-544	18	2′30″	
15b	Koga	s(132)	545-549	5	2′40″	
	Hina's death	p,rs(144),1	550-568	19		
subtotal				**42**		5
16	Sada	p,1(60),s(104)	569-587	19	3′51″	
	Dai	s(96)	588-595	8	40″	
	Sada	p,s(112),p	596-605	10	31″	
subtotal				**37**		5
17	fushigoto	1(52)	606-615	**10**	4′53″	5
18	head gift	1(58/104)	616-622	**7**	2′05″	2
19a	Daihanji	rs(120),s(108),p	623-644	22	2′07″	
19b	Sadaka	rs(104),s,rs,1	645-667	23	3′40″	
subtotal				**45**		6
20	Finale	rs(116),1,rs(106),1	668-695	**28**	4′25″	4
Total				**695**		**112**

It takes almost two hours to perform the entire *dan*. The graph of figure 1 abstracts the data of table 1 in terms of time (overall time rounded to the nearest minute) and the number of lines of text in each unit. Note that the introduction of the plot and of the two lovers consumes the greatest number of lines and time (22 minutes). The dialogue between the lovers completes the first major section of the play in the next longest unit (17 minutes). Thus, 25 percent of the units (1–5) and 28 percent of the lines (193 of 695) have consumed some 35 percent of the time (39 minutes of a 112 total).

The increasing intensity of the drama and the density of its sounds emerge before your eyes as you follow the graph into part II. The units get ever shorter in time though not necessarily in the number of lines.

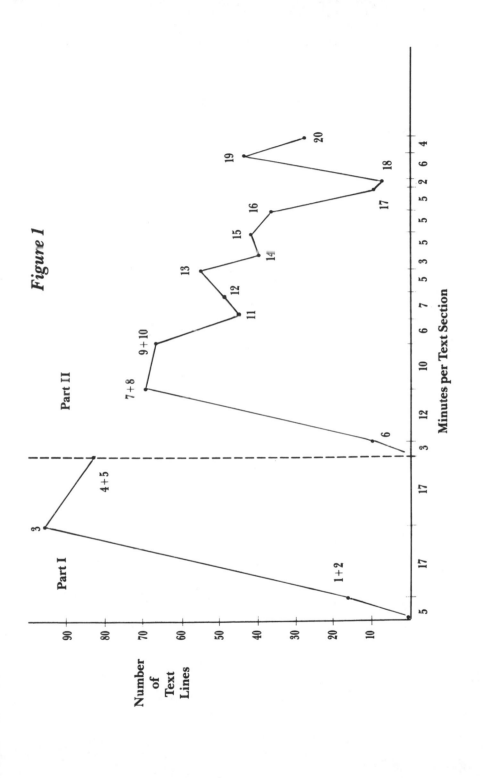

Figure 1

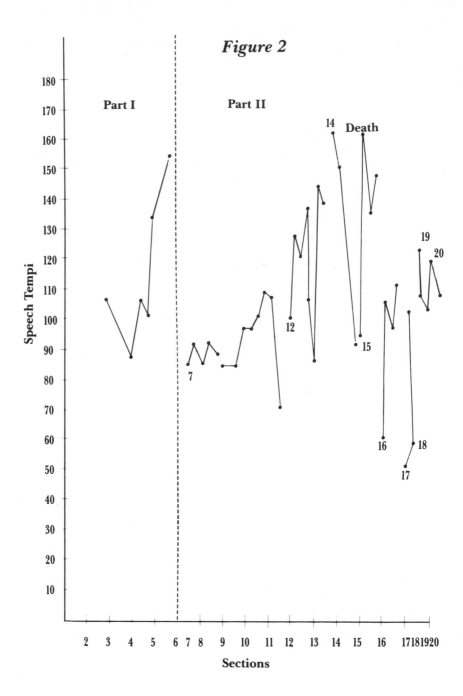

Figure 2

Section 12 is impressive in its density as Daihanji expounds the deeper problems from the overall plot of the play, while Hinadori's decision to die (unit 13) is equally dense. Lines and units rapidly change as the *dan* moves toward its tragic end. The whole second part seems to be following some giant form of a traditional dramatic or musical convention. It takes some fifty-one minutes to build to the suicides and twenty-two minutes afterward to console the parents and the audience and to tie up the scene. That is a classical music/theater formula: two-thirds time to the climax and one-third to the close. Readers with a sense of theater and a keen eye for numbers will be able to build substructures on the same model, such as the parents' lament from unit 16 to unit 20 with its climax at unit 19. However, these efforts tend to absorb the art of *gidayū* into general theatrical patterns. The unique quality in *gidayū* is its particular balance of words, parlando music, and music.

Figure 2 removes us for the moment from the more obvious musical characteristics of *gidayū*. The tempi of speech sections longer than two lines for the entire play have been graphed in metronome marks and section numbers. The maids high strung tempi have been left out of the graph lines as they are part of character acting rather than part of the long-range tempi design. Note how the first part builds to a climax in terms of speech alone. If we translate this abstraction in relation to table 1, we discover that the spoken lines of given characters tend to be delivered at "appropriate" speeds until intense moments. A clever eye looking at figure 2 can almost guess whether the speaker is the hero or heroine by the place of the dot on the graph without reference to the data in table 1. Note the general build up toward the moment of death (section 16). The time drop thereafter is powerful. However, to be consistent with the overall theories of conventions in this narrative tradition, note the manner in which renditions of the text alternate between slow (17) and fast (19) at the finale.

This preliminary analysis is of only one scene from one brilliant music/drama composition that in turn is part of a repertoire of hundreds of plays. Still, by understanding the basic conventions and formal designs of *gidayū* as they operate in this single musical microcosm, we will be able to travel further through the macrocosmic world of the Japanese puppet theater and its music.

Chapter Five   Notes

1   If A becomes the pitch center, G, B, and B flat are the leading tones (see example 1).

2   In our examples the convention of showing the lowest pitch on the shamisen as B is followed regardless of the tuning of an actual performance. In the recording from which the examples are transcribed, the shamisen tuning is heard as starting on G sharp or A depending on the quality of the listening machine.

3   A study of such conventions in *nagauta* is found in the author's "The Four Seasons of the Old Mountain Women," *Journal of the American Musicological Society*, 31.1 (1978): 102–9.

4   See further the author's *Six Hidden Views of Japanese Music* (Berkeley: University of California Press, 1986), Interlude, p. 43.

5   Compare Seigow Matsuoka, ed., *Ma Space and Time in Japan* (New York: Cooper-Hewitt Museum, 1981).

6   See Monica Beth and Karen Brazel, *Nō as Performance*, East Asia Program Papers 16 (Ithaca, NY: China-Japan Program, Cornell University, 1978).

Chapter Six   The History of Performance

C. Andrew Gerstle

"The Mountains Scene" was chosen for this study because it was written at the end of the creative period and has been performed regularly to the present day. One supposes, in a tradition where rote learning from the master is the rule, that today's performance should be close to the staging in 1771. Yet, can we trace the performance tradition when our oldest sound recordings of this scene are post-1950? The only early materials we have are texts—the original *maruhon* text published at the time of first performance, various practice texts from around 1800 to the 1920s, and chanters' and shamisen players' handwritten or marked up texts—and an unwritten rule guards them from reflecting changes: chanters do not alter the notation set out in the first edition, even when performance changes. The written text is considered sacred.

The performance, on the other hand, is flexible and has changed. That tradition and its changes are preserved orally. For example, Sadaka's lines, 577–578, are listed as *kotoba* in Yūda's book (from Takemoto Tsunatayū's hand-written text, which is the same as the original *maruhon*), meaning that they are spoken not sung, and without shamisen accompaniment.[1] Tsunatayū's performance on record, however, is certainly not *kotoba* and has a considerably complex musical accompaniment.[2] The chanter sees no paradox in this, and no one questions it because it is traditional to copy texts from one's teacher or from published *maruhon*, and because that text does not necessarily reflect the performance. Appendix A reflects a new Japanese text in which the notation does match today's performance as on the cassette of Tsunatayū and Tsudayū, and the notes discuss its variation from the original *maruhon* and other texts.

A more accurate source of past performances is the notation used by shamisen players and written on published texts or their own manuscripts. As far as I know, no one (except professional musicians) has systematically studied these texts, some of which have become available publicly in the last decade or so, to trace the development of performance from the late 18th century. In some cases, texts by different performers for the same play exist from the late 1700s to the present day. Unfortunately, texts with shamisen notation for "The Mountains Scene" are not as abundant. Nevertheless, there is one early text, probably dating around 1800, as well as another dated 1863 and others from the late 19th and early 20th centuries. The following is a list of important texts with shamisen notation: *Mameushi*, around 1800 (in Matazō notation)[3]; *Nagakodayū* (Yadayū V) (1837–1906), dated 1853[4]; *Nagatodayū* (1800–1864), dated 1863[5]; *Yadayū V* (1837–1906)[6]; *Kichibei V* (1841–1911)[7]; *Seiroku III* (1868–1922)[8]; *Shinzaemon II* (1867–1943)[9]; *Seihachi II* (1879–1970), dated 1931.[10]

The *Mameushi* text is of particular interest because it is not in the Seishichi style of notation but the earlier Matazō system.[11] This is significant because Tsuruzawa Matazō was, with Bunzō, responsible for "The Mountains Scene" music. Matazō played with Takemoto Harutayū (d. 1784), who performed the female Mt. Imo roles.[12] Though it is not in his hand, the text's lineage can be traced directly to Matazō. Mameushi appears to have been an amateur performer in the Matazō line, and his text most likely dates to around 1800, within thirty years of the first performance and twenty-odd years from Matazō's death.[13] Since amateurs would be unlikely to innovate, we can suppose with some certainty that the *Mameushi* text gives us a picture of how "The Mountains Scene" was performed in the last decades of the 18th century. How is it different from the 1771, 1930, or 1980s productions?

On 7 August 1984, Inobe, Malm, and Gerstle visited the shamisen player Nozawa Kizaemon (Katsuhei) at his home in Osaka and requested that he play various passages of "The Mountains Scene" according to different texts, beginning with the *Mameushi* down to the 20th century.[14] The results were intriguing. In general, the greatest difference exists between the *Mameushi* text and the 1863 *Nagatodayū*, which is much closer than the *Mameushi* to present practice, though still with some difference. The opening lines (1–15) of the *Mameushi* text are similar to later versions, but less dramatic and complicated. The Mt. Imo opening (beginning with line 16), however, is considerably, if not fundamentally, different from today. Lines 132–135 and lines 141–146 (the emotional climax of the first part of the scene) in *Mameushi* are similar to present performance but less complicated and with considerably fewer notes, whereas the *Nagatodayū* is similar to today's performance. Lines 194–198 in *Mameushi*, when Daihanji first appears, are extremely different from *Nagatodayū*, which is like today. The shamisen in the *Mameushi* text is light compared to the intensity of later performance. The effect is starkly different. In present performance the shamisen and chanter strive for the severest intensity to portray the seemingly harsh character of Daihanji. This intensity is absent in the *Mameushi* text.

Why would there be such significant change at Daihanji's entrance? The *Gidayū nenpyō—kinsei-hen* (Chronology of Edo-period *gidayū*) provides a hint.[15] Today, Daihanji is always played by a senior chanter who makes his first appearance with Daihanji's opening in line 194. The *tayū* must, with only a few lines, set the mood for the last part of the play. Until the mid-1820s, however, one chanter played both Koganosuke and Daihanji, and likewise, one man took the female roles. These senior *tayū*, therefore, would set the mood from the first lines of the play and would not need to "show off" when the parents appeared. The division into four performers provided the impetus for further development: each *tayū* needed to make his part more powerful, and the senior chanters needed to command the spotlight. Daihanji's entrance would not be satisfying for either the chanter or audience unless the senior performer was superior to the *tayū* playing Koganosuke. The roles of Daihanji and Sadaka were strengthened to outshine those of Koganosuke and Hinadori. For similar reasons, lines 141–146, the climax of Hinadori and Koganosuke's scene, have become more complicated after the split into four *tayū* because the younger chanters' performance must peak here before they are relegated to the shadows. Before 1823, however, the two chanters would not have wanted to peak this early. They needed to pace their performance for effect and tradition, which demanded that the climax come in the latter half of the scene.

Lines 267–274 have undergone similar change. The *Mameushi* text has less complicated shamisen, with fewer notes and less intensity, while, in contrast, the *Nagatodayū* version is similar to later texts. These lines are the end of the parents' introduction, and the performer must bring the audience to a measured peak before Daihanji and Sadaka go inside to meet their children. The intense music expresses the tortured hearts of the parents. The change of *tayū* before these lines allows, or rather demands, more effort be put into the passage. The genius of Hanji's text is that it can accommodate such amplification of performance.

The greatest changes to the performance have come in the music for the two female roles. In all cases the *Mameushi* text is much simpler than later versions. Shamisen players and chanters continually added flourishes to have the female Mt. Imo side contrast more vividly with the male Mt. Se. This contrast is fundamental from the first performance in the parallel stage organization: Mt. Se is in the *nishi* (west) style, which refers to the masculine, reserved chanting of the Takemoto theater; while Mt. Imo is chanted in the *higashi* (east) feminine, more melodic, style of the Toyotake theater. Later performers made the contrast more striking. An example is lines 578–579, which in the original *maruhon* are in *kotoba* without shamisen; in the *Mameushi* text simple shamisen has been added; in *Kichibei*, the music is more complicated; in *Shinzaemon* and *Seiroku*, it has become extremely complicated—in *Seiroku's* case more complicated than today. These lines now are a musical flourish and a high point of the drama, which was not originally the case in 1771.

An even more striking example is lines 644–648, which are *kotoba* in the *maruhon*, *Mameushi*, and even in the *Kichibei* text of the late 19th century. Today the lines have powerful shamisen accompaniment, an apparent development late in the 19th century. In this case, in particular, the effect is marvelous. Sadaka and Daihanji face each other in opposition. Daihanji declaims and Sadaka sings, each taking turns back and forth until the emotional intensity peaks and their voices are joined in song (line 663) as they express parents' love for children. All enmity has dissipated. This later development adds to the "reading" and effectiveness of Hanji's text.

The different versions of the *dangiri* finale (lines 667 to the end) follow a similar pattern of development. Though lines 668 and 669 are in *kotoba*, the early *Mameushi* text has some simple notation, and in later versions the notation becomes increasingly complex until the ending becomes a musical flourish in which one can hardly hear the words of the chanter. The passage reaches a crescendo of song and shamisen, expressing emotion without reference to meaning. The shamisen came to dominate the ending, a situation unthinkable in the 1750s.

What can we conclude about the development of Jōruri theater from about 1770 to the present day? To get a clearer picture we need to look at several major pieces in the repertoire for which we have shamisen notation dating from the late 18th century to at least 1930. Nevertheless, "The Mountains Scene" has given us some insight into the process of change in a lively performing tradition. A startling revelation is that the 1771 performance was only the germ of what was to grow into a musical masterpiece. The evidence shows that performance began to change soon after, or even during, the first run, and accelerated during the mid-19th century under the hands and voices of Tsuruzawa Seishichi III (d. 1856) and Takemoto Nagatodayū, and those of Nozawa Kichibei III (1821–1862) and Takemoto Harutayū V (1808–1877). Both Seishichi III and Kichibei III are in the Seishichi I lineage leading directly to Bunzō. Between 1771 and 1871 great changes occurred in the tradition, developments that made the experience of each performance considerably different.

"The Mountains Scene" stands at an important crossroads in the history of Bunraku. The success of the play gave Bunzō and his disciples greater freedom to create music for the text. Previously, *fushigoto* song passages had become the domain of the shamisen; during Bunzō's time the shamisen invaded the entire text, every line sung by the chanter. After Bunzō, *tayū* and shamisen players worked together to transform the repertoire during the 19th century. Both the chanter's voice and the accompanying shamisen music became increasingly sophisticated, pushing Bunraku to become the intensely dramatic theater that it is today. Post-1945 shamisen music, however, is generally less complicated than that of the 1920s.

One figure whose influence must be examined in greater detail is Toyozawa Danpei II (1827–1898), who from 1847 until his death played for seven important chanters, namely, Toyotake Wakatayū V (d. 1850?), Toyotake Tomoedayū III (d. 1860), Toyotake Sankōsai I (ca. 1830–1859), Takemoto Nagatodayū III, Takemoto Sometayū VI, Takemoto Harutayū V, Settsudaijō, and Takemoto Ōsumitayū. Many of today's shamisen pieces have come through his creative hands. Danpei's work merits a separate study. How deep and wide his influence extends has yet to be documented. Fortunately, we now have ample materials available to attempt this fascinating task.

Chapter Six   Notes

1   Yūda Yoshio, *Bunraku jōruri shū* (1965), p. 273.

2   *Imoseyama onna teikin*, King Record KH49–50 (1976).

3   Matazō-style notation added to woodblock text, provided to Gerstle by Yoshinaga Takao. On Mameushi's dates see Inobe Kiyoshi, "Gidayū-bushi ni okeru ishukei no shamisen shusho," *Ōsaka ongaku daigaku kenkyū kiyō* 7 (1968), pp. 20–24.

4   Hand-written text with shamisen notation for Mt. Se side, provided to Gerstle by Yoshinaga Takao. Nagakodayū (Yadayū V) was only sixteen years old at the time.

5   Shamisen notation for Mt. Se side added to woodblock text; no. 799 in *Takemoto Yadayū* collection of Ōsaka Ichiritsu Toshokan.

6   Shamisen notation added to woodblock text; no. 800 in *Takemoto Yadayū* collection of Ōsaka Ichiritsu Toshokan.

7   Hand-written text; no. 1366 in *Nozawa Kichibei* collection of Ōsaka Ichiritsu Toshokan.

8   Shamisen notation added to woodblock texts; nos. 290 and 445 in *Tsuruzawa Seiroku* collection of Ōsaka Ichiritsu Toshokan.

9   Hand-written texts; nos. 11–531, 11–647, and 11–663 in *Toyozawa Shinzaemon* collection of Waseda Engeki Hakubutsukan.

10 Shamisen notation added to woodblock text; no. 2073 in Ōsaka Ongaku Daigaku collection.

11 See Inobe, "Gidayū-bushi ni okeru ishukei no shamisen shusho."

12 Takemoto Harutayū was not a regular member of the Osaka Takemoto theater, performing more often in Kyoto and elsewhere.

13 See Inobe, "Gidayū-bushi ni okeru ishukei no shamisen shusho."

14 Inobe transcribed the Matazō notation into modern style.

15 *Gidayū nenpyō—kinsei-hen* (1980), vol. 2, p. 531.

Chapter Seven Playwrights and Performers

C. Andrew Gerstle

The discussion thus far has primarily been on Bunraku in contemporary performance. This final "historical" chapter will examine the relationship between playwrights and performers before and during the period when *Mt. Imo and Mt. Se* was first staged. Bunraku has always been a collaborative art—both in composition and in performance—and the particular relationships among playwrights, chanters, puppeteers, and musicians (all working in hierarchies of experience and talent within each category) has determined directly the kind of play produced at any given moment. *Mt. Imo and Mt. Se* stands as a monument to an especially fruitful moment of collaboration that consequently set the course for the development of Bunraku as we know it today. We turn first to the position of the playwright in a well-established genre.

The Playwright Chikamatsu Hanji

By the early 1760s when Chikamatsu Hanji became senior Takemoto playwright, he bore a heavy burden of the past, not only in the hundreds of plays already written but also in being well-trained by masters as an apprentice for more than a decade. Connoisseur audiences did not expect new themes, but they demanded innovation (*shukō*) in technique and style. Originality or creativity in theme or character, therefore, was necessarily sought within the bounds of tradition.

As a teenager Hanji witnessed the golden age of Jōruri before becoming an apprentice to Takeda Izumo II in the 1750s. The aspiring playwright, consciously or not, would have found himself in a similar situation to many Japanese artists of the past and present who strive to create original works in well-established traditions. In Japan, once a tradition is established, it is able (or forced), partly due to the insular nature of the culture, both to stay alive and to remain creative within its own rigid forms and conventions. As in the arts of painting, poetry, calligraphy, judo, and so forth, tradition demands first of all a technical mastery of the craft before any spontaneity is permitted. This rigorous training, then, instills respect for the thematic and technical limits of the art. Waka poetry must be one of the longest lasting poetic forms practiced today, though its strict rules on length, diction, and imagery may make it appear sterile at first glance. The Japanese enjoy taking well-worn material and fashioning it into something new. It is both a difficult task and a task difficult to appreciate unless one is steeped in the tradition. One must know the allusion before savoring the significance of a variation. All artists, of course, build on the work of predecessors, but the Japanese are extreme in their preservation of form, whether it be in poetry, music, painting, or drama.

In Japan during the mid-to-late 18th century, it was common for the many artists of the dominant and anti-commercial *bunjin* (literati) mold in the Kyoto-Osaka area to try their hand at various fields from calligraphy and painting, to tea ceremony and poetry, to philosophy and philology. Though Ueda Akinari, Hiraga Gennai (in Edo), Yosa Buson, and many other painters, poets, and scholars of like mind were Chikamatsu Hanji's contemporaries, he confined his talents within a narrow, well-established genre. Perhaps he could not succeed in these other pursuits, as he modestly contends (echoing Chikamatsu Monzaemon's last testament) in his posthumously published *Hitori sabaki* (One man's judgment, 1787):

> Since I was born with no talent, no matter what I took lessons in, nothing came of it. Because of my failings, I am weak-kneed and always get bored after two or three days of any pursuit. And so I've never mastered any art. Realizing my hopelessness, I decided against trying to learn from others, and follow only the feelings of my heart. No matter what anyone said, I satisfied myself and stuck to my opinions.[1]

Though he states that he got bored doing anything for even a few days, he spent more than thirty years writing plays, the first ten as an apprentice, and then from about 1762 as the senior playwright of the

Takemoto theater. Today, of course, we have no idea if he sensed that he was at the end of a tradition; we can, however, surmise that he certainly knew he was following in good company.

Hanji was born within a year of Chikamatsu Monzaemon's death and began writing when Namiki Sōsuke (Senryū) and Takeda Izumo II were at the end of their careers. We know little about his early life or even the details of his career. His name (only rarely alone) appears on fifty-five plays, the first dating from 1751, and the last, 1783. Except for a brief foray, he spent his entire energies in the service of the Takemoto theater.

Hanji's father, Hozumi Ikan (1692–1769), probably influenced his decision to enter the theatrical world. Ikan, a Confucian scholar of some repute, is well-known in the history of Japanese theater for his work *Naniwa miyage* (Souvenir of Naniwa, 1738), a commentary on puppet plays, which shows an in-depth knowledge of the drama and contains Chikamatsu's famous words on the art of Jōruri drama. Ikan could have told his son Hanji much about his friend Chikamatsu Monzaemon. Ikan certainly respected the playwright; above the portrait of Chikamatsu in *Naniwa miyage* is a eulogy in Chinese:

> He was a warm and upright man who even at seventy was full of youthful vigor. Everyone who met him was struck by his depth of heart. He read with a clear mind a myriad of books, and in his plays mixed skillfully the language of the sages with popular songs. At the touch of his brush even ordinary words gain the power to take our breath away.[2]

In following the "god of writers," as Chikamatsu was revered after his death, and other illustrious dramatists who had humbled the rival Kabuki theater by producing an array of masterpieces rivaling any theatrical tradition, Hanji might have been intimidated. He managed, however, to create a host of "original" plays, neither as erudite nor poetic as his predecessor's, but theatrical gems nevertheless.

Chikamatsu Hanji's plays are, some might say ironically, the most performed on the Bunraku stage and the most loved by connoisseurs (not necessarily scholars) and performers. His plays are excellent on stage, even on first view, yet at the same time cannot be fully appreciated without a familiarity with the tradition. Self-sacrifice—the most important theme in Bunraku, whether it be a man dying for his lord, a woman dying for her husband or lord, a parent sacrificing a child for a higher cause, or a pair of young lovers committing suicide for a life together in the next world—is the central theme in his popular plays as well. By the time Hanji began writing, all the *sekai* (world, historical setting) were well established. His audience knew the outline of the major stories, knew the major characters, and even knew generally what must happen in each act. They came to see performance: how familiar themes are presented more powerfully and with greater effect. What Hanji did most successfully, as all great dramatists do, was to write for performers: the puppeteers and musicians as well as the chanters, to give them good characters to interpret and portray, good situations to stretch their talents and skills.

Modern scholars have focused on Hanji's genius for theatricality, for creating twists and novelty in familiar settings. Tsubouchi Shōyō (1859–1935), the most famous member of the Waseda Chikamatsu Association (Chikamatsu Kenkyūkai), gives credit to Hanji's talent as a skillful dramatist who produced "opera-like" works successful on both the puppet and Kabuki stages.[3] The group chose Hanji's popular play *Mt. Imo and Mt. Se: An Exemplary Tale of Womanly Virtue* as his masterpiece. Other scholars have focused on Hanji's talents as a dramatist to criticize him for bringing the puppet theater too close to Kabuki and thereby ruining its chances for further development.

Yokoyama Tadashi has argued that almost no changes are needed to transform Hanji's Jōruri text into a Kabuki play.[4] As one example he uses "The Mountains Scene," which is a good Kabuki drama with almost no alteration—in the words at least. The total Kabuki performance, however, is greatly altered because the music is significantly reduced in the Kabuki version, particularly in the dialogue. One reason Chikamatsu Monzaemon's plays generally require considerable rewriting to become Kabuki is the amount of third-person narrative that must be eliminated to put the actor, rather than the chanter, in the limelight. In Kabuki, music, as well as the other theatrical elements of the stage, must support the actor, who is always the focus of attention. In Bunraku, the puppet is only one among three equals.

There is no doubt that Hanji's colloquial plays are more "theatrical" than the earlier works of Chikamatsu, Sōsuke, or Izumo. We must return again, however, to the introduction of more sophisticated three-man puppets in 1734 to understand the transition from Jōruri as primarily narrative in which the entire story is of interest to the audience, as in Chikamatsu's plays, to the middle ground of Sōsuke and

Izumo where the whole story is still important but the fragments begin to command a greater share of attention, to Hanji's world where the story is to be toyed with—twisted—for the purpose of the fragments that have grown independent of the whole. More lifelike puppets challenged playwrights to see them as characters; the audience, then, began to become fascinated by the characters (on the stage) rather than the overall story. This description of the changes in Jōruri playwriting explains why Chikamatsu Monzaemon's plays are the most successful as literature when removed from the theater (and the least successful on the contemporary stage); why Sōsuke and Izumo's dramas are good as long tales and powerful as fragments on the stage; and why Hanji's plays, though perhaps unable to stand alone as literature, are marvelous in the theater. Of the many plays Hanji wrote or collaborated on, parts of fourteen are still alive in Bunraku. These have proved themselves over two centuries to be enduring and engaging theater.

Tsuruzawa Bunzō and the Changing Role of Shamisen Players, 1744–1784

During the 18th century the relationship among playwrights, chanters, puppeteers, and musicians was fluid. It depended on the talents and personalities of individuals, and on the backing of patrons. Chanters have always held the spotlight in the public eye, and since Yoshida Bunzaburō's rise to fame, puppeteers, too, have commanded their share of attention. Relatively little, however, has been written about the shamisen players who populate the history of Jōruri.[5] We know the names of a few early shamisen performers. Takezawa Gon'emon (active in the first quarter of the 18th century), Nozawa Kihachirō (active in the first quarter of the 18th century), and Tsuruzawa Tomojirō (d. 1749) are famous as the founders of *gidayū* shamisen, but we know little about their lives or careers.

Although *banzuke* (playbills) advertising performances had from at least the 1720s contained lists of both chanters and puppeteers, not until 1744 did shamisen players' names begin to appear.[6] Since the playbills clearly reflect the status of performers in the eyes of both troupe and public, we cannot but conclude that shamisen players were considered insignificant until Jōruri's golden period. The early, influential chanters Uji Kaganojō and Takemoto Gidayū had made it clear that the shamisen was subservient: Kaganojō states that the chanting is the "needle," the shamisen the "thread"; the chanter always leads.[7]

Gidayū describes the relationship unequivocally as "master-servant" and states that private recitals can be held without shamisen accompaniment.[8] The shamisen in this early period must have given only simple accompaniment.

Until the 1740s (and some much later) shamisen players were usually blind, putting them into a low position in society, and at a disadvantage within the hierarchy of the troupe. Tsuruzawa Tomojirō was, as first shamisen in the Takemoto theater, involved in the performances of many famous plays. He had, however, no authority over chanters Harima no shōjō (1691–1744), Takemoto Konotayū (1700–1768), or Takemoto Masatayū II (1710–1765), the stars at the time. Though Tomojirō dutifully retired in 1744 when his partner of many years, Harima no shōjō, died, he was persuaded to become active again and gained due fame during the last five years of his life.[9] No doubt, however, his blindness kept him in a limited role within the troupe.

The situation of puppeteers was different, however, with the maverick Yoshida Bunzaburō successfully challenging the star chanter Konotayū in the historic *Chūshingura* incident in 1748 (see chapter one). Jōruri theaters were, of course, commercial ventures, and the decision to keep Bunzaburō happy at the expense of the first chanter meant that Bunzaburō, as a star, brought in crowds and patrons. His popularity was enormous and his rank in the critique books of the late 1740s is above any chanter.[10] His ego seems to have been inflated as well. He was a successful playwright (under the name Yoshida Kanshi) and even broke away from the Takemoto theater to found his own troupe, though without success. To reach full expression, his genius as an actor pushed puppet technology to great lengths and spawned the sophisticated acting techniques for three-man puppets, ushering in the golden age of popularity.[11] He forced playwrights to consider the puppets as actors. Though Tomojirō did achieve a status in the critiques equal to or above chanters, this was only during the last few years of his life.[12] No superstar with influence equal to Bunzaburō emerged among shamisen players until two decades later.[13]

Although shamisen players during the mid-18th century gradually began to assume a more prominent role, and although the music was certainly becoming more sophisticated, especially *fushigoto* (*michiyuki*, etc.) song sections, the putting of a text to music (*fushi o tsukeru*) was still the prerogative of senior chanters. The first treatise on Jōruri shamisen appeared in 1757, more than seventy years after the first treatise on chanting.

Jōruri shamisen hitori keiko (Do it yourself shamisen lessons) is an important work showing the increasing sophistication of the music as well as the growing interest among nonblind musicians.[14] The treatise explains the basics of the *gidayū* shamisen and gives us an insight into the role of shamisen in performance. It refers only to musical patterns, beginnings and endings, with no reference to specific plays, as contemporary shamisen notation does. One gets the sense that the shamisen's role as punctuator of the drama had become very sophisticated, though it had yet to invade the body of the "dramatic" (as opposed to "song") sections of the text and fully express their essence.

The shamisen notation that developed from the 1770s onward has usually been fixed to the lines of a particular text.[15] Historians of music tell us that from the 1720s, shamisen music in general became increasingly sophisticated. This trend is certainly evident in Jōruri as well, particularly in the 1750s when musicians are praised in critiques as talented performers; they came to command individual attention for the first time. The crucial difference in the shamisen playing after the 1760s is not necessarily due to the greater skill or genius of the musicians but to a fundamental change of attitude among them.

The earlier storytelling tradition of the *biwa hōshi* (blind minstrels), from which Jōruri emerged, had musical accompaniment to the narrative, but for the most part voice and music were kept separate except at beginnings and endings of musical paragraphs. This style of accompaniment was basic to early Jōruri as well. Music punctuated the narrative but, however sophisticated, remained fundamentally separate from it.

Until the late 1760s, when a new text was presented to the troupe by an author, it was the chanter who set the new work to music. He composed music for the voice without reference to the shamisen. The musician then filled in his part when the chanter and shamisen player began to practice. A chanter could be the primary composer because the voice was independent of the instrumental music. Therefore, though shamisen music became increasingly sophisticated, it was limited in range by the absolute authority of senior chanters over the preparation of the text for the stage. A lack of sight, as well as traditional practice, kept the musician from getting to the text ahead of the chanter. The above account makes the shamisen-chanter relationship sound antagonistic, but, in fact, only a cooperative arrangement produced a successful product. Nevertheless, the chanter totally dominated the relationship.

The 1760s was a traumatic decade in the history of Jōruri with the deaths of star performers such as Yoshida Bunzaburō (1760), Echizen no shōjō (1764, retired 1745, founder of the Toyotake theater), Masatayū II (1765), Yamatonojō (1766, retired 1763), Chikuzen no shōjō (Konotayū, 1768, retired 1757), and the consequent collapse of the Toyotake (1765) and Takemoto (1767) theaters. A star-studded generation was passing and the theaters were in trouble. Though younger chanters were certainly talented, they were unable to draw audiences on the scale of their masters; furthermore, Kabuki had regained its strong position in the Osaka theatrical world and challenged Bunraku for audiences.

It is well known that this trying decade was the time when Chikamatsu Hanji had finished his apprenticeship and, in 1762, was the senior playwright for the Takemoto theater. On the other hand, it is almost unknown that Tsuruzawa Bunzō (retired 1784–1785, d. 1807), who had been performing from about 1744, was in the early 1760s playing for the senior chanter Masatayū II and was listed in 1763 as first shamisen in the Takemoto theater, a position he held until his retirement.[16] Bunzō was not only first shamisen but also the most experienced member of the troupe. It is therefore essential to consider Bunzō's role in the presentation of Hanji's plays in general and *Mt. Imo and Mt. Se* in particular.

How could Bunzō suddenly command such a major role when shamisen players had been relatively insignificant in his own youth? Four factors stand out: one, the ability to see; two, that Bunzō was the most experienced performer in the troupe; three, that he gained recognition in critiques as a superstar—even outshining chanters; and finally, that he remained throughout his long career, as did Hanji, in the same Takemoto troupe at a time of frequent movement.

Bunzō's master, Tomojirō, had paved the way for his disciple's fortunes by gaining recognition on his own after the death of Harima no shōjō, his partner of many years. Although the earliest critique of Jōruri performers, *Ongyoku saru-gutsuwa* (Music of gagged monkeys, 1746), contains sections on *tayū* and puppeteers, not one shamisen player is mentioned. In the 1747 *Naniwa sono sueba* (Leaves of Naniwa) Tomojirō is listed as first shamisen but is ranked far below the top chanter and Bunzaburō. In the 1751 *Sōkyoku Naniwa no ashi* (Reeds of Naniwa) he is, along with Bunzaburō, in the highest rank—above the chanters.[17] Yet this text gives no significant detail on shamisen players, only on chanters. Even though Tomojirō in his last few years was appreciated as a shamisen superstar—the first time for such fame in the history of Jōruri—it is as if critics did not yet have the vocabulary to discuss shamisen music. Tomojirō had broken the ice, but it wasn't until two decades later that musicians began again to rise to the level of Tomojirō's brief glory.[18]

There is a gap between 1766 and 1781 in the Osaka critiques, making it difficult to trace the process, but in the 1781 *Yami no tsubute* (Stones in the dark), Bunzō had suddenly vaulted far above the *tayū* and was set upon a pedestal, with the puppeteer Yoshida Bunzaburō II (1732–1790), as a superstar in the troupe.[19] Since the famous chanters had passed from the stage long before, we can be certain that Bunzō had achieved his fame at least by 1771 with the success of *Mt. Imo and Mt. Se*. After Bunzō became first shamisen, he was listed as the star performer for nearly all of Hanji's new plays. To a great extent, Bunzō's skills in performance and composition helped to make Hanji's plays successful on the stage.

Only Hosokawa Kagemasa, in his slender, privately published book *Tōryū jōruri shamisen no hitobito* (Jōruri shamisen players, 1953),[20] has given Bunzō such prominence. He credits Bunzō with influencing Matsuya (Tsuruzawa) Seishichi, the creator of the modern code of notation, and suggests that after the late 1760s due to Bunzō the right of composing music for new plays passed from the *tayū* to the shamisen performer.[21] In his own time, however, Bunzō was recognized as "the founder of modern shamisen music."[22] His composition was considered unique, and he was praised as having had a "tremendous knowledge of songs" and being

able to answer any questions on the tradition. The late Kanetayū (1730–1779) was said to have been a star, but was it due to Bunzō's talents?—when he performed at the Toyotake Theater he made little impression, but when he moved to the Takemoto and performed with Bunzō, he blossomed and produced his best performances, all of which have remained part of the repertoire.[23]

Awareness of Bunzō's influence had become common by this time, and credit was given for his work: "It was Bunzō who made *Mt. Imo and Mt. Se* a success from act one to the finish."[24] The *Yami no tsubute* lists many of the plays for which he wrote the music and praises his loyalty in "never serving two masters, remaining at the Takemoto Theater all his career."[25]

The ultimate artistic compliment for a shamisen musician (particularly one with sight) is to receive praise from blind shamisen players. Toyozawa Danpei (1827–1898), the most famous musician of recent times, often was the recipient of such attention from *kengyō*, blind shamisen musicians, who would come only to listen to Danpei play.[26] Bunzō had gained such fame a century earlier. Three works from the period (*Naniwa kenbun zatsuwa* [Miscellaneous records of Naniwa, 1750s–1817], *Hanawarai*, [Sneering, 1803], and *Naniwa kidan*, [Strange tales from Naniwa, 1835]), refer to blind musicians coming to listen and praise his shamisen playing.[27]

Does this mean that Bunzō had become the authority in the troupe? The author of *Yami no tsubute* suggests as much. On Sometayū, the senior Takemoto chanter from early in the 1770s for whom Bunzō played, the writer states: "It's no wonder Sometayū's a star with a general like Bunzō taking care of him."[28] A slightly later critique, *Shiroto jōruri hyōbanki* (Critique of amateur Jōruri performers, 1786), states unequivocally: "Bunzō is the saint of shamisen performers— Sometayū is the insect (a talented performer) of Jōruri; Sometayū does not stand above Bunzō, nor does Bunzō stand beneath Sometayū."[29]

Our best sources for the time between 1766 and 1781, when there is a lack of critiques, are two works of satirical fiction, the 1770 *Ana saguri* (Hunting for holes) and the 1777 *Tōsei shibai katagi* (Characteristics of modern theater), about the theatrical worlds of Osaka and Kyoto.[30] The first chapter of *Tōsei shibai katagi* opens with extreme praise of *gidayū* shamisen as able with only three strings to express all the feelings of human experience: "neither the biwa, the koto, nor any music can match its unique sound."[31] Such praise, however exaggerated, suggests that appreciation of Jōruri shamisen music, on its own merits, had developed greatly among audiences of the time. Further, such an attitude would imply a considerable change from the earlier period when Jōruri "music" meant primarily vocal music. The first story contains an argument between a young shamisen player and a novice chanter:

Chanter:	"The shamisen is supposed to be subordinate to the *tayū*."

| Shamisen: | "That's how it was in the old days. Now the shamisen must be the leader." |
| Chanter: | "Then does the shamisen get to the text ahead of the chanter? Furthermore, is it the practice for the *tayū* to have the shamisen compose the music for the *tayū* to chant?"[32] |

The argument is left unsettled. In the next section, however, an answer is implied. A chanter is arguing with a playwright about the words of a new play.

| Chanter: | "How do you expect me to chant this line? How can I set it to music?" |
| Playwright (laughing): | "Fine talk—though actually the shamisen players write the music for you, you still pretend you had composed it yourself."[33] |

The text becomes even more explicit: "Today *tayū* can't chant a line without the shamisen player composing the music."[34] "Musical composition" had come to mean both vocal and instrumental composition.

The earlier *Ana saguri*, which has been described as an advertisement for the playwright Hanji, also refers to the current situation of shamisen performers. Tsuruzawa Tomojirō, Chikamatsu Monzaemon, Takemoto Gidayū, and Yoshida Bunazburō I are discussing, from the netherworld, the present situation of playwrights and performers at the Takemoto theater. Each takes his turn in criticizing performers. Tomojirō says of the shamisen:

> Nowadays shamisen players are different too. Originally the chanter was the father and the shamisen the mother who helps the father; these days, however, they are pushy and overwhelm like a wife who has brought a huge dowry.[35]

He is, of course, referring humorously to Bunzō, by that time well established as first shamisen in the troupe.

This is a radical change from the early period when the chanter was the lord and the shamisen the servant; a revolution has quietly taken place. Chikamatsu Monzaemon wrote his plays to be interpreted and performed by chanters; Takeda Izumo and Namiki Sōsuke wrote plays for chanters to set to music but with the talents of puppeteers in mind. Hanji wrote for all three roles. However, the shamisen had become the first to interpret the new text; he then composed the music for the chanter and puppeteers to perform. The shamisen player thus replaced the *tayū* as primary "reader" of a new work, and his interpretation appeared in the music (both voice and shamisen).

Hanji appears not to have liked this situation. In the *Naniwa nikkikō* (Diary of a journey to Naniwa, 1780) of the writer Fukumatsu Tōsuke, Hanji complains: "There are no expert chanters anymore; rather, there is more talent among amateurs. Therefore, it does no good to write plays [for them]."[36] Hanji is speaking not only of their voices but also of their talents at interpreting his words and giving them life through song. It is probable that he was writing for Bunzō instead, whether he liked it or not. Furthermore, it seems clear that Hanji wanted to revive the theater's fortunes on the strength of fine texts regardless of the particular performer, but that he found it impossible.[37] He seems to be complaining of the increasing importance of shamisen music (over literary content) for the audiences of the time.

Bunzō's name last appears on a program in 1784; with Chikamatsu Hanji's death in 1783 and Sometayū's in 1785, he retired from the stage, though he lived on until 1807. With both Sometayū and Hanji gone, Bunzō gave his time to teaching, leaving this poem:

> Put wisdom, benevolence, and valor into the three strings.
> Play the shamisen with your heart, not your hands.
> *Play* the notes, don't just pluck the strings; let your heart remain
>   open and gentle.[38]

Bunzō was confident in his ability to express the actions and emotions of Jōruri on the shamisen. Another of Bunzō's sayings, recorded in the *Setsuyō kikan* (The wonders of Setsuyō [Osaka], 1833), gives further insight into his attitude toward the art: "Even during *kotoba* sections [when the shamisen normally does not play], one should hold the shamisen and continue to play in one's heart."[39] This attitude is not unusual among shamisen players of the last 100 years, but was articulated first by Bunzō. Before he died, Bunzō performed publicly one final time around the year 1803 with Sometayū III.[40]

Bunzō's posthumous name of "Never-ending" (*mushū-oki*) is especially apt because of his many disciples. Two in particular, Tsuruzawa Matazō (d. 1778) and Matsuya (Tsuruzawa) Seishichi (d. 1829), developed systems of notation for shamisen music. Though Matazō died a young man, he gained fame as a partner with Bunzō in the composition of the music for *Mt. Imo and Mt. Se*.[41] His method of notation, however, gave way to that of Seishichi, who over his long career developed the system that is the basis for the notation used today. It is likely that Bunzō developed some system of notation, and it was certainly Bunzō's talent that spurred these two disciples to invent systems to record their master's work.[42]

This development may have occurred because of the increasing sophistication of the music and the larger number of pieces in the repertoire. It is probably false, however, to contend that the change from blind to seeing musicians during the mid-to-late 18th century led to the increasing complexity of the music. The difference is that the music was no longer separate from, or subordinate to, the words; the shamisen invaded the text and began independently to express the essence of the words along with the chanter's voice. This is fundamentally different from pre-1760 Jōruri when the shamisen was subservient to the chanter. Notation, as in *Jōruri shamisen hitori keiko*, without reference to a text was no longer satisfactory. From Bunzō's time onward the musician was expected not only to accompany the chanter but also to express the essence of the text.

Bunzō's career had been a period of transition, during which puppet technology had become sophisticated, and the shamisen too had become an indispensable element. Though much work still needs to be done on the many manuscripts dating from the late 18th and 19th centuries, since most of 18th-century Jōruri music has filtered through Seishichi's hand, we can speculate that much of the music we have today was composed or revised by Bunzō during his long career of over half a century. Through his influence shamisen players came to be considered the repositories of the tradition and therefore the primary teachers in the organization.

The process of composition, however, did not end with Bunzō or with the proliferation of the use of notation by shamisen players in the early 19th century. Plays once set to music and recorded in notation continued to change. Though certainly the foundations of the music were laid by 1800, changes, amplifications, and refinement found their way into performance through the talents of star chanters and musicians, at least until about 1930, after which there has been a retreat from the complicated music of the early 20th century.

Though Bunzō and other shamisen players usurped the authority to write music for the text, the process of composition was necessarily cooperative, and later influential chanters are known to have been able to play the shamisen and read the notation,[43] probably because the new "secret" notation was a threat to their control of the medium. To be creative, chanters had to understand the changes introduced during Bunzō's period of influence. After the division between chanting and shamisen ceased to exist, chanters could no longer compose music and ignore the shamisen. To set a text to music one had to understand the conventions of both chanting and shamisen. Furthermore, it was convenient, if not necessary, for chanters to be able to play the shamisen when giving lessons to amateurs—an increasingly common practice from the last quarter of the 18th century.[44]

Nevertheless, the shamisen performer's role as composer became more and more firmly entrenched during the 19th century when composition became the unquestioned domain of the musician. The chanter must be the "star" in Bunraku, because the tayū is the most important role in performance; puppeteers and shamisen players, no matter how talented, depend on the chanter. It is, however, perhaps not an accident that the growing importance of the shamisen meant the diminishing of the "literary" element in Bunraku. As in Western opera, where music dominates, the libretto need be only the skeleton of a literary work to be successful on the stage. Hanji's wish, to have his text alone bring about a revival, had become impossible. But the developments in puppet technology and then shamisen music, in combination with the text, changed Bunraku into the powerful three-pronged theatrical art that it is today.

Chapter Seven   Notes

1 Yoshinaga Takao, "Chikamatsu Hanji *Hitori sabaki* no honkoku ni atatte," *Hagoromo Gakuen Tanki Daigaku kiyō* 8 (January 1972): 83–84. Also printed in *Jōruri sakuhin yōsetsu (3): Chikamatsu Hanji-hen* (1984), pp. 725–26. Hanji was supposed to have treasured the inkstone that his father had received as a gift from Chikamatsu Monzaemon.

2 *Jōruri sakuhin yōsetsu (3): Chikamatsu Hanji-hen*, p. 8.

3 *Chikamatsu no kenkyū* (1898), chapter on *Imoseyama onna teikin*.

4 Yokoyama Tadashi, "Jōruri sakusha Chikamatsu Hanji: Jōruri-kabuki no setten ni okeru," *Geinōshi kenkyū* 58 (1977): 1–12.

5 Shamisen music has been mentioned frequently in passing by scholars, but few have examined it in detail. Recently, Uchiyama Mikiko (in *Jōruri Kabuki*, ed. Toita Yasuji [Kanshō Nihon koten bungaku 30; Tokyo: Kadokawa, 1977], pp. 446–47) acknowledges the importance of Tsuruzawa Bunzō in the creation of the music for *Imoseyama* but offers no more. Kurata Yoshihiro (notes to *Hasse Takemoto Tsunatayū daizenshū* King Record [1981], pp. 35–37) suggests that Bunzō was the most important performer in the troupe but gives little to support this claim. Since his hypothesis, also in this article, that the three-man puppets developed much later than the generally accepted date of 1734, has been solidly refuted by Tsunoda Ichirō ("Jōruri ayatsuri sannindō no sōshi to fukyū ni tsuite," *Kokugakuin zasshi* 85.11 [1984]: 163–75), Kurata's hypothesis on Bunzō would naturally be questioned, along with other points in the article (Kamakura Keiko, "Hōgaku no gihō 'Jūshūkō' no dan yori," *Rikkyō Daigaku Nihon bungaku* 29 [1972]: 92–105). Yūda Yoshio's work in *Bunraku jōruri shū* (1965) shows great concern with the importance of music in Bunraku, though more on the voice than the shamisen.

6 There are earlier isolated cases of shamisen players being listed on *banzuke*, but only individually: 1736 Tomojirō (*Gidayū nenpyō—kinsei-hen*

[1979], vol. 1, p. 108); 1742 (Edo) Takezawa Tōshirō (*Gidayū nenpyō—kinsei-hen*, vol. 1, p. 136). In the ninth month of 1744, shamisen players as a group are listed on a *banzuke* of the Toyotake theater (*Gidayū nenpyō—kinsei-hen*, vol. 1, p. 150). The Takemoto theater follows suit the next month (*Gidayū nenpyō—kinsei-hen*, vol. 1, p. 151; see also Nozawa Kizaemon's *Nozawa no omokage* [1934] in *Nidai Nozawa Kizaemon* [1977], p. 32).

7   *Takenokoshū* (1678) in *NSBSS*, vol. 7, p. 126; translated in the appendix of Gerstle, *Circles of Fantasy: Convention in the Plays of Chikamatsu* (1986). Though Kaganojō also says that when chanting *ji-iro* passages one does not follow the shamisen notes, this does not necessarily imply that the shamisen plays along with the chanter throughout.

8   *Jōkyō yonen gidayū danmonoshū* (1687) in *NSBSS*, vol. 7, p. 132; translated in the appendix of Gerstle, *Circles of Fantasy: Convention in the Plays of Chikamatsu* (1986).

9   *Sōkyoku Naniwa no ashi* (1751) in *NSBSS*, vol. 7, p. 389. Tomojirō is given the highest rank of all—above both chanters and puppeteers, though this is posthumous praise (*Nami no uneri kanae-uwasa* [1748?] in *NSBSS*, vol. 7, p. 395).

10   *Naniwa sono sueha* (1747) in *Naniwa sōsho* (1927), vol. 15, p. 14. *Sōkyoku Naniwa no ashi* in *NSBSS*, vol. 7, p. 390. *Nami no uneri kanae-uwasa* (1748?) in *NSBSS*, vol. 7, p. 396.

11   *Tōkanzasshi* (1759) in *NSBSS*, vol. 7, p.37: "His roles are never unpopular. At that time since the popularity of the puppeteers was so great, he became proud of his talents and tried to set up a new theater troupe. . . . but had to give up in the end." This work portrays Bunzaburō as the superstar who fundamentally changed puppet technique. *Chikuhō koji* (1756) in *NSBSS*, vol. 7, p. 31: "Yoshida Bunzaburō is the greatest puppeteer of all time."

12   Tomojirō is below the top chanter and puppeteer until after the 1747 *Naniwa sono sueha*.

13   It must be stated, however, that even puppeteers did not achieve equal status with chanters as head of a troupe (*monshita*) until 1872 in the early Meiji period when Yoshida Tamazō joined Takemoto Harutayū as head of the Bunraku troupe (*Gidayū nenpyō—Meiji-hen* [1956], pp. 26–27).

14   *Jōruri shamisen hitori keiko* (1757) in *NSBSS*, vol. 7, pp. 196–206.

15   Even in the earliest (1664) introductory text, notation is included for each syllable of shamisen songs. See *Shichiku shoshinshū* (1664) in *Nihon kayō shūsei* (1942), vol. 6, pp. 197–201.

16   *Gidayū nenpyō—kinsei-hen*, vol. 1, pp. 330, 340.

17   *Ongyoku saru gutsuwa* (1746) (Edo) in *NSBSS*, vol. 7, pp. 363–83. In the *Naniwa sono sueha* (1747) (*Naniwa sōsho*, vol. 15, p. 14), Tomojirō is far

below top chanters or Bunzaburō, though there is a small section of comment on shamisen. See also *Nami no uneri kanae-uwasa* (1748?) in *NSBSS*, vol. 7, pp. 393–96; *Sōkyoku Naniwa no ashi* in *NSBSS*, vol. 7, pp. 384–92.

18 Shamisen players have significantly lower rankings in the following works, which are in *NSBSS* vol. 7 unless otherwise noted: *Ayatsuri awase kendai* (1757), pp. 396–407; *Onna daimyō tōzai hyōrin* (1758) in *Naniwa sōsho*, vol. 15, pp. 32–57; *Take no haru* (1761), pp. 407–12; *Shin-hyōban kawazu no uta* (1761), pp. 412–16; *Hyōban hana-zumō* (1763), pp. 417–22; *Hyōban tsuno-gumu awase* (1764), pp. 423–27; *Hyōban tori awase* (1765), pp. 428–33; *Hyōban sangokushi* (1766), pp. 433–38.

19 *Yami no tsubute* (1781) in *NSBSS*, vol. 7, pp. 444–63.

20 Hosokawa Kagemasa, *Tōryū jōruri shamisen no hitobito* (1953). Kurata also suggests that Bunzō was important for Hanji. See note 5.

21 Hosokawa, pp. 52–61.

22 *Yami no tsubute* in *NSBSS*, vol. 7, p. 449. In the work *Hanawarai* (1803) (*Ongyoku sōsho* [1915, reprint 1973], vol. 2, p. 16) Bunzō is praised as the most brilliant player in Jōruri history. He is listed (the only shamisen player mentioned) as the founder of shamisen in *Jōruri hottan* (1825) (*NSBSS*, vol. 7, p. 286).

23 *Yami no tsubute* in *NSBSS*, vol. 7, pp. 449–50.

24 Ibid., p. 450.

25 Ibid. This critique is, however, not isolated in its praise. In the earlier *sharebon* (satiric fiction), *Naniwa ima hakkei* (Eight contemporary views of Naniwa, 1773), he is said to have been like an aristocrat in word and manner, unlike usual shamisen players (*Sharebon taisei* [1979], vol. 6, pp. 38–39). In the essay *Ōsaka kichin domari* (Collection of strange happenings in Osaka, 1780–1781), he is reported to have intervened in an argument between Takemoto Sometayū and Takemoto Sumitayū in order to have the production go on smoothly (*Ōsaka Furitsu Naka no Shima Toshokan kiyō* 11 [1975]: 47). The author also notes an interesting incident that further reflects the gentlemanly nature of Bunzō's personality. A young shamisen player apprenticed himself to Takezawa Yashichi, taking the name Take-zawa Komakichi. Yashichi left Osaka, however, and for some time Komakichi was learning from Bunzō, eventually changing his name to Tsuruzawa Komakichi. When Yashichi finally returned, Komakichi was told to change his name back to Takezawa, but the young man refused. Bunzō, however, told him to play in his heart as if he still had the Tsuruzawa name, but to follow the wishes of his master (Ibid., p. 37). Bunzō also had services held and a memorial stone built for his mentor Tomojirō.

26 See Kōnoike Yukitake, *Dōhachi geidan* (1944), pp. 51–52 and Chatani Hanjirō, *Bunraku kikigaki* (1946), pp. 55–56.

27 See *Naniwa kenbun zatsuwa* (1750s to 1817) in *Zuihitsu hyakaen* (1980), vol. 7, p. 24; *Hanawarai* (1803) in *Ongyoku sōsho*, vol. 2, p. 16; and *Naniwa kidan (zokuhen)* (1835), vol. 4 (manuscript in Tenri library). I am thankful to Ōhashi Tadayoshi for pointing out this last reference, which is also interesting because it mentions that Bunzō would lower the shamisen pitch to suit Sometayū's voice.

28 *NSBSS*, vol. 7, p. 451.

29 *Shiroto jōruri hyōbanki* (1786) in *NSBSS*, vol. 7, p. 493.

30 *Ana saguri* (1770) in *Kinsei Ōsaka geibun sōsho* (1973), pp. 271–83. Nakamura Yukihiko (*Kinsei sakka kenkyū* [1961], p. 273) refers to this work as an advertisement for Hanji. In the text Chikamatsu Monzaemon says of Hanji, "He merits inheriting my name" (p. 278); see also *Tōsei shibai katagi* (1777) in *NSBSS*, vol. 6, pp. 431–59.

31 *Tōsei shibai katagi*, p. 433.

32 Ibid., p. 436.

33 Ibid.

34 Ibid., p. 437.

35 *Ana saguri*, p. 276.

36 *Naniwa nikkikō* (1780) in *Gobun*, March 1954, p. 9.

37 Ibid. The author of the satirical *Hanakenuki* (1797) in *NSBSS*, vol. 7, pp. 235–36 also says how regrettable it is that Hanji worked so hard to produce plays only to have them killed (*katari-korosaruru*) by poor chanters, and he complains of the "showy" style of contemporary (1790s) shamisen.

38 *Zōho jōruri ō-keizu* (1885), chapter 19, p. 35 in *Ongyoku sōsho* (1915; reprint, 1973), vol. 3.

39 *Settsuyō kikan* (1833) in *Naniwa sōsho* (1928), vol. 5, p. 406.

40 *Naniwa kenbun zatsuwa* in *Zuihitsu hyakaen*, vol. 7, p. 24. Sometayū III died in 1806 (*Gidayū nenpyō—kinsei-hen*, vol. 2, p. 234).

41 *Zōho jōruri ō-keizu*, chapter 19, p. 36 in *Ongyoku sōsho*, vol. 3. Furthermore, a number of texts in Matazō's style of notation survive from the late 18th or early 19th century. See Inobe Kiyoshi, "Gidayū-bushi ni okeru ishukei no shamisen shushō," *Ōsaka Ongaku Daigaku kenkyū kiyō* 7 (1968): 20–23. There is also the *Yama no dan* Mameushi text that Yoshinaga Takao provided me.

42 The late Nozawa Kizaemon told Inobe Kiyoshi that he had seen examples of shamisen notation in Bunzō's hand, but Inobe has not been able to confirm this himself.

43 The famous Takemoto Sometayū V (Echizen no daijō, 1792–1855) is known to have played the shamisen, unthinkable for a chanter before the last part of the 18th century (*Sometayū ichidaiki* [1851; printed in 1973], p. 34). I am thankful to Robert Rann for pointing out this reference to me. Furthermore, Takemoto Nagatodayū III (1800–1864), the star of the

early-to-mid 19th century, appears to have been able to read and play shamisen music since several texts exist in his name which include shamisen notation. The texts are in Ōsaka Ichiritsu Toshokan, cataloged in the *Yadayū* collection: numbers 847, 857, 859, 817, and 799. His disciple Takemoto Yadayū V (1837–1906) also could play the shamisen, as could the two most famous Meiji-period *tayū*, Takemoto Settsudaijō (1836–1917) and Takemoto Ōsumidayū (1854–1913).

44   *Shiroto jōruri hyōbanki* (1786) in *NSBSS*, vol. 7, p. 493–513. Amateur chanting was so popular and the level so high that this serious work evaluating amateur performers was published. The *Hanakenuki* (1797) (*NSBSS*, vol. 7, p. 232) records: "Amateurs are as common as ants."

Appendix A   "The Mountains Scene"

Translated by C. Andrew Gerstle

I.1 (*Makura*)

1   三重上
　（かけり行）

        sanjū kami

(Koganosuke) (kakeriyuku)

(. . . gallops off)

地ウキン
古への。

ji u gin

Inishie no.

In the ancient and mythical age

2   ハルスエテ　　中
　神代の昔　　山跡の。

haru suete　　naka

Kamiyo no mukashi yamaato no.

the land of Yamato

3   　　　　　ハル
　国は都の　始めにて。

　　　　　　haru

Kuni wa miyako no hajime nite.

was the first capital.

4   妹背の

Imose no

始め山々の。

hajime yamayama no.

Here between two mountains, Imo
(woman) and Se (man),

where conjugal love began,

5   ラ   中
中を流るる 吉野川。   flows the Yoshino River.
haru u   naka
Naka o nagaruru Yoshinogawa.

6   塵も芥も花の山。   Rushing waters wash all dirt and
Chiri mo akuta mo hana no yama.   grime away.

（ヲリ延シ）

(orinobashi)

7   実世に   Truly it is here
Ge ni yo ni

遊ぶ歌人の。   poets have often come
asobu utabito no.

8   本フシ   to cast verse among the grasses.
言の葉草の捨所。[1]
honbushi
Koto no hagusa no sutedokoro.

2

9   地中   ウ   Mt. Imo is the land of Dazai no
妹山は太宰の小弐   Shōni Ku'nindo.
ji naka   u
Imoyama wa Dazai no Shōni

ハル
国人の 領地にて。
haru
Ku'nindo no ryōchi nite.

10   中   Across the river Daihanji Kiyozumi
川へ見越の 下館。
naka
Kawa e mikoshi no shimoyakata.

11　背ウ山の方は大判事

u　　　　　　　　**u**

Seyama no kata wa Daihanji

清澄の領内。

Kiyozumi no ryōnai.

has a retreat on Mt. Se where

12　ハル
　子息清船日外より

haru

Shisoku Kiyofune itsuzoya yori

ウ　　　　　巾
ここに勘気の　山住居。

u　　　　**naka**

koko ni kanki no yamazumai.

（ハリマ）

(harima)

his son Koganosuke, disgraced, is
confined.

13　ハル　　　ウ
　伴ふ物は　巣立鳥

haru　　　　**u**

Tomonou mono wa sudachidori

中
こだまとわれと　ただ二つ。

　　　　　　naka

kodama to ware to tada futatsu.

（舞）

(mai)

His sole companion, the echo of
his voice intoning

14　経読鳥の音も澄て。

Kyō yomu tori no ne mo sumite.

the Lotus Sutra—the cry of a
young bird fleeing its nest.

15　フシ
　心ぼそくも哀れなり。

fushi

Kokorobosoku mo awarenari (nni).

Pity the fate of this young man.

（ユリ流シ）

(yuri nagashi)

3a

16　比ハルフシ
比は　弥生の

　　　　ji haru fushi

(Hinadori) Koro wa yayoi no

　ウ　　　中　²
初つかた。

u　　　naka

hajimetsukata.

The time is early spring, and

17　ウ　　　　　　　ウ
こなたの亭には　雛鳥

u　　　　　　haru u

Konata no chin ni wa Hinadori

の。³

no.

Mt. Imo prepares for the Dolls'
Festival

18　ハル
気を慰めの雛祭。

haru

Ki o nagusame no hinamatsuri.

（相ノ山）

(ai no yama)

to comfort a despondent
Hinadori.

19　ウ　　　ウ　　　　⁴
桃の節句の　備へ物。
の。

u　　　　u

Momo no sekku no sonaemono.

Sweet cakes are arranged by the
strait-laced

20　　ウ　　　中　　　⁵
萩のこは飯こしもとの

u　　　naka

Hagi no kowaii koshimoto no.

21 ハル 6
小菊。
haru
Kogiku.

maid Kogiku.

22 ウ　　　キン
ききょうが 配膳の
haru u　　　gin
Kikyō ganna　　haizen no
中 7
腰も。
naka
koshi mo.

Kikyō arranges the table setting,

23 　　ウ　　ウヲクリ
すふはり 春風に
u　　　u okuri
Suuwari　　harukaze ni
柳の。
yanagi no.

her hips slim and willowy as branches

24 フシ
楊枝はし近く。
fushi
Yōjihashi chikaku.

bending to the spring wind.

3b

25 詞
ノウ小菊。
kotoba
Nō Kogiku.

(Kikyō) "Kogiku,

26 いつものお雛は御殿で
Itsumo no ohina wa goten de
お祭りなさるれど。
omatsuri nasaruredo.

Hinadori has always gone to the palace for this festival,

27   姫様のおしつらひで。
 Himesama no oshitsuraide.

but perhaps this doll

28   此山岸の仮り座敷。
 Kono yamagishi no karizashiki.

display and

29   谷川を見はらし桜の
 Tanigawa o miharashi sakura no

splendid blossoms along the stream

 見飽。
 miaki.

30   雛様も一入お気が
 Hinasama mo hitoshio o ki ga

will delight her even more.

 晴てよからふのふ。
 harete yokarōnō.

31   地色ウ
 こちらも追付よい殿御
 ji iro u
 Kochira mo ottsuke yoi tonogo

With a good husband

 持たら。 [8]
 mottara.

32   ハル ウ
 常住あの様に　引ついて居たら
 haru u
 Jōju ano yō ni hittsuite itara

she could live here forever."

 色
 嬉しかろ。 [9]
 iro
 ureshikaro.

33   詞
 ノウききょうの何云やるやら。
 kotoba
 Nō Kikyō no nani iyaruyara.

(Kogiku) "Kikyō, what's you on about!

34　何ぼ女夫ならんで居ても。　　　　Even if she were married,
　　Nanbo myōto narande itemo.

35　あのやうに行儀にかしこまつて　　if she was still so chaste and
　　Ano yō ni gyōgi ni kashikomatte　proper,

　　斗居て。
　　bakari ite.

36　手を握る事さへならぬ。　　　　　they'd never even hold hands.
　　Te o nigiru koto sae naranu.

37　窮屈な契りはいや　　　　　　　　I hate such stuffiness.
　　Kyūkutsu na chigiri wa iya.

38　地ハル　　　　　　　　　　　　　Having to sleep apart,
　　肝心の寝る時は

　　ji haru
　　Kanjin no neru toki wa

　　　　　　　　　ウ　　　　10
　　放ればなれの　箱の中。

　　　　　　　　　u
　　hanarebanare no hako no naka.

39　色　　　　　　　　　　　　　　　no relief for her longing."
　　思ひの絶る間は有まいと。
　　iro
　　Omoi no tayuru ma wa arumai to.

40　(地)ハルウ　　　　　　11　　　　Idle chatter strikes Hinadori's
　　仇口々も　雛鳥の。　　　　　　　heart.
　　(ji) haru u
　　Ada kuchiguchi mo Hinadori no.

41　ウ　　　　　　中　　　　　　　　She looks away bashfully to hide
　　胸にあたりの人目せく。　　　　　from staring faces,
　　u　　　　　　　**naka**
　　Mune ni atari no hitome seku.

42 ウ

つらひ恋路の其中に親と

u

Tsurai koiji no sono naka ni oya to

ウ　　　　12
親とは昔より。

u

oya to wa mukashi yori.

her love blocked by the barrier of
feuding parents.

43 ウ　　　　ウ

御中不和の関と　成

u　　　　　　　u

Onnaka fuwa no seki to nari

あふ事さへも片糸の。

au koto sae mo kataito no.

Lovers' hearts, knotted by
unrelieved longing,

44 長地ハル

むすぼれとけぬ我思ひ

nagaji haru

Musuboretokenu waga omoi

ウ　　　　　13
恋し　床しい清船様。

u

koishi yukashii Kiyofunesama.

grasping, clinging to an ephemeral
string of hope.

(Hinadori) "Dearest Koganosuke,

45 ウ　　　上　　　14
此山の　あなたにと。

u　　　kami

Konoyama no anata ni to.

having heard you'd come here,

46　　　色　　　15
聞たを便り母様へ。

iro

Kiita o tayori hawasama e.

I begged mother to send me

47 詞
お願ひ申て此仮屋。

to this retreat,

kotoba
Onegai mōshite kono kariya.

48 お顔が見たさの出養生。
Okao ga mitasa no deyōjō.

hoping to be revived by gazing
upon your face,

49 ここ迄は来たれ共。
Koko made wa kitaredomo.

but this river divides us.

50 山と山とが領分の。
Yama to yama to ga ryōbun no.

51 境の川に隔られ。
Sakai no kawa ni hedaterare.

Desire thwarted!

（カカリ）
(kakari)

52 地ハル   ウ
物云かはす事さへも

Tormented more than ever,

jiharu   **u**
Mono iikawasu koto sae mo

中   16
ならぬ我身のままならぬ。
        naka
naranu wagami no mama naranu.

53 ウ   ウ   17
今は中々思ひの種。

it is better to be far away,

u   **u**
Ima wa nakanaka omoi no tane.

54 上
いつそ隔て恋詫びる。

kami
Isso hedatete koiwabiru.

55 ウ
逢れぬ昔がましぞかし
u
Awarenu mukashi ga mashi zokashi

と。[18]
to.

alone, with no hope of meeting."

56 ウ　　　　中　　　[19]
切なる思ひかきくどき。
u　　　　　　naka
Setsunaru omoi kaki kudoki.

Grief flows from her tortured heart;

57 ハルフシ 中　ハル　　　　　[20]
嘆けば　ともにこしもと共。
haru fushi naka haru
Nagekeba tomoni koshimotodomo.

the maids sympathize.

3c

58 色　　　　　　　　[21]
お道理でござります。
iro
Odōri de gozarimasu.

(Kikyō) "You have every reason to complain.

59 ハル
ほんにひよんな色事で
haru
Hon ni hyonna irogoto de

A strange affair,

ウ　　　ウ　中　[22]
隣同志の　紀国大和。
u　　　u　naka
Tonaridōshi no Kinokuni Yamato.

caught between a squabble over land.

60 ハル　　　色　　　　[23]
御領分の　せり合で。
haru　　　iro
Goryōbun no seriyaide.

61 詞
    お二人の親御様はすれすれ。

    kotoba
    Ofutari no oyagosama wa suresure.

Parents at odds, and

62 雛鳥様と久我様の。
    Hinadorisama to Kogasama no.

the river divides your love.

63 妹背の中を引分る
    Imose no naka o hikiwakuru

    妹山背山。
    Imoyama Seyama

Boats and rafts are forbidden,

64 船も筏も御法度で。
    Fune mo ikada mo gohatto de.

but it's only a little stream

65 たつた此川一つ。
    Tatta kono kawa hitotsu.

66 つい渡られそふな物。
    Tsui watarareso̅ na mono.

simple to ford.

67 小菊瀬踏して見やらぬか。
    Kogiku sebumishite miyaranu ka.

Kogiku, won't you step in and test the depth?"

68 ヲヲめつそふな。
    Oo messo̅na.

(Kogiku) "Are you out of your mind! A stumble and I'd be dragged

69 此谷川の逆落し。
    Kono tanigawa no sakaotoshi.

70 紀州浦へ一てきに流て居たら
    Kishū ura e itteki ni nagarete itara

    鮫の餌食。
    same no ejiki.

by the current all the way to the bay of Kishū—I'll not be shark bait!

71 したが申雛鳥さま。
    Shita ga mōshi Hinadorisama.

But listen, Miss Hinadori,

72 お前の病気をお案じなされ。
    Omae no byōki o oanji nasare.

your mother is not a dull-wit; she's sharp and sensitive.

73 此仮屋へ出養生さしなさつた
    Kono kariya e deyōjō sashinasatta

    は。
    wa.

She sent you here to recuperate,

74 余所ながら久我様に。
    Yosonagara Kogasama ni.

didn't she? She must have intended for you

75 お前を逢す後室様の粋
    Omae o awasu kōshitsusama no sui

    なお捌き。
    na osabaki.

to meet Koganosuke.

76 女夫にして下さりませと。
    Myōto ni shite kudasarimase to.

Why don't you just put it to her straight;

77 直にお願ひ遊ばしたら。
    Jiki ni onegai asobashitara.

ask her to let you get married.

78 よもやいや　とは岩橋
            地ハル
            ji haru
    Yomoyaiya to wa Iwahashi

    の渡る事こそならず共。[24]
    no wataru koto koso narazutomo.

More than likely she won't object. Even if you can't cross a bridge

79 ウ　　ウ
    せめて遠目に　お姿を　と。[25]
    u   u
    Semete tōme ni osugata o to.

for a rendezvous, at least take a look at him from the window."

80　　ウ　　　　　　ウ　　　　　²⁶
　障子ぐはらりと　えん端に。
　　u　　　　　**u**
　Shōji guwararito enbanani.

Kogiku flings open the window
and both maids step out onto the

81　ウ　　　ユリ　　　²⁷
　覗こぼるるこしもと共。
　u　　　　**yuri**
　Nozoki koboruru koshimotodomo.

　（七ツユリフシ）
　(nanatsu-yuri fushi)

veranda and stare across the river.

82　地中
　久我之助はうつうつと
　ji naka
　Koganosuke wa utsuutsu to

　ウ
　父の行末身の上を。
　u
　chichi no yukusue minoue o.

Koganosuke sits gloomily, praying
that his father is safe.

83　スエテ　　　　中　　　²⁸
　守らせ給へと　心中に。
　suete　　　**naka**
　Mamorasetamae to shinchū ni.

His face speaks concern as he

84　キン
　念悲観音の経机。
　gin
　Nebikannon no kyōzukue.

seeks solace in the Kannon Sutra.

85　　　　ウ
　案じ入たる顔形。
　　　u
　Anjiittaru kaokatachi.

　（ハリマ）
　(harima)

86   地ハル
　　　手に取様に

ji haru

Te ni toru yō ni

　　　色
　　　ノウあれあれ。 [29]

iro

nō areare.

As if taking his face in her hands,

(Hinadori) "Oh look,

87   詞
　　　机にもたれて久我様の。

kotoba

Tsukue ni motarete Kogasama no.

look at his distraught face as he leans on the desk.

88   物思はしいお顔持。

Mono omowashii okaomochi.

89   地ハル　　　　色
　　　おしゃくがな　起りつらん。

ji haru   iro

Oshaku gana okoritsuran.

He must be sick and feverish.

90   詞
　　　エエお傍へ行たい。

kotoba

Ee osoba e yukitai.

I must go to him.

91   コレここに居るはいなと

Kore koko ni iruwaina to

　　　地ハル
　　　云へど。

ji haru

iedo.

Look! I'm over here!"

92   ウ　　　　　　キンウ
　　　招けど谷川の　みなぎる

u   gin u

Manekedo tanigawa no minagiru

But her beckoning cries are swallowed in the roar of the swollen stream.

音に　紛れてや。
中
　　　　　　30
naka
oto ni magirete ya.

93　ウ　　　　　　31
聞へぬつらさ。
u
Kikoenu tsurasa.

Her pain—all the greater knowing he cannot hear.

94　詞
エエしんき。
kotoba
Ee shinki.

(Kogiku) "How vexing!

95　こちらが思ふ様にもない。
Kochira ga omou yō ni mo nai.

Things just won't go right.

96　コレこっちや向て見たがよいと。
　　　　　　　　　　　　　32
Kore kotcha muite mita ga yoi to.

Hey! Look this way, over here!"

97　地ウ　　　　フシ　　　33
あせるお傍に気のつきづきんに。
ji u　　　　　　　**fushi**
Aseru osoba ni ki no tsukizukin ni.

Both maids wave wildly, stirring Hinadori, who gets an idea.

3d

98　詞
ほんに夫よ。
kotoba
Hon ni sore yo.

(Hinadori) "That's it!

99　口で云れぬ心のたけ。
Kuchi de yuwarenu kokoro no take.

Spoken words can't express my heart."

100　地ハル　　　　ウ
兼て認め奥山の
ji haru　　　　　　　**u**
Kanete shitatame okuyama no

Tender love flows through the deer-hair brush

鹿の巻筆　封じ文。

ハル

haru

shika no makifude fūjibumi. [34]

101　ウ

恋しい小石にくくり添。 [35]

u

Koishi koishi ni kukurisoe.

into a missive, strong as the stone she ties it to.

102　ウ

女の念の通ぜよと祈願を

u

Onna no nen no tsūzeyo to kigan o

込て打つぶて。

komete utsu tsubute.

With all her heart, she hurls the rock;

103　ウ

からりと川に落滝津。

haru u

Karari to kawa ni ochitakitsu.

tumbling, splashing, it falls into the rapids.

104　ウ　フシ

浪に　せかれて流れ行。 [36]

u　fushi

Nami ni　sekarete nagareyuku.

（フシタタキ）

(fushitataki)

It is caught in a whirlpool, carried away by rushing waves.

3e

105　詞

エエ　どんな。

kotoba

Ee donna.

(Hinadori) "How irritating!"

106　心の念は届いても。

Kokoro no nen wa todoitemo.

No matter if my heart will fly to him,

107 地ハル　　　　　ウ
女力の届かねば
ji haru　　　　　u
Onnajikara no todokaneba

思ふた斗り片便り。[37]
omoota bakari katadayori.

my arm hasn't the strength.
Unrequited love. Doomed to
wait—

108 ウ
返事を松浦佐用姫の。[38]
u
Henji o Matsurasayohime no.

could I but become Princess
Matsurasayo

109 上
石に成共なりたいと。
kami
Ishi ni naritomo naritai to.

and turn to stone pining for my
husband's return!"

110 ヲ　　入　　フシ
ひれ伏　山の　かひもなき。[39]
haru u iru　　fushi
Hirefusu　yama no　kai mo naki.

（車フシ）
(kuruma bushi)

As fruitless as Mt. Hirefusuyama,
which lay down and wept, tears
bring no results.

4a

111 地ウ　　　　　色
久我之助川に　目を
　　　ji u　　　　iro
(Koga) Koganosuke kawa ni me o

付。
tsuke.

Koganosuke looks over at the river.

112 詞
何国よりか水中に打たる石
kotoba
Izuku yori ka suichū ni uttaru ishi

(Koganosuke) "Although that rock
just tossed in the water is surely
heavy,

は重けれど。
wa omokeredo.

113   逆巻水の勢ひに沈み
Sakamakimizu no ikioi ni shizumi

もやらず流るるは。
mo yarazu nagaruru wa.

caught in the rushing whirlpool, it was carried downstream without

114   ムム重き君も入鹿といふ
Mumu omoki kimi mo Iruka to yuu

逆臣の水の勢には。
gyakushin no mizu no ikioi ni wa.

sinking—hm . . . our weighty lord, Emperor Tenchi, too is caught in

115   敵対がたき時代のならひ。
Tekitai gataki tokiyo no narai.

the force of Iruka's revolution. Seeing that the time is not ripe to be

116   夫を知て暫しの中。
Sore o shitte shibashi no uchi.

openly hostile,

117   敵に従ふ父
Teki ni shitagau chichi

大判事殿の心。
Daihanjidono no kokoro.

my father must suffer and pass his days serving the enemy Iruka.

118   　　地ウ　　　ハル
　善か　悪かを　三つ柏。
　　ji u　　　haru
Zen ka aku ka o mitsugashiwa.

Will righteousness or evil win out? If this bog myrtle

119   中ウキン
　水に沈めば　願ひ
　naka u gin
Mizu ni shizumeba negai

sinks in the water, my hopes are dashed; should it float, all shall be well,

叶はず　浮む時は
ウ　　ハル
u　　　　**haru**
kanawazu ukamu toki wa

願成就。
ganjōju.

120
ハル
吉野を仮の御そぎ川
haru
Yoshino o kari no misogi gawa

太神宮へ朝拝せん　と。 ⁴⁰
daijingū e chōhaisen to.

and I'll use the Yoshino River as a purification stream and offer prayers to the imperial shrine."

121
ウ　　　　　　　⁴¹
柏の若葉つみとつて。
u
Kashiwa no wakaba tsumitotte.

He takes three young leaves

122
ウ　　　　　中　　⁴²
谷をつたひに水の　面。
u　　　　　**naka**
Tani o zutai ni mizu no omo.

and sets them on the water's surface.

123
地ハル　　　　色
見やる女中が　申申。
ji haru　　　　**iro**
Miyaru jochū ga moshimoshi

(Kogiku) Kogiku spots him near the river. "Hello, hello!

124
詞
今の小石が届いたか。
kotoba
Ima no koishi ga todoita ka.

Did the rock make it to you?

125　久我様が川へ下りなさるる。
Kogasama ga kawa e orinasaruru.

Koganosuke is going down to the river—

126 あの岩角のおり曲が。
Ano iwakado no orimagari ga.

it's narrowest just where those
rocks make a curve.

127 川端がいつち狭ひ。
Kawahaba ga itchi semai.

This is such a fortunate chance to
meet!"

128 幸のよい逢せと。
Saiwai no yoi oose to.

129 地ハル   ハル
いふに嬉しさ雛鳥の
ji haru   haru
Yuu ni ureshisa Hinadori no

Hearing her words Hinadori,
flushed with happiness, flies

飛立斗 ウ振袖も。 43
          u
tobitatsubakari furisode mo.
(霞)
(kasumi)

130 ウ   中
裾もほらほら 坂道を
haru u   naka
Suso mo horahora sakamichi o

toward him, her long sleeves and
skirts fluttering. She rushes down
the slope, among the blossoms

折から風に ハル散花の。 44
          haru
orikara kaze ni chiru hana no.
(併ビ)
(narabi)

131 ウ
桜が中の立すがた
u
Sakura ga naka no tachisugata

blown about by the wind; she
stretches to reach him, undaunted
at the danger of the river.

ウ
しどけ難所も厭ひなく。[45]

u

shidoke nanjo mo itoinaku.

132　上
ノウ久我様かなつかしやと。[46]　(Hinadori) "Oh, Koganosuke, how
good it is to see you!"

kami

Nō Kogasama ka natsukashiya to.

133　(地)ハルウ
　　いふに思はず清船　Hearing her words he too
unconsciously calls out.

　　　(ji) haru u

(Koga) Yuu ni omowazu Kiyofune

も。

mo.

134　色　　　　　　　　ハル
　　雛鳥無事でと　　顔と　(Koganosuke) "Hinadori, have you
been well?"

iro　　　　　　　　**haru**

Hinadori buji de to kao to

顔。

(Hina) kao.

135　ハル
　　見合す斗　Their eyes meet and can only
caress from a distance, but their

　　　　　　　haru

(Koga & Hina) Miyawasubakari

遠間の。[47]

(Koga) tōai no.

136　ウ
　　心斗がい　hearts reach out to grasp and
squeeze the other.

　　　haru u

(Hina) Kokorobakari ga i

だ　き
(Koga) da (Hina) ki

あ　い
(Koga) a (Hina) i

フシ
詮方涙
fushi
(Koga & Hina) senkata namida

さき立り。⁴⁸   Hopeless tears.
sakidateri.

4b

137   詞   (Hinadori) "Koganosuke, I feigned
　　　申清船様。   sickness just to see you,
　　　kotoba
　　　Mōshi Kiyofunesama.

138   わしやお前に逢たさに。
　　　Washa omae ni aitasa ni.

139   病気と云立ここ迄は来て   but I can't slip
　　　Byōki to iitate koko made wa kite

　　　居れど。
　　　iredo.

140   地ハル   past this barrier forged by
　　　親の赦さぬ中垣に   disapproving parents. The star-
　　　ji haru   lovers in
　　　Oya no yurusanu nakagaki ni

　　　ウ
　　　忍んで通ふ事叶わず。⁴⁹
　　　u
　　　shinonde kayou koto kanawazu.

141   ラ   the Chinese legend get to meet at
　　　女雛男雛も年に一度   least once a year.
　　　haru u
　　　Mebina obina mo toshi ni ichido

は七夕の。

wa tanabata no.

142　ラ
あふせは有に此様に。
haru u
Ōse wa aru ni kono yō ni.

How cruel!

143　ラ　　　　　　　　　50
お顔見ながら添事の。
haru u
Okao minagara sou koto no.

While I can see your face, I can't
be in your arms.

144　上　　ウ　　　キン　　51
　　ならぬは　何の　　報ぞや
kami　　u　　　gin
Naranu wa nan no mukui zo ya.

（尻持）
(shiri-mochi)

Is there no magpie bridge

145　中ウ
妹背の山の。
naka u
Imose no yama no.

to join the Imo and Se
mountains!?"

146　ウ　　ハル　　52
中を隔つ　吉野の。
u　　　haru
Naka o hedatsu Yoshino no.

147　ウ　入　スエテ
川にかささぎの橋はない
u　　iru　　suete
Kawa ni kasasagi no hashi wa nai

　　　　中
かと　くどき言。
　　　naka
ka to kudokigoto.

（サハリ）

(sawari)

4c

148　地ハル　　　　ウ
聞清船もかじ　有ば
ji haru　　　　　u
Kiku Kiyofune mo kaji araba

早渡りたき床しさを。
haya watariaki yukashisa o.

（ハリマ）　　（ハリマ）

(harima)　　(harima)

Her sorrowful pleas press
Koganosuke's heart. Were there an
oar to row,

149　ハル
胸に包て。
haru
Mune ni tsutsumite.

he'd rush across the stream.

150　色　　　　53
道理　道理。
iro
Dōri dōri.

(Koganosuke) "How desperate our
plight!

151　詞
我も心は飛立ど。
kotoba
Ware mo kokoro wa tobitatedo.

My heart also flies to you,

152　**此川の法度厳しきは**
Kono kawa no hatto kibishiki wa

親親の不和斗でない。
oyaoya no fuwa bakari de nai.

but the strict ban on crossing this
river is not only from

153　**今入鹿世を取て君臣上下**
Ima Iruka yo o totte kunshin jōge

our parents' quarrel. Iruka has
taken the reins of government,
and lords and retainers—high and

心心。
kokorogokoro.

low—all think differently about the crisis.

154 隣国近辺といへ共。
Ringoku kinpen to iedomo.

Though we're neighbors, if it appears we're becoming friendly, the court

155 親しみ有ば徒党の企
Shitashimi areba totō no kuwadate

有んかと。
aranka to.

would suspect conspiracy, and so travel between our territories is forbidden.

156 互に通路を禁しめて船を
Tagai ni tsūro o imashimete fune o

とめたる此川は。
tometaru kono kawa wa.

Since all ferries have been banned,

157 領分を分る関所も同然。
Ryōbun o wakeru sekisho mo dōzen.

it's an official barrier.

158 命だに有ならば又逢事
ji u
Inotta ni arunaraba <u>mata au koto</u>

も　有べきぞ。
haru
<u>*mo arubekizo.*</u>

(筑前)
(chikuzen)

If we live through this, we'll surely meet again.

159 今流したる水の柏。
iro
Ima nagashitaru mizu no gashiwa.

Those myrtle leaves I just dropped into the stream have

160 詞
波にもまれて浮みしは
kotoba
Nami ni momarete ukamishi wa

心の願ひ叶ふ知せ。
kokoro no negai kanau shirase.

been swept up by the waves and are floating downstream—

161 地ウ
入鹿がおきて厳しければ
ji u
Iruka ga okite kibishikereba

ハル
我も世上をはばかりて。
haru
ware mo sejō o habakarite.

a sign my wish shall be granted. Iruka's proscriptions are severe; I too

162 ハル
此山奥の隠れ住
haru
Kono yamaoku no kakurezumi

中　　54
心のままに　鴬の。
　　　　naka
kokoro no mama ni uguisu no.

(ハリマ)
(harima)

must hide from the world in this mountain retreat.

163 ウ　　　　ウ　　　　ウ
声は聞共　ろう鳥の雲井を
haru u　　　**u**　　　**u**
Koe wa kikedomo rōchō no kumoi o

ウ
慕ふ身の上を。
u
shitau minoue o.

Though to listen to the bush warbler's beautiful voice—

164 思ひやられよ雛鳥　と。
Omoiyarare yo Hinadori to.

Hinadori—feel for my plight. . . . I'm a caged bird longing for the heavens (court)."

The following photographs were taken during a 1986 Bunraku performance at the Osaka National Bunraku Theater. They are used with the permission and cooperation of the Bunraku Kyōkai and the Osaka National Bunraku Theater. The photographer was Miyake Seisuke.

During the performance, the cast included the following: puppeteers—Yoshida Bunjaku (Sadaka), Kiritake Ichō (Hinadori), Kiritake Kanju (Kogiku), Yoshida Minotarō (Kikyō), Yoshida Sakujurō (Daihanji), Yoshida Tamamatsu (Koganosuke); chanters—Takemoto Sumitayū (Mt. Se), Takemoto Oritayū (Mt. Imo); shamisen players—Tsuruzawa Seiji (Mt. Se, first part), Nozawa Kinshi (Mt. Se, second part), Takezawa Danroku (Mt. Imo, first part), Tsuruzawa Enza (Mt. Imo, second part).

Hinadori speaking to Koganosuke across the river

Koganosuke speaking to Hinadori across the river

Hinadori speaking to Koganosuke across the river

Koganosuke speaking to Hinadori across the river

Sadaka speaking to Daihanji across the river and holding the cherry
blossom branch that will signal whether Koganosuke has chosen death or
life

Daihanji speaking to Sadaka across the river and holding the cherry blossom branch that will signal whether Hinadori has chosen death or life

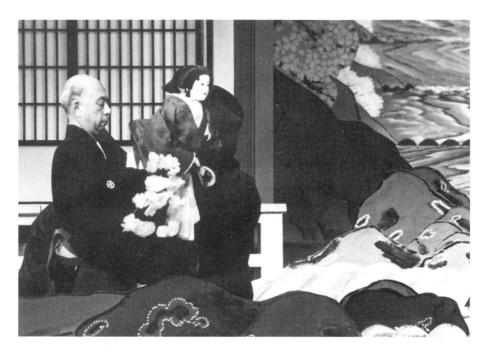

Sadaka holding a cherry blossom branch and speaking to Daihanji across
the river

Sadaka after Hinadori's death, with Kikyō (*left*) and Kogiku (*right*)

Hinadori (*left*) and Sadaka (*right*), holding sword

Koganosuke (*left*) and Daihanji (*right*), holding sword

165 スエテ　　　　中
ままならぬ世を　恨なき。
suete　　　　**naka**
Mamanaranu yo o uraminaki.

Bitter tears, cruel world.

4d

166 詞
ノフ又逢事も有ふと
　　kotoba
(Hina) Nō mata aukoto mo aroo to

は。
wa.

(Hinadori) "Words, 'We'll surely meet again,' are lightly said

167 別るる時の捨詞。
Wakaruru toki no sutekotoba.

to cheer a final farewell.

168 たとへ未来のとと様に
Tatoe mirai no totosama ni

御勘当受る共。
gokandō ukerutomo.

Though father in heaven disown me,

169 わしやお前の女房じや。
Washa omae no nyōbō ja.

I'm your wife!

170 地ハル
とても叶はぬ浮世なら法度
ji haru
Totemo kanawanu ukiyo nara hatto

を破つて　此川の。
　　　　ウ
　　　u
o yabutte kono kawa no.

If our love be not accepted in this cruel world,

171 　　　入　　　　　　　55
早瀬の　浪も いとふまじ。
　　iru
Hayase no nami mo itoumaji.

I'll break the ban and brave the rapids.

172 ウ
何国いかなる方へなと
u
Izuku ikanaru kata e na to

ウ
連て退て下さんせ。
u
tsurete noite kudasanse.

Please take me away anywhere—

173 色   56
私はそこへ行ますと。
iro
Watashi wa soko e yukimasu to.

Here I come."

174 地ウ
既に飛込川岸に。
ji u
Sude ni tobikomu kawagishi ni.

She rushes to the river's edge ready to dive in,

175 ウ
あはて驚きとどむるこしもと。
u
Awate odoroki todomuru koshimoto.

and the maids hurry to restrain her.

176 色   ハル
イヤイヤ放しやと泣入
iro   **haru**
Iyaiya hanasha to nakiiru

娘。
musume.

(Hinadori) "No, no! Let me go!"

177 詞
ヤレ短慮なり雛鳥。
kotoba
Yare tanryo nari Hinadori.

(Koganosuke) "Listen, Hinadori, don't be foolish!

178 山川の此早瀬。
Yamakawa no kono hayase.

Even a strong swimmer

179 水練を得たる者だに
Suiren o etaru mono dani

渡りがたき此難所。
watarigataki kono nanjo.

couldn't cross this rushing mountain stream. You'd lose not only

180 忽命を失ふのみ
Tachimachi inochi o ushinoo nomi

か母後室に歎をかけ。
ka haha kōshitsu ni nageki o kake.

your life but also grieve your widowed mother.

181 我にも弥憎しみ
Ware ni mo iyoiyo nikushimi

かかる。
kakaru.

I'd be blamed and hated for your death.

182 科に科を重る道理アア
Toga ni toga o kasanuru dōri aa

コレコレコレコレ。
korekore korekore.

Now, now, listen! Please, please, you mustn't do

183 詞 地ハル上 中   57
必早まり 召れなと。
kotoba ji haru kami naka
Kanarazu hayamari mesarena to.

(ハリマ)
(harima)

anything rash."

184 ウ   58
せいする詞一筋に。
u
Seisuru kotoba hitosuji ni.

His forbidding words fall heavily on the maiden's weary

185 ウ
思ひ詰めたる 女気も
        haru u
(Hina) Omoitsumetaru onnagi mo

heart, weakening it even further.

フシ
今更よはる折こそ有。[59]

fushi

imasara yowaru ori koso are.

5

186   詞
大判事清澄様御入

kotoba

Daihanji Kiyozumisama on'iri

[なり]としらする声。[60]

[nari]to shirasuru koe.

(Voice) "Lord Daihanji has returned!" comes the cry from outside.

187   地ハル   中
はつと驚き　久我之助

　　ji haru   naka

(Koga) Hatto odoroki Koganosuke

帰るを名残。

kaeru o nagori.

(染太夫)

(sometayū)

Koganosuke starts in surprise but regrets to leave his love.

188   上   ウ
押とむるも　我身を我身

kami   u

Oshitomuru mowagami o wagami

のままならず。

no mama narazu.

Hinadori tries desperately to hold him:

189   ウ   色
コレのふ待て　の　声斗。

u   iro

Kore nō matte no koe bakari.

"Please wait!" but when

190   詞
後室様御出と。

　　　　kotoba

(Voice) Kōshitsusama on'ide to.

"Madame Sadaka has returned!" is announced,

191 地ハル　　　ウ
　　告る下部に詮方も。
　　ji haru　　　　　**u**
　　Tsuguru shimobe ni senkata mo.

her hopes melt into tears.

192 キン　　　　ウ
　　なくなく　庵りの打しほれ
　　gin　　　**u**
　　Nakunaku iori no uchishiore

Crestfallen, she must brave the
slope and return.

　　ウ　　　　中
　　登る坂さへ別路
　　u　　　　　**naka**
　　noborusaka sae wakare ji

　　　色ヲクリ　ウ
　　は　　力　難所を行
　　　iro okuri　u
　　wa   chikara   nanjo o yuku

　　　　　フシ　　　61
　　心地　　空に。
　　　　fushi
　　kokochi sora ni.

193 ハル
　　しられぬ花ぐもり。
　　haru
　　Shirarenu hanagumori.

Her heart, a flower clouded in
darkness, lacks strength to bear
this cruel parting.

6

194 地ハル
　　花を歩めど
　　　　　　ji haru
　　(Daihanji) Hana o ayumedo

Daihanji walks among the
blossoms,

　　武士の心のけんそ
　　mononofu no kokoro no kenso

　　　　　62
　　刀して。
　　katana shite.

195

中
削るが如き　物思ひ。
naka
Kezuru ga gotoki monoomoi.

tortured by thoughts that—

196

ウ
思ひ逢瀬の　中をさく。
u
Omoi oose no naka o saku.

like a sharp sword—scrape away at his samurai heart.

197

ウ
川辺伝ひに　大判事
u
Kawabezutai ni Daihanji

清澄。
Kiyozumi.

(ソナエ)
(sonae)

The river hides these thoughts

198

ウ　　　　　　　ウ
こなたの岸より
u　　　　　　　u
(Sadaka) Konata no kishi yori

太宰の後室。
Dazai no kōshitsu.

from Lady Sadaka on the other bank.

199

ウ　　ハル　ウ
定高に　夫と　道分の
u　　　haru　u
Sadaka ni sore to michiwake no

石と　意地とをむかひ合。
ishi to iji to o mukaiau.

(ハネル)
(haneru)

She stops at the milestone defiantly to face Daihanji.

200 　ウ
　　川を隔て。
　　u
　　Kawa o hedatete.

201 　色　　　　63
　　大判事様。
　　iro
　　Daihanjisama.

"Lord Daihanji,

202 　詞
　　お役目御苦労に存じますと。
　　kotoba
　　Oyakume gokurō ni zonjimasu to.

service at court has kept you quite busy."

203 　地ハル　　　　　　　　ウ
　　声うちかけをかい取の　夫
　　ji haru 　　　　　　　**u**
　　Koe uchikake o kaidori no <u>tsuma</u>

　　のたましい。
　　<u>*no tamashii.*</u>

She holds tight her long skirt and offers cool greetings,

204 　フシ
　　放さぬ式礼。
　　fushi
　　<u>*Hanasanu shikirei.*</u>

　　（重ネフシ）
　　(kasane bushi)

without letting go of her husband's sword.

7

205 　地ハル　　色
　　清澄も　一ゆうし。
　　　　　　ji haru 　　**iro**
　　(Daihanji) Kiyozumi mo ichiyū shi.

Daihanji offers his greeting.

206 　詞
　　早かりし定高殿。
　　kotoba
　　Hayakarishi Sadakadono.

(Daihanji) "You've certainly returned in a hurry, Lady Sadaka."

207 御前を下るも一時 参る
Gozen o sagaru mo ittoki mairu

所も一つ成共。
tokoro mo hitotsu naredomo.

It's been but hours since we left the palace. Though our destinations be the same,

208 此背山は身が領分。
Kono seyama wa mi ga ryōbun.

Mt. Se is my land,

209 妹山は其元の御支配。
Imoyama wa sonomoto no goshihai.

and Mt. Imo, yours.

210 川向ひの喧嘩とやら
Kawamukai no kenka to yara

にらみ合て日を送る此年月。
niramioote hi o okuru kono toshitsuki.

We've squabbled over this territory—glaring daily at each other from the banks of the river—

211 心解るか解ぬかはけふ
Kokoro tokeru ka tokenu ka wa kyō

の役目の落去次第。
no yakume no rakkyo shidai.

for many months and years. Whether we finally settle the matter or not

212 二つ一つの勅命。
Futatsu hitotsu no chokumei.

depends on the outcome of today's orders. Only two choices: follow or rebel.

213 地ウ
狼狽た捌召るな。
ji u
Urotaeta sabaki mesaru na.

Don't be hasty with your decision!"

214 ハル   フシ
とまじり くしやつく茨道。 [64]
haru   fushi
To majiri kushatsuku ibaramichi.

A menacing scowl and words sharp as thorns.

8a

215　地ウ　ハル　　　色
脇へ　　かはして　仰の通り。
ji u　haru　　iro
Waki e kawashite ōse no tōri.

Sadaka evades the force of his speech.

216　詞
入鹿様の御じょう意は。
kotoba
Irukasama no gojōi wa.

(Sadaka) "Truly as you say, we've both agreed to accept Lord Iruka's

217　お互に子供の身の上。
Otagai ni kodomo no minoue.

orders for our children's fate.

218　受合ては帰りながら。
Ukeyoote wa kaerinagara.

Yet, though born of our flesh,

219　身腹は分ても心は
Mihara wa waketemo kokoro wa

別々。
betsubetsu.

their hearts are all their own.

220　若あつと申さぬ時は。
Moshi atto mōsanu toki wa.

If they refuse to abide,

221　マアお前にはどふせふと
Maa omae ni wa dooshoo to

思し召。
oboshimesu.

what do you intend to do?"

222　テ知た事。
Te shireta koto.

(Daihanji) "You know well the answer!

223　御前で承つた通り。
Gozen de uketamawatta tōri.

Just as we agreed at the palace—

224 首打放す分の事さ。
Kubi uchihanasu bun no koto sa.

cut off his head.

225 不所存なせがれは有て
Fushozon na segare wa atte

益なくなふて事かけず。
eki naku noote koto kakezu.

A worthless son won't be missed.

226 身の中の腐は殺で
Mi no uchi no kusari wa soide

捨るが跡の養生。
sutsuru ga ato no yōjō.

One can cut away a rotten limb—
so long as you take care of the
wound.

227 畢意親の子のと名を
Hikkyō oya no ko no to na o

付けるは人間の私。
tsukeru wa ningen no watakushi.

After all, it's only a mere human
like me who calls him son.

228 天地から見る時は同じ
Tenchi kara miru toki wa onaji

世界にわいた虫。
sekai ni waita mushi.

From heaven's vantage he's just
another worm.

229 ヤモ別に不便とは 存じ
Yamo betsu ni fubin to wa zonji

申さぬ。
mōsanu.

No . . ., I don't feel especially sad
about the matter."

230 きつい思し切。
Kitsui oboshikiri.

(Sadaka) "Well, certainly a cold
assessment!

231 私は又 いかふ了簡が
Watakushi wa mata ikoo ryōken ga

My feelings are quite the contrary.

違ます。
chigaimasu.

232 女子の未練な心
Onago no miren na kokoro

からは。
kara wa.

My feminine heart can't help

233 我子が可愛ふて成ませぬ。
Wagako ga kawayuute narimasenu.

but pity my child.

234 其かはりに　お前の
Sono kawari ni omae no

御子息さまの事は。
goshisokusama no koto wa.

But I actually care nothing for your son.

235 真実何共存じませぬ。
Shinjitsu nantomo zonjimasenu.

236 只大切なはこちの
Tada taisetsu na wa kochi no

娘。
musume.

I only know that my daughter is precious.

237 添い入鹿様のお声の
Katajikenai Irukasama no okoe no

かかつた身の幸。
kakatta mi no saiwai.

Now, having the good fortune of an invitation from kind

238 たとへどふ申さふ共。
Tatoe doo mōsoo tomo.

Lord Iruka—no matter what she may say—

239 母が勧て入内させ。
Haha ga susumete judaisase.

I intend to have her go to court.

240 お后様と多くの人に。   Just the thought of having her
     Okisakisama to ōku no hito ni.   respected and waited

241 敬ひ伝かそふと思へば。   upon as the empress—
     Uyamai kashizukasoo to omoeba.

242 此様な嬉しい事は   simply nothing could make me
     Kono yō na ureshii koto wa   happier.

    ごさりませぬ。
    gozarimasenu.

243 ホホホホホホホホホ   Ho, ho, ho, ho, ho, ho. . . ."
     hohohohohohohohoho   Hollow laughter.

    フシ
      と　　空笑ひ。
    fushi
    to <u>*sorawarai*</u>
    (雛形フシ
      [or 柳])
    (hinagata-bushi
    [or yanagi])

8b

244 詞   (Daihanji) "But what if she
    ムムシテ又得心せぬ   refuses?"
    kotoba
    Mumu shite mata tokushin senu

    時は。
    toki wa.

245 ハテそりやもふ是非に及ばぬ。   (Sadaka) "Then there's no way to
     Hate sorya moo zehi ni oyobanu.   avoid it.

246 枝ぶり悪い桜木は。   If a cherry tree's branches are bad,
     Edaburi warui sakuragi wa.

247 切て継木を致さねば。
Kitte tsugiki o itasaneba.

then it must be cut down and a
new successor planted,

248 太宰の家が立ませぬ。
Dazai no ie ga tachimasenu.

or the Dazai house will perish."

249 ヲヲそふなくては叶ふまい。
Oo soo nakute wa kanaumai.

(Daihanji) "It's what must be done.

250 此方のせがれとても　得心
Kono hō no segare totemo tokushin

If my son agrees to serve, then
he'll be a success

すれば身の出世。
sureba mi no shusse.

251 栄花を咲す此一枝
Eiga o sakasu kono hitoeda.

and blossom in the world. A
cherry branch in the river

252 川へ流すがしらせの
Kawa e nagasu ga shirase no

will signal my reply.

返答。
hentō.

253 盛ながらに流るるは
Sakarinagara ni nagaruru wa

A branch full-flowered will be an
auspicious sign;

吉左右。
kissō.

254 花を散して枝斗
Hana o chirashite edabakari

if a naked branch flows down the
stream,

流るるならば。
nagarurunaraba.

255 せがれが絶命と思はれよ。
Segare ga zetsumei to omowareyo.

then know it's the end of my boy."

256　いかにも。
　　　Ikanimo.

(Sadaka) "Agreed.

257　此方もサ此一枝。
　　　Kono hō mo sa kono hitoeda.

I'll do the same.

258　娘の命生花を。
　　　Musume no inochi ikebana o.

I'll make sure my daughter will
live by sending a branch in full
blossom."

259　ちらさぬやうに致しませふ。
　　　Chirasanu yō ni itashimashoo.

260　ヲヲサ今一時が互の
　　　Oosa ima hitotoki ga tagai no

(Daihanji) "Fine. This next hour
we must ford the rapids.

　　　瀬ごし。
　　　segoshi.

261　　カカリ　地
　　　此国境は生死の
　　　kakari　　　　ji
　　　Kono kunizakai wa shōji no

The border of our lands is the line
between life and death.

　　　色　　　詞　　　65
　　　ハハハハさかい。
　　　iro　　kotoba
　　　hahahaha sakai.

262　詞
　　　返答の善悪に寄て。
　　　kotoba
　　　Hentō no zennaku ni yotte.

Depending on their replies . . .,

263　遺恨に遺恨を重るか。
　　　Ikon ni ikon o kasanuru ka.

will we be forced to pile malice on
old grudges?"

264　サア　是迄の意趣を流して。
　　　Saa kore made no ishu o nagashite.

(Sadaka) "Will past enmity be
washed away?"

265 中吉野川と落合か。
Nakayoshinogawa to ochiyoo ka.

266 先それ迄はそう方の
Mazu sore made wa sōhō no

領分。
ryōbun.

(Daihanji) "First we must settle our own houses."

267 お捌きを待ております　と。
Osabaki o matte orimasu to.

(Sadaka) "I await the judgment."

268 地ハル
詞そばだつ
ji haru
(Both) Kotoba sobadatsu

Their words sharp . . .

ウ
親
u
(Daihanji) Oya

As parent . . .

と ……親。[66]
(Sadaka) to ...... oya.

And parent . . .

269 ウ
山と。
u
(Daihanji) Yama to.

To each mountain return,

270 大和路分かれても。
(Sadaka) Yamatoji wakarete mo.

And though they part, the road of Yamato . . .

271 かわらぬ紀の路
(Both) Kawaranu kinoji

And of Ki are the same . . .

恩愛の。[67]
(Daihanji) onnai no.

As the love . . .

272 ウ
胸は霞に

u
(Sadaka) *Mune wa kasumi ni*

埋れし ヲクリ 庵り

okuri
uzumoreshi iori

イイ。
(Daihanji) *Ii.*

In their hearts . . .

273 の。
(Sadaka) *No.*

274 ヲ ヲ   ヲヲヲヲヲヲ
(Daihanji) *Oo*   (Both) *Oooooo*

おお   ヲクリ
内に
okuri
(Daihanji) *Oo* (Sadaka) *Uchi ni*

別れ入。 68
wakareiru.

Each to his own cottage . . .

they part.

9a

275 地ウ
立派にいひは

ji u
(Sadaka) <u>*Rippa ni ii wa*</u>

放しても定かにしらぬ 子 ハル

haru
<u>*hanashitemo*</u> *Sadaka ni shiranu ko*

の心。 69
no kokoro.

(ハリマ)
(harima)

Though she spoke so assuredly,
Sadaka has in fact no idea

276　ハル　　　　中
覚束なくも　呼子鳥。

haru　　　naka

Obotsukanakumo yobu kodori.

of the feelings in her child's heart, and though doubtful of the outcome,

277　色　　地ウ　　ハル
娘　娘　と　谷の戸に。

iro　ji u　　haru

Musume musume to tani no to ni.

she beckons her darling— "daughter, daughter!"—at the door of the house.

278　中　　　　　　ウ
音なふ初音　雛鳥

**　　　　naka　　　u**

(Hina) Oto noo hatsune Hinadori

も。

mo.

From within Hinadori straightens her kimono and offers her greeting,

279　ハル　フシカカリ
母の　　　　機嫌をさし足に.

haru　　fushi kakari

Haha no kigen o sashiashi ni.

hoping to please her mother.

9b

280　詞
かか様よふぞ今日は。

kotoba

Kakasama yoo zo konnichi wa.

(Hinadori) "Mother, today is such a fine day

281　お目出たふ存じますと。

Omedetoo zonjimasu to.

for the Dolls' Festival."

282　フシ　　　　　　　　　70
武家の行義の三つ指に。

fushi

Buke no gyōgi no mitsuyubi ni.

（雛形フシ〔柳〕）

(hinagata-bushi[yanagi])

With hands to the floor, she bows in samurai fashion.

10a

283　地ウ
　　かたい程なお親子
　　　　ji u
　　(Sadaka) Kataihodo nao oyako

　　　色　　　　⁷¹
　の　したしみ。
　iro
　no shitashimi.

The more stiff the greeting, the more intimate mother and child.

284　詞
　　ヲヲよふ飾が出来ました。
　　kotoba
　　Oo yoo kazari ga dekimashita.

(Sadaka) "The doll display looks marvelous,

285　けふはそなたの顔持も
　　Kyō wa sonata no kaomochi mo

　　よさそふで。
　　yosasoo de.

and your color is much improved.

286　一入目出たい。
　　Hitoshio medetai.

Certainly something to celebrate!

287　母も祝ふて献上の此
　　Haha mo ioote kenjō no kono

　　花。
　　hana.

Use these flowers as my offering.

288　備へてたも。
　　Sonaetetamo.

No matter how old one grows, how wonderful is this festival.

289　いくつに成ても雛祭は
　　Ikutsu ni nattemo hinamatsuri wa

　　嬉しい物。
　　ureshii mono.

290 女子共　何成と。
Onagodomo nannari to.

You girls must somehow find amusements to suit my daughter's pleasure

291 娘が気にあふ遊びをして。
Musume ga ki ni au asobi o shite.

292 随分と諫めてくれと。
Zuibun to isametekure to.

and make her feel even better."

293 地ウ
いつに勝れし後室の。
ji　u
Itsu ni sugureshi kōshitsu no.

Seeing the mistress in rare spirits, Kogiku considers it a

294 ハル
機嫌は訴訟のよい
　　　　haru
(Kogiku) Kigen wa soshō no yoi

出汐．
deshio.

choice moment to broach the request and prods Hinadori.

295 詞
今のをちやつと乗出して
kotoba
Imano o chatto noridashite

地ハル
御らふじませとこしもとに。
　　　　ji haru
gorōjimase to koshimoto ni.

(Kogiku) "Now is a great time to bring up the subject."

296 ウ　　　　　　中
腰押れてもとやかふと。
u　　　　**naka**
Koshi osaretemo toyakoo to.

But though encouraged, she misses the chance; her heart,

297 フシ　　　　　　72
云そそくれのもつれ髪。
fushi
Iisosokure no <u>motsuregamin ni</u>.

too distressed, tangled like hair all dishevelled.

（三ツユリ）

(mitsu yuri)

10b

298　詞
イヤのふ雛鳥。

kotoba

Iya noo Hinadori.

(Sadaka) "Now, Hinadori, if a mother binds a grown daughter with her

299　背丈延た娘を。

Setake nobita musume o.

300　親の傍に引付て置ば。

Oya no soba ni hikitsukete okeba.

apron strings, it'll only be seed for sickness.

301　結句病の種。

Kekku yamai no tane.

302　それで急に思案を極め。

Sore de kyū ni shian o kiwame.

So I've decided

303　そなたによい殿御を持す。

Sonata ni yoi tonogo o motasu.

you're to marry a fine man.

304　嫁入さすが嬉しいか。

Yomeiri sasu ga ureshii ka.

Doesn't that make you happy!"

305　エエ。

Ee.

(Hinadori) "What?"

306　ハテ気遣仕やんな。

Hate kizukai shiyanna.

(Sadaka) "Now don't worry.

307　可愛娘の一生を任す

Kawaii musume no isshō o makasu

I could never entrust my precious daughter

夫。
otto.

308 そなたの気に入ぬ男を。
Sonata no ki ni iranu otoko o.

to someone she didn't like.

309 何の母が持そふぞ。
Nan no haha ga motasoo zo.

Isn't that true, girls?"

310 ナアこしもと共。
Naa koshimotodomo.

311 ハイハイ 左様でござります。
(Kikyō) Haihai sayō de gozarimasu.

(Kikyō) "Yes, yes, of course, madam.

312 お気の通った後室様。
Oki no tōtta kōshitsusama.

Lady Sadaka understands well the feelings of young people.

313 嫁入の先は大かた今の。
Yomeiri no saki wa ōkata ima no.

Yes, the groom must be the gentleman

314 ナ こがるる君で
Na kogaruru kimi de

ごさりませふと。
gozarimashoo to.

Hinadori has such affection for."

315 地ウ
押推あてども得手勝手。
ji u
Oshizui atedomo etekatte.

Her hint falls on deaf ears.

316 ハル
誰にか縁を
haru
(Sadaka) Tare ni ka en o

To whom will the conjugal ties be knotted?

組紐に。
kumihimo ni.

317 スエカカリ 中
胸は　　真紅の。
sue kakari naka
Mune wa shinku no.

Sadaka's heart is inflamed with worry, but she disguises her

318 ハル　　　色
ふさがる箱　取出し。
haru　　　　iro
Fusagaru hako toriidashi.

anxiety in the action of taking out a brightly wrapped box.

10c

319 詞
妹瀬をならぶる雛の日は
kotoba
Imose o naraburu hina no hi wa

嫁入の吉日。
yomeiri no kichinichi.

(Sadaka) "This festival of aligning girl and boy dolls shall be

320 此箱の主は極る
Konohako no nushi wa kiwamaru

殿御。
tonogo.

the wonderful day of matrimony. The presents of this box represent

321 雛の御前で夫定め。
Hina no gozen de tsumasadame.

Hinadori's new husband; he offers this to the doll display

322 コレ　そなたの夫といふは誰
Kore sonata no otto to yuu wa tare

有ふ。
aroo.

as a nuptial pledge. Can you guess who the groom is?

323 入鹿大臣様じやはいの。
Irukadaijinsama jawaino.

He is none other than the great Minister Iruka!"

324 エエ そんならわたしを嫁入
Ee, sonnara watashi o yomeiri

さすとは。
sasu to wa.

(Hinadori) "What! Then your plans to have me married are . . ."

325 ヲヲ太宰の小弐が娘
Oo Dazai no Shōni ga musume

雛鳥。
Hinadori.

(Sadaka) "The great Iruka has heard of the beauty of the daughter

326 美人の聞へ叡分に達し。
Bijin no kikoe eibun ni tasshi.

of Dazai Shōni and wishes to make her his empress.

327 入内させよと モ有難い
Judaisaseyo to mo arigatai

勅じょ。
chokujo.

This is an imperial decree to cherish."

328 エエ ハアハア
Ee   haahaa

地上
はつとびっくりうろうろと
ji kami
Hatto bikkuri urouro to

スヱテ   73
詞は涙。
suete
kotoba wa namida.

(Hinadori) "Wha . . . Wha . . . No . . . What!"

Hinadori is aghast, unable to utter a word;

329 中
ぐむ斗。
naka
Gumubakari.

all are washed away in rushing tears.

10d

330   詞
　　　ヲヲ肝が潰れる筈。
kotoba
Oo kimo ga tsubureru hazu.

(Sadaka) "Oh, you have good reason to be overwhelmed. It is enough

331   夫と申すも恐れ多い。
Otto to mōsu mo osoreōi.

excitement for a young girl to get married.

332   一天の君をむこに取家の
Itten no kimi o muko ni toru ie no

面目。
menboku.

And it is an even greater

333   日本国に此上のない
Nippongoku ni kono ue no nai

嫁入の随一。
yomeiri no zuiichi.

honor for a family to have the emperor for its son-in-law.

334   果報な娘。
Kahō na musume.

This is the greatest blessing in all Japan!

335   此様なめでたい事が
Kono yō na medetai koto ga

有物か。
aru mono ka.

What a fortunate daughter! Could there be a more auspicious happening?

336   ナア女子共。
Naa onagodomo.

Right, girls?"

337   ハイハイおめでたいと申そふか。
Hai hai omedetai to mōsooka.

(Kogiku) "Yes, yes. Should I offer congratulations or . . . No, this is

338 イヤモいつそ乱騒ぎで
Iya mo isso ransawagi de
ござりますと。
gozarimasu to.

going to bring the house down."

339 地ウ
ji u
工合違ひの嫁入に。
Guwaichigai no yomeiri ni.

At the revelation of these
unexpected marriage plans,

340 ハル
haru
菊もききょうも投首の。
Kiku mo Kikyō mo nagekubi no.

both Kogiku and Kikyō bow and

341 フシ
fushi
二人は小腹立て行。
Futari wa kobara tatte yuku.

leave angrily with heads drooping.

11

342 地ウ
ji u
母の心も
(Sadaka) Haha no kokoro mo
色々に。[74]
iroiro ni.

Sadaka's heart too is torn asunder.

343 ハル   色
haru   **iro**
咲分の枝 差出し。
Sakiwake no eda sashiidashi.

She takes down the flowered
branch from the shelf.

344 詞
kotoba
親の赦さすぬ云かはし。
Oya no yurusanu iikawashi.

(Sadaka) "For an affair
unsanctioned by the parents, even
should

345 徒はしかつて返らず。
Itazura wa shikatte kaerazu.

one scold the tryst, facts can't be altered.

346 一旦思ひ初た男。
Ittan omoisometa otoko.

A virtuous woman must always

347 いつ迄も立て通すが女
Itsu made mo tatetōsu ga onago
の操。
no misao.

stand with the man she has given her heart.

348 破りやとは云ぬが。
Yaburya to wa iwanu ga.

I won't suggest you break your vow,

349 貞女の立やうが有そふな物。
Teijo no tateyō ga arisō na mono.

but there is such a thing as a woman's proper duty.

350 コレ　とつくりとよふ思案仕や。
Kore tokkuri to yō shian shiya.

Listen and consider carefully what I have to say.

351 此花は八重一重。
Kono hana wa yae hitoe.

On this branch there is a mixture of single and

352 互ひに不和なる親々の。
Tagai ni fuwa naru oyaoya no.

multi-layered blossoms—

353 心揃はぬ二つの花。
Kokoro sorowanu futatsu no hana.

354 一つ枝に取結び。
Hitotsueda ni torimusubi.

enemies grafted onto one branch.

355 切放すにはなされぬ悪縁
Kirihanasu ni hanasarenu akuen

Though we may try to sever them, such flowers are fated to fall.

の仇花。

no adabana.

356　今そなたの心次第で。

Ima sonata no kokoro shidai de.

The choice is yours.

357　当時入鹿大臣の深山嵐

Tōji Irukadaijin no miyama oroshi

に吹散され。

ni fukichirasare.

In the tempest roaring from Iruka's palace, blossoms will scatter.

358　久我之助はコレ腹を

Koganosuke wa kore hara o

切ねば成ぬぞや。

kiraneba naranu zoya.

Koganosuke may very well be driven to suicide, or he may

359　雛鳥と縁をきつて入鹿様

Hinadori to en o kitte Irukasama

へ降参すれば。

e kōsan sureba.

sever ties with you and submit to Iruka's demands, thus saving his life.

360　清船も命を助る。

Kiyofune mo inochi o tasukaru.

Your answer shall float down the river.

361　知せは川へ流す桜。

Shirase wa kawa e nagasu sakura.

Full-blossomed or

362　散かちらぬが身の

Chiru ka chiranu ga mi no

納まり。

osamari.

naked branch will tell the fate.

363　時に従ふ風になびき。

Toki ni shitagau kaze ni nabiki.

These are times to bend with prevailing winds.

364 君が手生の花になれば。
Kimi ga teike no hana ni nareba.

If you become a flower of the court.

365 八重も一重もつつがなふ。
Yae mo hitoe mo tsutsuga noo.

both the many layered

366 九重の内に伝るる
Kokonoe no uchi ni kashizukaruru

互の幸ひ。
tagai no saiwai.

and single-petal blossoms will be spared destruction. By going to the palace you'll both be saved.

367 恋しと思ふ久我之助。
Koishi to omou Kogonosuke.

Koganosuke whom you dearly love—

368 たすけふと殺さふと今の返事
Tasukyoo to korosoo to ima no henji

のたつた一つ。
to tatta hitotsu.

with your answer you'll save or kill him.

369 貞女の立て様。
Teijo no tateyō.

Do your duty as a virtuous woman.

370 サアサアサササササ見たいと。
Saa saa sasasasasa mitai to.

Well . . . well . . . what'll it be. Your answer?"

371 地色ハル   75
恋も　情も弁へて。

ji iro haru
Koi mo nasake mo wakimaete.

Her words distinguish desire and true affection.

372 地上
義理の柵みせき留ても

ji kami
Giri no shigarami sekitometemo

The strictures of duty may trap love in its meshes,

涙せき上せき上 ハル
haru
(Hina) namida sekiage sekiage

but they cannot restrain rushing tears.

ながら母様段々 色
iro
nagara hahasama dandan

(Hinadori) "Mother, I've gradually come to perceive the meaning of your words. I shall not thwart your wishes."

聞訳ました お詞は 地ハル ウ 色
ji haru   u   iro
kikiwakemashita okotoba wa

背きませぬ。 76
somukimasenu.

373 詞
そんなら得心して入内仕て
kotoba
Sonnara tokushin shite judai shite

(Sadaka) "Then you've agreed. You'll go to court?"

たもるか。
tamoru ka.

374 アイ（アイ）。
Ai (ai).

(Hinadori) "Yes. Yes."

375 ヲヲ嬉しや。
Oo ureshiya.

(Sadaka) "Oh, how happy that makes me! You've chosen bravely.

376 出かしやつた 出かしやつた。
Dekashatta dekashatta.

377 それでこそ貞女なれ。
Sore de koso teijo nare.

Now you're truly a mirror of virtue.

378 馴ぬ雲井の宮づかへ。
Narenu kumoi no miyazukae.

You're not accustomed to life at

379 武家の娘と笑われな。
　　　Buke no musume to warawarena.

（カカリ）
（kakari）

the 'court above the clouds.' We'll
not let them laugh

380 地中　　　ハル
　　　けふより内裏　　上ろうの。
　　　ji naka　　　haru
　　　Kyō yori dairi jōrō no.

at a warrior's daughter. From today
your hair

381 詞
　　　髪も改めすべらかし。
　　　kotoba
　　　Kami mo aratame suberakashi.

will be in the flowing style of court
ladies.

382 祝ふて母が結直して
　　　Ioote haha ga yuinaoshite

やりましよと。
yarimasho to.

We'll celebrate; I'll arrange your
coiffure myself."

383 長地ハル
　　　いそいそ立は立ながら
　　　nagaji haru
　　　Iso iso tachi wa tachi nagara
　　　ヲ　　　　　　　77
　　　娘の心思ひやり。
　　　haru u
　　　musume no kokoro omoiyari.

Sadaka slowly stands up, in
sympathy with

384 ヲ
　　　別れの櫛の　　はかなさも。
　　　haru u
　　　Wakare no kushi no hakanasamo.

the pain that racks her daughter's
heart. The comb, to tie Hinadori's

385 ウキン　　　　　　中　　　78
　　　ときほどかれぬ憂　思ひ。
　　　u gin　　　　　naka
　　　Toki hodokarenu uki omoi.

hair for her marriage to
Koganosuke, is now loosened for
court.

386 ウフシ
　　重き背山の。

　　　　　u   fushi
　　(Koga) Omoki seyama no.

No relief for Hinadori's agony.

12a

　　　　　　　　　79
387 庵の内。

　　Iori no uchi.

Across on Mt. Se

388 地ハル　　色
　　父が前に　謹で。

　　ji haru　　　iro
　　Chichi ga mae ni tsusshinde.

Koganosuke is reserved before his father's formal bow.

389 詞
　　久我之助が心底聞し

　　kotoba
　　Koganosuke ga shintei kikoshi

　　召分られ。

　　meshiwakerare.

(Koganosuke) "For Iruka to have kindly considered my feelings in

390 切腹御赦免下さるる

　　Seppuku goshamen kudasaruru

　　事。

　　koto.

the Uneme incident and given the command of *seppuku* is

391 身に取ていか斗大慶至極

　　Mi ni totte ikabakari taikei shigoku

　　と手をつけば。

　　to te o tsukeba.

the greatest joy possible for me."

392 地ハル
　　黙然たる大判事。

　　　　　ji haru
　　(Daihanji) Mokunentaru Daihanji.

A silent Daihanji opens his eyes dimmed with tears.

393   良打うるむ。
Ya ya uchiurumu.

394   フシ
目を開き。
fushi
Me o hiraki.

（染太夫中フシ）
(sometayū naka fushi)

12b

395   詞
今朝入鹿大臣此大判事を
kotoba
Konchō Irukadaijin kono Daihanji

召出し。
o meshindashi.

(Daihanji) "This morning when summoned for an audience with Iruka,

396   先帝寵愛の采女。
Sentei chōai no Uneme.

the subject in question was grave. He revealed that

397   身を投げ死たりとは
Mi o nageshishitari to wa

偽。
itsuwari.

the drowning of Uneme, former emperor Tenchi's favorite, was a lie and

398   其方がせがれ久我之助。
Sono hō ga segare Koganosuke.

that my son had helped her flee into hiding.

399   人知ぬ方へ落しやりしに
Hitoshirenu kata e otoshiyarishi ni

極れば。
kiwamareba.

He even accused me of

400 必定汝らが方に
Hitsujō nanjira ga kata ni

かくまひ有べしとの難題。
kakumai arubeshi to no nandai.

harboring her. I had no idea of

401 元来知ぬ大判事。
Motoyori shiranu Daihanji.

all these happenings, and the

402 よくよく思へば采女の御難
Yokuyoku omoeba Uneme no gonan

をさけん為。
o saken tame.

more I thought about it, the plan

403 猿沢の池に入水のていに
Sarusawa no ike ni jusui no tei ni

もてなして。
motenashite.

to have Uneme elude death by a fake

404 密に落し参らせしは。
Hisoka ni otoshi mairaseshi wa.

drowning and secret escape was too grand a scheme

405 中中久我之助が智恵で
Nakanaka Koganosuke ga chie de

ない。
nai.

for young Koganosuke's talents.

406 鎌足公の差図を受ての
Kamatarikō no sashizu o ukete no

計ひと。
hakarai to.

I realized for the first time that

407 知たは身もけふが始。
Shitta wa mi mo kyō ga hajime.

you had taken orders from Kamatari.

408 地色中 ハル [80]
親にもかくし包みしは
ji iro naka **haru**
Oya ni mo kakushi tsutsumishi wa

大事を洩さぬ心の金打。
daiji o morasanu kokoro no kinchō.

You kept it buried in your heart, secret even from your father.

409 ウ
若輩者には神妙の
u
Jakuhaimono ni wa shinmyō no

仕かた。
shikata.

Such fortitude is honorable in the spirit of a true samurai.

410 ハハア出かしたりと
Hahaa dekashitari to

フシ [81]
思ふに付。
fushi
<u>*omou ni tsuki.*</u>

（一ツユリ）
(hitotsu yuri)

What magnificent behavior! Just as I was gloating over your heroic actions

12c

411 詞
邪智ふかき入鹿。
kotoba
Jachi bukaki Iruka.

that cunning Iruka said,

412 久我之助が降参せば命を
Koganosuke ga kōsan seba inotto

助ん連来れと。
tasuken tsurekitare to.

'If Koganosuke submits to me, I'll pardon him.'

413 情の詞は釣よせて。
Nasake no kotoba wa tsuri yosete.

These kind words were tossed out as bait to bring you to court.

414　拷問にかけん謀。[82]

Gōmon ni kaken hakarigoto.

（カカリ）

(kakari)

But it's a sly trick, and you'll be
tortured to reveal Uneme's
hideaway.

415　地色ハル
責殺さるる苦しみより

ji iro haru

Semekorosaruru kurushimi yori

切腹さすれば 采女の詮議
　　　　　　ウ
　　　　　u

seppuku sasureba Uneme no sengi

Rather than face a painful death
within his grasp, commit *seppuku*

の根を断 大功。[83]
　　ナカ
　　naka

no ne o tatsu taikō.

and achieve a great deed by
cutting away the root

416　ウ
天下の主の 御為には。[84]

u

Tenga no aruji no ontame ni wa.

leading to Uneme. For the
emperor's sake it is a

417　ハル
何せがれの一人など。

　　haru

Nani segare no ichinin nado.

samurai's duty never to begrudge
an only son's life.

418　ラ
律に生る草一本

haru u

Mugura ni ooru kusa ippon

引抜よりもさ細な事と。

hikinuku yori mo sasai na koto to.

It's only a trifling more than
pulling out a creeping weed
among the grass.

419　涙一滴こぼさぬは 武士の表。

*Nanda itteki kobosanu wa bushi no
omote.*

Never to shed a tear is the
warrior's code. Yet could there

420   上
　　子の可愛ない者が凡。

kami

Ko no kawayuu nai mono ga oyoso.

ever be a parent who loves not his child!

421   入　　　　　　　　85
　　生有者に有ふか。

iru

Shō aru mono ni arooka.

Ashamed to have a son too

422   余り健気な子に恥て。　86

Amari kenage na ko ni hajite.

brave, the father acts as his second in *seppuku*—cutting off his head.

423   色
　　親が介錯　してくれる。

iro

Oya ga kaishaku shitekureru.

424   地色ハル　　　　　87
　　侍の奇羅をかざり。

ji iro haru

Samurai no kira o kazari.

A wonderful example of samurai valor! I never dreamed in

425   丂
　　いかめしく横たへし大小。

haru u

Ikameshiku yokotaeshi daishō.

all my fifty years that these two swords would be called upon

426   せがれが首を切刀

Segare ga kubi o kiru katana

　　　　地上　　　　　88
　　とは五十年来しらざりしと。

ji kami

to wa gojū nenrai shirazarishi to.

（クドキ）

(kudoki)

to sever the head of my son."

427 ウ
老の悔に清船
u
Oi no kuyami ni (Koga) Kiyofune

も。 ^89
mo.

For his aged father's grief and
merciful heart,

428
親の慈悲心有難涙。 中
　　　　　naka
Oya no jihishin arigatananda.

Koganosuke weeps tears of
gratitude.

429 ハル
命二つ有ならば君に
haru
Inochi futatsu arunaraba kimi ni

は死て忠義を立。
wa shishite chūgi o tate.

(Koganosuke) "Had I two lives, I'd
die to serve my sovereign and

430 ウ
父には生て養育の御恩を
u
Chichi ni wa ikite yōiku no goon o

送り申さんに。
okurimōsan ni.

live for my father's love, but

431
今生の 色 残念 地上 是一つ と。 ^90
　　　　iro　　　　ji kami
Konjō no zannen kore hitotsu to.

regretfully I have but one to give."

432 ハル
顔を見上 見下して
haru
Kao o miyage (Daihanji) mioroshite

He looks up, and Daihanji down;
together they weep

入
わつと
iru
(Both) *watto*

^{スエ中}
ひれ伏　　親子の誠。⁹¹
sue naka
hirefusu oyako no makoto.

and collapse, truly father and son.

13a

433　地ハル
こなたの亭には
ji haru
(Sadaka) *Konata no tei ni wa*

^中
母　後室。
naka
haha kōshitsu.

At the other house Sadaka says happily,

434　詞
サアサア目出たい。
kotoba
Saasaa medetai.

"Well, well, congratulations!

435　そなたの名の雛鳥を。
Sonata no na no Hinadori o.

Your name Hinadori, altered a bit,

436　其ままの内裏雛。
Sonomama no dairibina.

becomes 'Dairibina' the empress doll.

437　装束の付様も。
Shōzoku no tsukeyō mo.

We'll fashion your

438　此女雛と見合せて。
Kono mebina to miyawasete.

robes to suit your role as queen.

439　地ハル　　　フシ
　　サアサア早ふ　と有ければ。
ji haru　　　fushi
Saasaa hayoo to arikereba.

Yes, let's hurry and get ready."

13b

440　地ハル　　　中　　　92
　　恨めしげに　打守り。
　　　　ji haru　　naka
(Hina) Urameshige ni uchimamori.

But her words are heard in anger.
(Hinadori takes the doll in hand.)

441　地ウ　　　　　　ハル
　　女大一対いつ迄も　添とげる
　　ji u　　　　　haru
Myōto ittsui itsumade mo soitogeru

こそ雛の徳。
koso hina no toku.

(Hinadori) "A virtuous woman
should manage somehow to be
with her husband.

442　ウ
　　思ふお人に引放され。
　　u
Omou ohito ni hikihanasare.

Torn away from my love, how can
I look forward to life as the
empress!

443　詞
　　何楽しみの女御后。
　　kotoba
Nani tanoshimi no nyōgo kisaki.

444　茨の絹の十二一重。
Ibara no kinu no jūnihitoe.

The fine, many-layered silks will be
thorns.

445　雛の姿も恨しと。
Hina no sugata mo urameshi to.

Even the sight of this empress doll
angers me!"

446　地ウ　　　　　93
　　取て打付えん板に。
　　ji u
Totte uchitsuke en'ita ni.

She tosses the doll aside, and

447 ウ
ころりと落し女雛の首。

u

Korori to ochishi mebina no kubi.

it rolls onto the veranda, its head breaking off.

448 ハル
驚く母の胸板に。 [94]

haru

Odoroku haha no munaita ni.

Sadaka is shocked.

449 必死と極る。

Hisshi to kiwamaru.

In her heart she now realizes

450 地入 [95]
娘の命。

ji iru

Musume no inochi.

that her daughter must die.

451 包めどせきくるはらはら

Tsutsumedo sekikuru harahara

涙。 [96]

namida.

Tears restrained for too long burst forth.

452 詞
娘入内さすといふたは

kotoba

Musume judai sasu to yuutta wa

偽り。

itsuwari.

(Sadaka) "It's all a lie; sending you to court's a lie! Just as this

453 真此様に首切て。

Ma kono yō ni kubi kitte.

doll's head was severed, so must be yours.

454 渡すのじやはいのふ。

Watasu no jawainoo.

I shall present your head!"

455 エエそんならほんぼんに。　　　　(Hinadori) "Wha . . . Wha . . .
　　Ee sonnara honbon ni.　　　　　　Then . . . Then you'll

456 貞女を立さして下さりますか。　　let me truly be virtuous.
　　Teijo o tatesashite kudasarimasu ka.

457 アアかたじけない。　　　　　　　How happy I am!
　　Aa katajikenai.

458 有がたいと。　　　　　　　　　　Thank you dear mother."
　　Arigatai to.

459 地ハル　入　　　　　　　　97　　Sadaka takes Hinadori's hand.
　　ふし　　拝む　手を取て。
　　ji haru iru
　　Fushiogamu (Sadaka) te o totte.

460 上　　ウ　　　　　　　　　　　　(Sadaka) "Could I possibly not
　　ノウ入内せずに死るのを　　　　know that my daughter would be
　　kami u　　　　　　　　　　　happier
　　Nō judai sezu ni shinuruno o

　　　　　　　　　　98
　　それ程に嬉しがる。
　　sorehodo ni ureshigaru.

461 ウ　　色　　　　　　　　　　　　to die rather than go to court?
　　娘の心　知いで
　　u　　　　　　iro
　　Musume no kokoro shiraide

　　ならふか。
　　naroo ka.

462 詞　　　　　　　　　　　　　　　While I knew you'd be ready to
　　あつと受ても自害して。　　　　sacrifice
　　kotoba
　　Atto uketemo jigaishite.

463 死る覚悟は知ながら。
Shinuru kakugo wa shirinagara.

yourself and perish, when your
dear Koganosuke heard of your
death,

464 そなたの死る事聞たら。
Sonata no shinuru koto kiitara.

465 思ひ合た久我之助。
Omoioota Koganosuke.

he would surely follow you.

466 倶に自害召れふもしれぬ。
Tomo ni jigai mesaryoo mo shirenu.

It was my wish to save at least

467 せめて一人は助けたさ。
Semete hitori wa tasuketasa.

one of you that pushed me to try
persuasion.

468 一旦得心したにして。
Ittan tokushin shita ni shite.

The hair your mother was to

469 母が手づからといた髪は。
Haha ga tezukara toita kami wa.

arrange was not the flowing style
for the court,

470 下髪じやない。
Sagegami ja nai.

but the raised style

471 成敗のかき上髪。
Seibai no kakiagegami.

for execution.

472 介錯の介錯の
Kaishaku no kaishaku no

支度じやはいの。
shitaku jawai no.

I was preparing to cut your head
off! Princesses or

473 地上
尊いも卑いも姫ごぜの。
ji kami
Takai mo hikii mo himegoze no.

peasants have but one husband.

474　ウ
　　夫といふはたつた一人。
haru u
Otto to yuu wa tatta hitori.

Could any mother be happy to see her

475　けがらはしい玉の輿
　　Kegarawashii tama no koshi

　　　入　　色　　　　　99
　　何の母も　嬉しかろ。
　　　iru　　iro
　　nan no haha mo ureshikaro.

daughter in a jeweled palanquin— tainted with the filth of a traitor!

476　詞
　　祝言こそせぬ。
kotoba
Shūgen koso senu.

You won't be able to celebrate a wedding,

477　心斗は久我之助が。
　　Kokorobakari wa Koganosuke ga.

but are you willing to die

478　宿の妻と思ふて死にや。
　　Yado no tsuma to omoote shiniya.

as Koganosuke's wife?"

479　アイ
　　Ai.

(Hinadori) "Yes."

　　ヤ。　100
　　Ya.

(Sadaka) "Can you?"

480　アイ。
　　Ai.

(Hinadori) "Yes."

　　ヤ。
　　Ya.

(Sadaka) "Are you certain?"

481　アイ。
　　Ai.

(Hinadori) "I am."

482　エエ是程に思ふ中。
　　Ee kore hodo ni omou naka.

(Sadaka) "You love him that much—

483 一日 半時添しもせず。

Ichinichi hantoki sowashimosezu.

and I can't let you be with him for one day, even an hour.

484 地上
さいの河原へやるかいのと。[101]

ji kami

Sai no kawara e yaru kai no to.

Instead, I must send you to a cruel death!"

485 ウ
引寄引寄雛鳥

u

Hikiyose hikiyose (Hina) Hinadori

キン
も　　膝に取付抱付。[102]

　　gin

mo hiza ni toritsuki idakitsuki.

She hugs her daughter tightly. Hinadori squeezes her mother's knees in gratitude.

486 ウ
かたじけなさと嬉しさと逢で

u

Katajikenasa to ureshisa to awade

　　　　ウ
別るる 名残の涙。[103]

　　　　u

wakaruru nagori no namida.

Tears of joy and of agony, to part without seeing him,

487 　　フシ
一つに　　落る

　　　　fushi

(Both) Hitotsu ni otsuru

三つ瀬川。[104]

mitsusegawa.

（三ツユリクドキ)

(mitsu yuri kudoki)

flow together into the Three Rivers of hell.

14

488 地ウ
川を隔て 清船

　　　ji u

(Koga) Kawa o hedatete Kiyofune
が。[105]
ga.

Across the river Koganosuke faces his final moments

489　最後の観念　わるびれず。
　　ハル　　　中
　　haru　　naka
　　Saigo no kwannen warubirezu.

106　with unflinching composure while
his father reads the sutra.

490　焼刃直なる魂の。
　　ウ
　　u
　　Yakiba sugunaru tamashii no.

Well-tempered, both his spirit and
the eleven-inch blade he carefully

491　九寸五分取直し。
　　Kusun gobu torinaoshi.

492　腹にぐつと突立る。
　　Hara ni gutto tsukitatsuru.

takes in hand—and thrusts into
his stomach!

493　ヤレ暫く引廻すな。
　　詞
　　kotoba
　　Yare shibaraku hikimawasu na.

(Daihanji) "Wait, don't pull it
across yet! No need

494　覚悟の切腹せく事は
　　Kakugo no seppuku seku koto wa
　　ない。
　　nai.

to rush when you're determined.

495　コリヤ冥土の血脈
　　Korya meido no kechimyaku
　　読さしの無量品。
　　yomisashi no muryōbon.

Listen, while I'm reading

496　親が読じゅする間。
　　Oya ga dokuju suru aida.

this treasured sutra why don't you
glance even once at the

497　一生の名残女が頬。
　　Isshō no nagori onna ga tsura.

498 一目見てなぜ死ぬ。
     Hitome mite naze shinanu.

face of the woman you will leave
behind? Why?"

499 イイヤ存じも寄ず。
     Iiya zonji mo yorazu.

(Koganosuke) "I . . . I don't know
myself.

500 此期に及んで左程狼狽た
     Kono go ni oyonde sahodo urotaeta

     未練な性根はござりませぬ。
     miren na shōne wa gozarimasenu.

At this point I've no particular
regrets

501 去ながら。
     Sarinagara.

to cloud my way.

502 今はの際の御願ひ。
     Ima wa no kiwa no onnegai.

But I do have one final request.

503 私相果しと聞ば。
     Watakushi aihateshi to kikaba.

     (カカリ)
     (kakari)

When she hears of my death,

504 地中
     義理に繋がれ雛鳥も。
     ji naka
     Giri ni tsunagare Hinadori mo.

trapped by our vows, she'll wish to
kill herself.

505 ハル   色
     倶に生害と　申べし。
     haru   iro
     Tomo ni shōgai to mōsubeshi.

506 詞
     左有時は太宰の家も
     kotoba
     Sa aru toki wa Dazai no ie mo

It will mean the end of the Dazai
line.

断絶。
danzetsu.

507 暫くの間ながら。
Shibaraku no aida nagara.

If only for a short while, please hide the fact of my death.

508 切腹の義は お隠しなされ。
Seppuku no gi wa okakushinasare.

509 降参承知致せしていに。
Kōsan shōchi itaseshi tei ni.

When Lady Sadaka gets word that I've decided to abide by Iruka's orders, Hinadori will be able

510 後室方へお知せ 有ば。
Kōshitsukata e oshirase areba.

511 女も得心仕り。
Onna mo tokushin tsukamatsuri.

to choose to go to court.

512 入内致せば彼が為。
Judai itaseba kare ga tame.

Though tainted with an adulteress's

513 地ハル
不義の汚名は受たれ共。
ji haru
Fugi no omei wa uketaredomo.

name, at least she will show a pure heart

514 ウ
是ぞ色に迷はぬ潔白。
u
Kore zo iro ni mayowanu keppaku.

unsullied by lust."

515 詞　　　色
ヲヲ出かしたよく気が付た。
kotoba　iro
Oo dekaita yoku ki ga tsuita.

[107] (Daihanji) "Oh, what a noble thought! You certainly are right. I'm proud of

516   詞
年来立ぬく武士の意地。
kotoba
Toshigoro tatenuku bushi no iji.

your samurai spirit, advanced
beyond your youth.

517   地ウ   ハル
不和な中程　　義理深し。
ji u   haru
Fuwa na nakahodo giri fukashi.

Our past disputes make us more
conscious of their welfare.

518   ウ
命を捨るは天下の為。
u
Inotto sutsuru wa tenga no tame.

Cast your life away for country,

519   色
助るは又家のため。
               iro
Tasukuru wa mata ie no tame.

and preserve it for her family.

520   詞
気遣ひせずと最後を清ふ。
kotoba
Kizukaisezu to saigo o kiyoo.

Don't worry, rest assured during
your final moments.

521   花は三吉野侍の。
Hana wa miyoshino samurai no.

On this Yoshino cherry branch
your pure heart will blossom.

522   手本に成と潔く。
Tehon ni nare to isagiyoku.

Die an example for all samurai."

523   地ハル   上
いへど心の　　乱れ咲。
ji haru   kami
Iedo kokoro no midarezaki.

Gallant words, but his heart is
torn, riddled by regrets,

524   あたら桜の若者を。
Atara sakura no wakamono o.

to witness his young blossom be
scattered by the storm.

525　ちらす惜さと不便さと小枝
　　　　　　　　　　ウ
Chirasu oshisa to fubinsa to koeda

入　　　　　フシ　　108
にそそぐ血の涙 落て。
iru　　　　　　　fushi
ni sosogu chi no namida ochite.

As he sets the branch afloat in the stream, loving tears of blood fall

526　なみ間に流れ行。
　　　　　　　　109
Namima ni nagareyuku.

into the rushing waves, carried away forever.

15a

527　地色ハル　　　色
夫共しらず 悦ぶ
ji iro haru　　　iro
(Hina) Soretomo shirazu yorokobu

110
雛鳥。
Hinadori.

Unaware of the blossoms true intent, Hinadori is filled with happiness.

528　詞
アレアレ花が流るるは。
kotoba
Are are hana ga nagaruru wa.

(Hinadori) "Look! Look at the blossoms floating downstream. What a joy!

529　嬉しや久我様のお身に
Ureshiya Kogasama no omi ni

つつがのないしるし。
tsutsuga no nai shirushi.

Koganosuke will be safe.

530　地ハル
私は冥土へ参じます。
ji haru
Watashi wa meido e sanjimasu.

I shall go ahead to the nether world.

531 ウ　　上　　　111
千年も万年も。
u   kami
Sennen mo mannen mo.

（あめ屋綱太夫のクドキ）
(ameya tsunatayū no kudoki)

Please, for a thousand, myriad
years live a healthy life

532 ウ
御無事で長生遊ばして。
u
Gobuji de nagaiki asobashite.

533 上
未来で添て下さんせ。
kami
Mirai de soote kudasanse.

and let us be together in the next
world."

534 と心でいふが暇乞。　112
To kokoro de iu ga itomagoi.

（サハリ）
(sawari)

These are the feelings of her
heart, and now her parting words:

535 詞
思ひ置事云置事。
kotoba
Omoioku koto iioku koto.

(Hinadori) "I've no more thoughts
to speak.

536 もふ何にもござんせぬ。
Moo nannimo gozansenu.

537 片時も早ふサアかか様。
Henshi mo hayoo saa kakasan.

We've not much time. Mother,

538 　　地ハル　　　113
切て　切てと身を惜まぬ。
　　ji haru
Kitte kitte to mi o oshimanu.

cut my throat, cut it!" Brave
words.

539 ハル
我子の覚悟
    haru
(Sadaka) Wagako no kakugo

に励され。
ni hagemasare.

（文弥）
(bun'ya)

Sadaka, encouraged by her daughter's determination,

540 胸を定めて取上れど。[114]
Mune o sadamete toriyagurodo.

（併ビ）
(narabi)

calms her mind and takes up the sword.

541 ハル
刀は鞘に錆付
haru
Katana wa saya ni sabitsuku

如く。[115]
gotoku.

But as if rusty from disuse,

542 ウ
離れ兼たる血脈のきずな。[116]
u
Hanarekanetaru chisuji no kizuna.

it sticks in the sheath tightly, as the bonds between mother and child.

543 ウ
今切殺す雛鳥を無事と
u
Ima kirikorosu Hinadori o buji to

知する返事の桜。[117]
shirasuru henji no sakura.

She too lets float a flowered branch,

544   フシ   中
同じく川に　浮ぶれば。
fushi   **naka**
Onajiku kawa ni ukaburebanna.
（三ツユリ）
(mitsu yuri)

sending false notice that Hinadori is safe.

15b

545   詞
ハハア嬉しや是ぞ雛鳥
kotoba
Hahaa ureshiya kore zo Hinadori
が入内のしらせ。
ga judai no shirase.

(Koganosuke) "What a wonderful sight! Hinadori will be going to court.

546   久我之助が心の安堵。
Koganosuke ga kokoro no ando.

Now I am truly at peace.

547   采女の方の御有家は
Uneme no kata no onnarika wa
最前申上る通。
saizen mōshiyaguru tōri.

Since earlier I told you of Lady Uneme's hideaway,

548   此世に心残りなし。
Kono yo ni kokoro nokori nashi.

I've no concerns left for this world.

549   御苦労ながら御介錯。
Gokurō nagara gokaishaku.

Though it be a dreadful task, please end my life."

550   サアサアかか様切ていの。
Saasaa kakasama kitteino.

(Hinadori) "Mother, mother, raise the sword.

551   詞ノリ
未練にござんす母様
kotoba-nori
Miren ni gozansu hawasama

Do you still have regrets?" Strong words from dry-eyed Hinadori.

地中
と泣ぬ顔するいぢらしさ。 [118]

ji naka

to nakanu kao suru ijirashisa.

552   ウ
   刀持手も

   u

   (Sadaka) Katana motsu te mo

   [119]
   大盤石。

   daibanjaku.

Sadaka holds up the sword but it is leaden,

553   地色ハル   [120]
   思ひは同じ大判事。

   ji iro haru

   Omoi wa onaji Daihanji.

leaden as Daihanji's thoughts;

554   子よりも親の四苦八苦。 [121]

   Ko yori mo oya no shikuhakku.

neither parent can unsheath the sword. More than the young who die

555   命もちりぢり。 [122]

   (Sadaka) Inochi mo chirijiri.

the living parents suffer the twelve torments of hell.

556   日もちりちり。 [123]

   (Daihanji) Hi mo chirichiri.

Scattered by the winds, young lives follow the sun's setting course.

557   詞
   ハアそふじや。

   kotoba

   Haa sooja.

558   早西に入日輪は

   Hayanishi ni iru nichirinna

   むすめがお迎ひ。

   musume ga omukai.

(Sadaka) "Yes, that's perfect! Golden sunset rays will lead my

559 弥陀の来迎　西方浄土へ
Mida no raigō saihō jōdo e

導き給へ。
michibiki tamae.

daughter's path. Amida, take care to guide my child to the Western Paradise.

560 地ハル
南無あみだ仏と眼をとぢて。
ji haru
Namu Amida Butsu to me o tojite.

[124] All hail to Amida, Namu Amida Butsu."

561 ウ
思ひ切たる首諸共　入わつと
u　　　　　　　　**iru**
Omoikittaru kubi morotomo watto

中　125
泣声答ゆるこだま。
　　　　　　naka
nakukoe kotoyuru kodama.

Eyes closed, with all her might she strikes off Hinadori's head; the mother's cry of woe echoes through the hills,

562 ハル
肝に徹して
　　　　haru
(Daihanji) Kimo ni tesshite

大判事。
Daihanji.

startling Daihanji.

563 ウ
刀からりと落たる障子。　126
u
Katana karari to ochitaru shōji.

His sword drops and he thrusts open the door.

564 詞
ヤア雛鳥が首討たか。
kotoba
Yaa Hinadori ga kubi utta ka.

(Daihanji) "What! Did you cut off Hinadori's head!"

565 久我殿は腹切てか。
Kogadono wa hara kitte ka.

(Sadaka) "Did Koganosuke stab himself?"

566　地上　*127*
ハア
ji kami
Haa

(Both) "Oh, no!"

しなしたりとどふど座し。
shinashitari to dōdozashi.

(Daihanji) "What have we done!"

567　上ウ
悔むも泣も一時に
kami u
Kuyamu mo naku mo ittoki ni

Both collapse in shock.
Thunderstruck by the turn of
events,

スヱテ　　　　　*128*
あきれて詞も。
suete
akirete kotoba mo.

568　　　中
なか　りしが。
　　　　　　naka
(Daihanji) Nakarishiga.

no tears of regret or grief, no
words flow forth.

16

569　地ハル　　色　　*129*
良有て定高　声を上。
ji haru　　　　iro
Yaya atte Sadaka koe o age.

After a moment of silence Sadaka
raises her voice:

570　詞
入鹿大臣へさし上る雛鳥
kotoba
Irukadaijin e sashiaguru Hinadori

(Sadaka) "Please accept for
inspection Hinadori's head,

が首。
ga kubi.

571　御検使受取下されと。
Gokenshi uketori kudasare to.

（カカリ）
(kakari)

which I present to Lord Iruka."

572　地ハル
　　呼はる声を吹送る。
　　ji haru
　　Yobawaru koe o fukiokuru.

Her voice, carried by the winds,

573　　中　ウ
　　風の　案内に
　　naka u
　　Kaze no annai ni

　　　ウ
　　大判事歎きの。
　　u
　　Daihanji nageki no.

stirs a distraught Daihanji to attention.

574　ヲクリ　ハル
　　姿　　改て。
　　okuri　haru
　　Sugata aratamete.

He straightens the folds of his kimono

575　ハル
　　衣紋つくろひしづしづと
　　haru
　　Emon tsukuroi shizushizu to

　　中
　　おり立。
　　naka
　　oritatsu.

and slowly descends to

576　ウ　　ハル　　　*130*
　　川辺の　柳腰。
　　u　　haru
　　Kawabe no　yanagigoshi.

the river bank. Sadaka, too, gracefully walks down among the willows along the shore,

577　娘の首をかき抱き。　*131*
　　Musume no kubi o kaki idaki.

reverently carrying her daughter's head.

578　ハル
　　大判事様わけては何にも
　　haru
　　Daihanjisama wakete wa nannimo

(Sadaka) "Lord Daihanji, there is nothing left to say.

申ませぬ。[132]

mōshimasenu.

579　御子息の御命はどふぞと^ウ

u

Goshisoku no oinochi wa dōzo to

思ふたかひもない

omouta kai mo nai

あへない有さま。^上

kami

aenaiarisama.

> Even the effort to save your son has come to nought. A fate too cruel!

580　お前様のお心も推量^ウ

u

Omaesama no okokoro mo suiryō

致しておりまする。

itashite orimasuru.

> I know your agony. We wished to achieve the impossible, to join this

581　添に添れぬ悪縁を。^{ハル}

haru

Sou ni sowarenu akuen o.

> ill-fated pair, but their love was blocked by karma.

582　思ひ合たが互の因果。^ウ

u

Omoioota ga tagai no inga.

> She wanted so much

583　此方の娘も添たい。^ウ

u

Kono hō no musume mo soitai.

> to be with him . . . 'to be with him' were her dying thoughts.

584　上　　　　色　　　133
そいたいと　思ひ死。
kami　　iro
Soitai to omoijini.

585　詞
余り不便に存じます。
kotoba
Amari fubin ni zonjimasu.

It is just too pitiful.

586　せめて久我之助殿の息有
Semete Koganosukedono no iki aru

中に。
uchi ni.

At least to have her head go to

587　此首を其方へ
Kono kubi o sono hō e

お渡し申すが。
owatashimōsu ga.

Koganosuke before he dies—

588　娘を嫁入さすこころ。
Musume o yomeiri sasu kokoro.

I send her as his bride."

589　実尤嫁は大和
Ge ni mottomo yome wa Yamato

むこは紀伊国。
muko wa Kinokuni.

(Daihanji) "Truly, she is my
daughter of Yamato; he is your
son of Kinokuni;

590　妹背の山の中に落る。
Imose no yama no naka ni otsuru.

the waters of Yoshino flowing
between Imo and Se will serve as
wedding saké.

591　吉野の川の水盃。
Yoshino no kawa no mizusakazuki.

592　桜の林の大島だい。
Sakura no hayashi no ōshimadai.

The cherry forest of Yoshino offers
bountiful wedding gifts.

593 めでたふ祝言さしませふはい。
Medetoo shūgen sashimashoo wai.

Let us celebrate this grand occasion."

594 そんなら是までの心も
Sonnara koremade no kokoro mo

とけて。
tokete.

(Sadaka) "Then you've forgiven the past."

595 ハテ互にあいやけ同士。
Hate tagai ni aiyakedōshi.

(Daihanji) "Certainly, we're relatives."

596 エエかたじけないと
Ee katajikenai to

(Sadaka) "Ah, how happy those words make me!"

地ハル   *134*
悦ぶも 跡の祭。
ji haru
yorokobu mo ato no matsuri.

Their joy all too late.

597 詞
ほんに背丈延た者を。
kotoba
Hon ni setake nobita mono o.

(Sadaka) "It is a parent's curse forever to consider

598 いつ迄も子供の様に。
Itsumade mo kodomo no yō ni.

599 思ふてくらすは親のならひ。
Omoote kurasu wa oya no narai.

a grown child as a baby.

600 地ハル
あまやかした雛の道具。
ji haru
Amayakashita hina no dōgu.

All these dolls I showered her with—what shall I do with them,

601 ウ
一人子を殺して何にせふ。
u
Hitorigo o koroshite nan ni shoo.

after I killed my only child!

602　ウ　色
　　跡に置程 涙の種。
　　u   iro
　　Ato ni okuhodo namida no tane.

Left here, they'll be seeds for future sorrow.

603　詞
　　こしもと共。
　　kotoba
　　Koshimotodomo.

Maids, take this whole display, every single doll, and float them

604　其一式。
　　Sono isshiki.

605　残らず川へ　流れ潅頂。
　　Nokorazu kawa e nagare kwanjō.

with Hinadori as memorial offerings."

(The drama stops as head and dolls are prepared to be sent on Hinadori's koto across to Mt. Se, where Koganosuke is still alive. The following sections 17 and 18 are a musical flourish.)

17

606　(地)ハルフシ　中
　　未来へ　送る。
　　(ji)haru fushi naka
　　(Sadaka) Mirai e okuru.

Gifts and trappings for the wedding will accompany her to the next world.

607　ウ　　　　　　135
　　嫁入道具行器。
　　u
　　Yomeiri dōgu hokai.

608　ハルウ
　　長持犬張子。
　　haru u
　　Nagamochi inuhariko.

Her hope chest is decorated with wild dogs to ward off

609 タタキ
小袖箪すの幾さおも。

tataki

Kosodedansu no ikusao mo.

evil spirits. Her wardrobe fills
many trunks;

610 命ながらへ居るならば。

Inochi nagarae irunaraba.

were she to live a full life,

611 ウキン　ハル
一世　一度の送り物。

u gin haru

Isse ichido no okurimono.

these would be gifts for an entire
lifetime.

612 中
五丁七丁続く程。

naka

Gochō shichichō tsuzuku hodo.

The many presents fill tens of
chests. How wonderful I thought

613 上　　　　　　　　　136
びびしうせんと楽しみに。

kami

Bibishūsen to tanoshimi ni.

this ceremony would be.

614 　　　ナヲス中
思ふた事　　　は引かへて。

  naosu naka

Omoota koto wa hikikaete.

All my care has come to nothing—

615 フシ
水になつたる水葬礼。

fushi

Mizu ni nattaru suisōrei.

(一ツユリ)

(hitotsu yuri)

disappearing bubbles in a rushing
stream.

18

616 中タタキ
大名の子の嫁入に。

naka tataki

Daimyō no ko no yomeiri ni.

Not even a palanquin for a daimyō
daughter's wedding.

617 上
乗物さへも中中に。
kami
Norimono sae mo nakanaka ni.

618 ウ   137
かたみも仇の爪琴に。
u
Katami mo ada no tsumagoto ni.

The koto she loved, a sweet remembrance, now is

619 中
首取乗る弘誓の船。
naka
Kubitorinosuru guzei no fune.

hateful, a hateful raft that steals my daughter away. Let it be the saving

620 フシヲクリ   138
あなたの岸より。
fushi okuri
Anata no kishi yori.

boat of Amida to bear her from this shore

621 ナヲス　ウ
彼岸に

　　　　　naosu　u
(Koganosuke) Kano kishi ni

流るる。
nagaruru.

to the other shore of Paradise over waves that wash away

622 フシ
血汐清船が。
fushi
Chishio Kiyofune ga.

（道具返シ）
(dōgugaeshi)

her blood, purifying her for Koganosuke.

19a

623 地ハル
今はの顔ばせ見る

ji haru

(Daihanji) Ima wano kanbase miru

親の。

oya no.

As Daihanji gazes at the poor girl's face, prayers form on

624 口に祝言心の称名。[139]

Kuchi ni shūgen kokoro no shōmyō.

his lips; he chants,

625 ワタイ　　　　地人
千秋万歳の　千箱の

utai　　　　ji iru

Senshū bansei no chihako no

地色ハル　　　[140]
玉の緒も切て。

ji iro haru

tama no o mo kirete.

"Happiness for many thousands of years' should be her wedding gift,

626 今はあへなき此死顔。

Ima wa aenaki kono shinigao.

but the life of this precious jewel has been cut. The pitiful face of death.

627 ウ
生て居る中此様に。

haru u

Ikite iru uchi kono yō ni.

If while still alive we could have called them son and daughter,

628 ウ
むこよ嫁よといふならば。

haru u

Muko yo yome yo to iunaraba.

629 　　地入　　[141]
いか斗　悦ばんに。

ji iru

Ikabakari yorokoban ni.

how happy they would have been.

630   地色ウ   142
領分の遺恨より。
ji iro u
Ryōbun no ikon yori.

The enmity of our

631   ハル   143
意地に意地を立通す。
haru
Iji no iji o tatetōsu.

feud made us stubborn. We had to
have our way.

632   ウ   ウ
其上重る入鹿の疑ひ
u   u
Sono ue kasanaru Iruka no utagai

中直るにも直られぬ。
nakanaoru ni mo naorarenu.

Iruka's suspicions made it
impossible to forget our quarrel,
even if we wanted.

633   ウ   色   144
義理に成たが二人が不運。
u   iro
Giri ni natta ga futari ga fuun.

Duty bound them to misfortune.

634   詞
あれ程思ひ詰た嫁。
kotoba
Are hodo omoitsumeta yome.

How could Hinadori ever submit
to Iruka,

635   何の入鹿に従はふ。
Nan no Iruka ni shitagaoo.

her devotion was so deep?

636   速も死ねば成ぬ子供。
Totemo shinaneba naranu kodomo.

These children had to die.

637   一時にころしたは。
Ittoki ni koroshita wa.

By killing them at the same time

638   未来で早ふ添はしてやりたさ。
Mirai de hayoo sowashite yaritasa.

we send them together to the next
life.

639　地色ハル　　　　　　　*145*
云合さねど後室にも。

ji iro haru

Iiyawasanedo kōshitsu ni mo.

Though we hadn't spoken before,

640　是迄不和な大判事を。

Kore made fuwa na Daihanji o.

for you to consider this former enemy

641　ウ
あいやけと思し召ばこそ。

u

Aiyake to oboshimesaba koso.

as the father of your child,

642　せがれに立て一人の娘。

Segare ni tatete hitori no musume.

and even more nobly to offer your only daughter in death for love of my son—

643　色
ヲヲよくぞお手にかけられし。

iro

Oo yoku zo ote ni kakerareshi.

no, I could never express

644　地ウ　　　　フシ　　　*146*
過分に　存る　　定高どの。

ji u　　　fushi

Kabun ni zonzuru Sadakadono.

（行義 [キヲイ]）

(gyōgi [kioi])

my gratitude, Lady Sadaka."

19b

645　地色ウ　　　　　*147*
アア勿たいない。

ji iro u

Aa mottainai.

(Sadaka) "No, no, your praise is unwarranted.

646　其お礼はあちらこちら。

Sono orei wa achira kochira.

I am the grateful one.

647 ウ
ふつつかな娘故大事の
u
Futsutsuka na musume yue daiji no

お子を御切腹。
oko o goseppuku.

Your son committed suicide for my ill-bred daughter.

648 器量筋目も勝れた殿御。
Kiryō sujime mo sugureta tonogo.

What a fine, brave and honorable husband;

649 夫に持た果報者。
Otto ni motta kahōmono.

it was her good fortune to marry him.

650 地ウ
とは云ながら。
ji u
To wa iinagara.

And now,

651 ハル
あれ程迄手しほにかけて
haru
Arehodo made teshio ni kakete

育た子を。
sodateta ko o.

this child you so dearly raised . . .

652 ウ
又手にかけて切心。
u
Mata te ni kakete kiru kokoro.

what must be your anguish before you, by your own hands, cut him down!"

653 詞
ササササ推量致しておる。
kotoba
Sasasasa suiryō itashiteoru.

(Daihanji) "Yes, I am ready.

654 武士の覚悟は常ながら。
Bushi no kakugo wa tsune nagara.

Though a samurai must always be

655　まさかの時は取乱し。
Masaka no toki wa torimidashi.

ready for the unforeseen,
confusion rules my heart. It is
shameful

656　介錯しおくれ面目ない。
Kaishaku shiokure menbokunai.

for me to delay his death."

657　地ハル
　イエイエ。
ji haru
Ie ie.

(Sadaka) "Never! Never!

658　夫でめでたい此祝言。
Sore de medetai kono shūgen.

Now it will be a

659　ウ
　是がほんの葬よ嫁入。
u
Kore ga hon no sō yo yomeiri.

true funeral, and a genuine
wedding.

660　ウ
　一代一度の祝言に。
u
Ichidai ichido no shūgen ni

On this once-in-a-lifetime
celebration,

　むこ殿の無紋の
mukodono no mumon no

the groom wears a white death
robe."

　上下。
kamishimo.

661　詞
　首斗の嫁御寮に
kotoba
Kubi bakari no yome goryō ni

(Daihanji) "I never dreamed I'd
face only the head of my son's
bride!"

　対面せふとは知なんだ。
taimen shoo to wa shirananda.

662　地ハルウ
　　それも子供が遁れぬ
　　ji haru u
　　Sore mo kodomo ga nogarenu

　　寿命。[148]
　　jumyō.

(Sadaka) "A fate they couldn't escape."

663　ハルウ
　　とにも角にも世の中の
　　haru u
　　Tonimokaku ni mo yo no naka no

　　子と云文字に死の声の。[149]
　　<u>*ko to yuu*</u> *moji ni shi no koe no.*

　　（ヒロイ）
　　(hiroi)

(Daihanji) "Indeed they are children of death."

664　矢上
　　有も定る宿業と。[150]
　　　　ya kami
　　(Both) Aru mo sadamaru shukugō to.

(Both) "All is determined by karma of past lives."

665　隔つる心親々の
　　Hedatsuru kokoro oyaoya no

　　積る思ひの山々は。
　　tsumoru omoi no yamayama wa.

The anger on each mountain, festering over many years of feuding,

666　矢上
　　解て流れて
　　　　ya kami
　　(Daihanji) <u>*Tokete nagarete*</u>

　　入上
　　吉野川いとど。[151]
　　　　iru kami
　　(Sadaka) <u>*Yoshinogawa itodo.*</u>

　　（大ヲトシ）
　　(ō-otoshi)

melts as tears flowing down the Yoshino River,

667　ハル　　フシ
　　　みなぎる　斗也。
　　　　haru　　　fushi
　　　(Daihanji) *Minagiru bakari nari*
　　　on.

overwhelming its banks.

20

668　地色ハル
　　　涙払ふて大判事首
　　　ji iro haru
　　　Namida haroote Daihanji kubi

　　　　　　　　　　¹⁵²
　　　かき上て 声高く。
　　　kakiagete koe takaku.

Daihanji wipes his eyes, looks up,
and exclaims in a loud voice,

669　詞ノリ　　　　　¹⁵³
　　　せがれ清船承はれ。
　　　kotoba-nori
　　　Segare Kiyofune uketamaware.

"Koganosuke, my dear son,
prepare yourself! For they say
one's

670　人間最後の一念に寄て
　　　Ningen saigo no ichinen ni yotte

　　　輪廻の生を引とかや。
　　　rinne no shō o hiku tokaya.

final thought determines rebirth.

671　地ウ
　　　忠義に死る汝が
　　　ji u
　　　Chūgi ni shisuru nanji ga

　　　ハル
　　　魂ぱく。
　　　haru
　　　konpaku.

Let your spirit die for loyalty and

672　　　　　ハル
　　　君父の影身に付添て。
　　　　　　　haru
　　　Kunpu no kagemi ni tsukisoote.

remain with your lord and father.

673   ウ
朝敵退治の勝軍を
u
Chōteki taiji no kachiikusa o

中
草薙の影より　見物せよ。
　　　　　　　　naka
kusaba no kage yori kenbutsu seyo.

From the shadows of the grasses
be spectator to our victory over the
enemies of the court.

674   ウ
今雛鳥と改て親が
u
Ima Hinadori to aratamete oya ga

ハル
赦して　　尽未来。
　　haru
yurushite jinmirai.

Once again I grant my blessing to
your marriage with Hinadori.

675   ハル　　　　　　　　中
五百生迄かはらぬ　夫婦。
haru　　　　　　　**naka**
Gohyakushō made kawaranu fūfu.

For ever and ever may you remain
together through five hundred
reincarnations.

676   ハル
忠臣貞女の操を
haru
Chūshin teijo no misao o

立死たる者と高声に。
tateshishitaru mono to kōshō ni.

Let this young pair pass through
the gates of death, exclaiming
loudly to Lord Enma

677   上ウ
焔魔の庁を名乗て通れ
kami u
Enma no chō o nanotte tōre

ウ　　　　　　154
南無成仏得脱と。
u
namu jōbutsu tokudatsu to.

that they are virtuous and loyal.

Praise be for their salvation and
attainment of Buddhahood."

678 ウ
唱ふる声の聞へてや
　　　u
(Koga) Tonouru koe no kikoeteya

物得云ねど合す手を。
mono eyuwanedo awasu te o.

His prayers stir Koganosuke, and
though unable to speak,

679 ウ
合せ兼たる此世の別れ。
u
Awasekanetaru kono yo no wakare.

he folds his hands, a final parting
from this world.

680 ウ
早日も暮て
　　　u
(Daihanji) Haya hi mo kurete

人顔も。
hitogao mo.

The day is quickly passing and
faces dim;

681
見へず庵の　中霧隠れ。
　　　　　naka
Miezu iori no kirigakure.

all hidden in the mist.

682 上
うづむ娘の
　　　kami
(Sadaka) Uzumu musume no

亡骸はこなたの山
nakigara wa konata no yama

に中どまれど。
naka
ni todomaredo.

Sadaka's daughter will be buried
on Mt. Imo, but her

683 合ウ
　首は背山に
　　　　ai u
　(Daihanji) Kubi wa seyama ni

　ハル　　色
　検使の　役目。
　haru　　iro
　kenshi no yakume.

head has gone to Mt. Se for
inspection.

684 (地)ハル
　我子の介錯
　　　　(ji) haru
　(Sadaka) Waga ko no kaishaku

　涙の雛。
　namida no hina.

Sadaka weeps for having killed her
child.

685 ウ
　よしや世の中憂事は。
　u
　Yoshiya yo no naka uki koto wa.

Though it is the cruel way of the
world,

686 ウ　　　色
　いつか　たへまの
　u　　iro
　Itsuka taemano.

some day the corruption will end.

687 ハル
　大和路や。
　　　　haru
　(Daihanji) Yamatoji yanna.

688 アア。
　(Sadaka) Aanna.

689 アア。
　(Daihanji) Aa.

合中ウ
跡に妹山。
    ai naka u
(Sadaka) Ato ni imoyama.

Their deaths will not be wasted!
Behind is Mt. Imo,

690 ハル
先立背山。
    haru
(Daihanji) Sakidatsu seyama.

ahead is Mt. Se.

691 ウ
恩愛義理をせきくだす。
    u
(Both) Onnai giri o sekikudasu.

Tears of love, gratitude, and duty
flood the river,

692 矢ウ   155
涙の川瀬。
    ya u
(Daihanji) <u>*Nanda no kawase.*</u>

rushing (Daihanji cuts off
Koganosuke's head) downstream,

693 上   156
三吉野の花を。
    kami
(Sadaka) <u>*Miyoshino no hana o.*</u>

〈尻持〉
(shiri-mochi)

694 ハル   157
見捨て。
    haru
(Daihanji) Misutete on.

leaving behind the fallen blossoms
of Yoshino.

695 出て行。   158
(Both) <u>*Idete yuku.*</u>

〈段切〉
(dangiri)

Appendix A   Notes

Inobe, Malm, and Gerstle met in June 1984 with Takemoto Mo-
jitayū (now Sumitayū) to analyze the record of "The Mountains
Scene." In these notes I have cited the variations in notation between
our text and the original *maruhon* and Tsunatayū texts used by Yūda
Yoshio in *Bunraku jōrurishū*. The notation in the text translated here
has followed the performance on the *Imoseyama onna teikin* King Record (1976) KHA49–50 (SKLB 386–389). The notation found below
the underlined words is normally "secret" and not included in the
printed text. In the following notes, this performance is compared to
those reflected in early texts with shamisen notation. (See chapter six,
"The History of Performance.") "M" is the original 1771 *maruhon*. "T"
is the Tsunatayū text.

1. *Haru* over "no sute-" in M and T.

2. *Fushi* not in M.

3. *Haru u* not in M.

4. *Haru u* in place of *u* over "momo"; *u* over "sonae-" not in M.

5. *U* over "hagi" is *haru u* in M and T. *Naka* over "koshi-" is *haru* in M and
    T.

6. No *haru* over "Kogiku" in M or T.

7. *Noru* over "koshi" in T.

8. *Naga(ji)* in M instead of *ji iro u.*

9. No *haru, u,* or *iro* in M.

10. No *u* over "hako" in M.

11. *Haru* instead of *haru u* in M, and *u* over "Hina-" in M.

12. No *u* over "tsurai" in M; *u* over "sono" in M.

13. *U* in place of *nagaji haru* in M; *u* over "waga" in M; no *u* over "yuka-" in M; *kami* over "Kiyo-" in M.

14. *Haru u* over "Kono-" in M; *haru* over "Kono-" in T. *Kami* not in either text.

15. *Kami* over "Kiita" in T; no notation in M.

16. *Naka* not in M.

17. *U* over "Ima" not in M; *u* over "omoi" not in T.

18. No *u* in M; *haru u* in T.

19. *Haru u* for *u* in M and T.

20. No *naka* or *haru* in T.

21. No punctuation mark in M. *U* over "-masu" in M.

22. No *haru* over "Hon" in M. *Haru* over "Yamato" in M; no notation over "Yamato" in T.

23. No *haru* over "Goryō-" in M or T.

24. *Ji u* in T.

25. *Haru u* over "Seme-" in M; *iro* over "Seme-" in T. No *u* over "osu-" in M.

26. *Haru u* over "Shōji" in M; *kami* in T. No notation over "enban-" in M or T.

27. No *u* over "Nozoki" in M; no *yuri* in T.

28. *Sue* in M; *haru* in T for *suete*.

29. *Haru u* in T.

30. M reads *u* over "mane-"; *haru u* over "tani-"; *gin u* over "minagi-"; *u naka* over "magire-."

31. No *u* in M.

32. No punctuation mark in T.

33. *Naka* for *ji u* in M. No *fushi* in T.

34. *Ji u* in M.

35. No *u* in M or T.

36. No *u* in M.

37. No *u* in M.

38. *Haru u* in M.

39. No *haru u* or *iru* in M.

40. No *haru* in M or T. *Au* over "miso-" in M.

41. No *u* in M or T.

42. *U* is *naka* in M and T; second *naka* is not in M.

43. *Ji u* in T; no *haru* in M or T.

44. No *haru u* in M.

45. *Haru u* over "Sakura" in M and T. *Haru u* over "itoi-" in M.

46. M has *kami haru u* for *kami*.

47. No *haru* in M or T.

48. M has Koganosuke chant "Kokorobakari ga i" and Hinadori until "i," after which they join together. This is one example of "stretching" the intensity that began after the 1820s. The earliest Mameushi (1800?) text has the divisions the same as M but has both *tayū* chant together from "ki." M has *iru* over "namida."

49. M has no *u*.

50. M has *kami* for *haru u*.

51. No *kami* in M.

52. *U gin* in T.

53. *Kotoba* for *iro* in M and T.

54. No *haru* in M or T. M has *u* over "-zumi."

55. *Kami* for *iru* in T.

56. *Kotoba* in M and T; no shamisen notation until 20th-century texts.

57. M and T have *ji haru* over "kanarazu," and no *kami*.

58. *Haru* for *u* in M and T.

59. No *haru u* in M and T; M has *naka fushi*.

60. Performance deletes "nari . . . koe."

61. *Kami* for *gin* in M; no *naka* in M. M and T have *yuri* over "nanjo." M has *u* over "yuku."

62. *Ji iro haru* in M and T.

63. *Kotoba* begins on "Daihanji-" in M and T.

64. No *haru* in M or T.

65. No *ji* over "shōji" in M or T. However, the earliest Mameushi text has this line as *kakari, iru* over "shōji," and *iro* over "no" and "sakai" and *kotoba* from "Hentō." M has no "ha . . . ha."

66. M has both sing entire line; Mameushi text is the same.

67. M and Mameushi have both sing entire line.

68. M and Mameushi do not have them sing this line together. *Fushi* for *okuri* in M. *Okuri* in Mameushi.

69. *Ji iro u* for *ji u* in M. Mameushi has *harima* from "ko no kokoro."

70. Mameushi has *yotsu yuri kakari tome.*

71. *Ji iro u* in M for *ji u.*

72. M has *haru* over "no motsu-."

73. M and T have *ji u.* Mameushi has *ji kami.*

74. M and T have *ji iro u* for *ji u.*

75. M and T have no *ji iro haru.* Mameushi has two shamisen notes on this line.

76. No *haru* in M and T over "namida." M and T have no *ji haru* over "kiki-," and *haru* over "okotoba."

77. *Ji haru u* in M and T.

78. No *gin* in M.

79. *Fushi* in M and T.

80. *Ji naka* in M and T.

81. Mameushi has *iro* over "Hahaa."

82. *Kakari* in Mameushi.

83. *Ji haru* for *ji iro haru* in M and T.

84. *Haru u* over "ontame" in M and T.

85. *U* for *iru* in M and T.

86. *U* over "Amari" in M and T.

87. *Ji haru* in M and T.

88. *Kami* over "Segare" in M and T; no *ji kami* over "gojū-" in M and T.

89. No *u* over "Oi" in M and T.

90. No *ji kami* over "kore" in M and T.

91. No *iru* in M and T.

92. *Ji iro haru* in M.

93. *Ji u* in M and T.

94. *Haru u* for *haru* in M and T.

95. No *iru* in M and T. T has *kami*.

96. *Haru u* over "Tsutsu-" in M and T.

97. No *iru* in M and T.

98. No *kami* or *u* in M and T.

99. No *iru* in M and T. *Haru u* over "kegara-" in M and T.

100. This section, lines 479–480, has shamisen accompaniment, but not in pre-20th-century texts.

101. T has *ji iru*.

102. *U* for *gin* in M and T.

103. No *u* in T over "Kata-"; no *u* in M over "nagori."

104. *Haru u* over "Hitotsu" in M and T.

105. *Haru* over "Kiyofune" in M and T.

106. *U* in M and T for *haru*.

107. No *iro* in M, T, or shamisen texts until 20th century.

108. No *iru* in M or T. *Kami* for *iru* in T.

109. *Gin* in T over "Nami-."

110. *Ji haru* in T.

111. No *kami* in M or T.

112. *Iro* over "itoma-" in M and T.

113. No *ji haru* in M or T.

114. *Naka* over "Mune" in M and T. *Haru* over "tori-" in M.

115. No *haru* in M or T. *U* in T.

116. *Kami* over "Hanare-" in M. *U* over "chisuji" in T.

117. No *u* in M over "Ima." *Haru u* over "buji" in M and T.

118. No *kotoba-nori* in M or T. Various shamisen texts show different amounts of notes, gradually becoming greater in number with time. No *ji naka* in M or T.

119. *Kami* in M. *Haru* in T.

120. *Ji haru* in M and T.

121. *Haru u* over "Ko yori."

122. *Haru u* in M over "Inochi"; *haru* in T.

123. *Haru* over "Hi" in M and T.

124. *Ji u* in T.

125. "Omoi-" has *kami* in M; *haru* in T. No *iru* in M. No *naka* in M or T.

126. No *u* in M or T.

127. Only Daihanji in M.

128. *Haru u* in M over "Kuyamu."

129. *Ji iro haru* in M and T.

130. No *u* in M.

131. *Iro* over "idaki" in M and T.

132. *Kotoba* in M and T from lines 578–580. This is a good example of adding music after the first performance. Mameushi text shows some notation for this passage.

133. No *kami* in M.

134. *Iro* in T over "ato."

135. *Haru* over "hokai." The shamisen notation *ai* has been left off lines 608, 609, 611, 612, and 619.

136. *Iro* over "tanoshi-" in T.

137. *Iru* over "ada" in T.

138. *Kami fushi okuri* in M and T. *Naka* over "yori" in M.

139. *U* over "shūgen" in M and T.

140. *Kotoba* for *utai* in M and T. No *ji iru* in M or T. *Ji iro haru* is *ji haru* in M and T.

141. No *ji iru* over "yoroko-" in M and T.

142.   No *ji iro u* in M or T.

143.   No *haru* in M.

144.   No *iro* in T. *Iro* in M is over "fuun."

145.   *Ji iro* in M and T.

146.   No *ji u* in M or T.

147.   Lines 645–649 are *kotoba* in M and T. This is the best example of later performers embellishing original music. This passage does not have shamisen accompaniment until the late 19th or 20th century. Sadaka's "song" voice contrasts with Daihanji's "spoken." *Kotoba* in Mameushi and Kichibei texts but *ji* in Yadayū text.

148.   *U* over "jumyō" in M.

149.   No *haru u* in M or T.

150.   *U* for *ya kami* in M and T.

151.   No *iru kami* in M or T. *Kami kuru* over "Yoshino-" in T. *Naka* over "itodo" in M and T.

152.   *Ji haru* in M and T. *Iro* over "koe" in M and T.

153.   *Kotoba* in M and T from lines 667–668.

154.   *Kami* for *kami u* in M. Nothing in T.

155.   *Kami* for *ya u* in M and T.

156.   *Gin* for *kami* in M and T.

157.   No *haru* in M and T.

158.   M has Sadaka sing the end.

Appendix B   Musical Comments on "The Mountains Scene"

William P. Malm

(The function of this section is to serve as a musical reference tool as one reads or listens to the *dan*.)

Section 1

Sanjū

Our musical journey begins with the shamisen prelude to the *dan*. It is based on a traditional opening passage called *sandanme no sanjū* (third-act *sanjū*). According to Inobe, it is played slowly and rather thickly in this piece because the scene is part of a period play (*jidaimono*) whose characters are of high rank.

Lines 1–6

The slow, rubato style of the first lines helps set the mood for following the story. The first two lines of this section are in *ji* style. The tonally static nature and low vocal entry of the first two words relates to the *gidayū* convention that each scene begins with the last words of the previous scene. The B and E pitch centers dominate most of the *dan* though F sharp, the fifth of B, can also become a pitch center. Note how the *tayū* often enters a passage in the lower leading tone (A or D) of one of these centers.

The pentatonic scale (E, F#, A, B, D) and general tonal movement represent the basic tonal style of much of *gidayū*. Like most of the world's music, however, art comes in skillfully bending the rules. The first new tonal material (C) is seen in the cadence of line 5.

Lines 7–8

The texture gradually changes with more shamisen activity and a greater use of the upper leading tones (C and F). Evidence of text setting may be the shamisen use of short, active motives as the text speaks of the poets who cast their verses among the grasses. A full cadence then occurs to mark the end of this general mood introduction. The cadences at the ends of lines 2, 5, and 8 might be considered formal markers of the *jo ha kyū* divisions of the introduction.

Section 2

Lines 9–11

The mood having been established, the story begins. C sharp is added to the tonal vocabulary on *Ku'nindo*. The word *shimoyakata* is declaimed to emphasize the importance of our awareness that there is another residence over the river. Daihanji's name is also given special emphasis as well, as he is the male protagonist in the story. The name is rendered, in fact, in the male warrior style that will be heard when Daihanji actually appears.

Lines 12–15

The cruelness of confinement is powerfully declaimed on the word *yamazumai* (mountain residence). This is preceded by a pause (*ma*) and shamisen shout (*kakegoe*) to enhance the power of the actual declamation. The loneliness of his companionship (*tomonou mono*) is drawn out in a long vocal phrase, while the reference to the young birds flown from their nest (*sudachidori*) is sung at low range with a high shamisen part "flying" above it and using an "exotic" pitch, G sharp. The use of unusual pitches in Edo-period theater music is a common convention for something odd like an animal. Perhaps the G sharp adds to the bird creature aspect of this moment. The echoing sound of the sutra chanting is played an octave lower by the shamisen. Since the last character of the sutra is the same *tori* as the word "bird," the shamisen plays one more quick "fluttering" before the cadence. Note at the ending of this section (line 15) and opening of the next how the upper leading tone of E is changed to F sharp at the cadence, perhaps in preparation for the change of music that follows.

Section 3a

Lines 16–18

As we move across the river we hear a new sound filled with F sharps. The shamisen passage represents the actions of servant-class women with both its rhythm and its new pentatonic sound. When Hinadori's sadness is mentioned, however, the half-step upper leading tone of E (F) appears (on the word *nagusame*), but the music returns to the brighter F sharp with the words "doll festival."

Lines 19–24

To keep up the lively pace of maids working, the music pauses only for a sensual moment at the end of line 22 when the maid's slim hips (*koshi*) are mentioned.

Section 3b

Lines 25–32

This section is done in a fast *kotoba* style of a country maid. Musically, it is noteworthy for the excellent quick transfer from *kotoba* to *ji iro* in line 31 and back to *kotoba* by line 32.

Lines 33–39

The sexy remarks of line 38 call for a musical setting in the midst of this dialogue section.

Lines 40–43

Music takes on a more standard parlando style as we turn to comments dealing with the princess herself rather than the maid. What is significant is the change of style and tempo for the lively servant section, which provides an important contrast and entertainment before we return to the sad story. As in most *gidayū*, the essential word is *to* (he/she said). This word is always performed in a manner that clearly marks a change from one style to another. Note that the first shamisen note is a half-step upper leading tone, so one is left in tonal suspense until the *dori* of Hinadori. The *tayū* rendition of the word "love" (line 42, *koi*) and the first use of the word "parent" (*oya*) are important conventions of this performer (note, not all). They remind us of the topic of the entire *dan*. The fact that the repetition of the word *oya* is not rendered in that fashion relates to a tradition in *gidayū* that one does not repeat the same word in the same style if the two uses are close. When the barrier (*seki no*) is mentioned, the shamisen makes a movement (against it?) and remains active throughout line 43.

Lines 44–50

The lover's knot (*musubore*) is sung unaccompanied, while the word love (*koishi*) is done in Nanbudayū's individual style. This leads to the highest pitch when the princess says "you" (*anata ni*). The change from a whole- to a half-step upper leading tone occurs in line 46 on the end of the word (*tayori*) just before the *tayū* declaims (not sings) the word "mother." This declamation leads to the princess's first dialogue. Even in this *kotoba* section note that there is a break between the two renditions of the word *yama* to give them a performance difference of the type mentioned earlier for the repetition of words.

Lines 51–57

This section again starts with a half-step upper leading tone on the shamisen. If there had been two, it would have been typical of a *kakari* opening. Since there is only one, professionals might have called it a *kakaru* to note the difference. It then moves to a really different tonal area a fifth away. The quicker action in the shamisen in line 52 seems more movement than word oriented. The sliding shamisen rendition of notes at *wagami* may relate to the torment in Hinadori's body. The tonal high point occurs in line 54 with the barrier (*hedatete*) of love (again performed as declamation). Only at the cadence of line 56 do we hear the whole-step upper leading tones that were more the *higashi-fū*, but it is followed by a full cadence of line 57.

Section 3c

Lines 58–60

The dialogue comes in before the shamisen ends, which creates a smooth transition. The freshness of the pentatonic sound of the shamisen accompaniment for line 59 is used because the characters in action are peasant-class maids rather than aristocratic persons. Thus, a more folk music sound is desired. The tempo relates to puppet movements that occur at this time. This brief mixture of musical and maid dialogues leads into the full dialogue that follows.

Lines 61–79

In this dialogue one can note the pause between the rendition of the two mountain names in line 63. Similar dramatic breaks in the fast tempo can be found elsewhere, such as between lines 75 and 76, this one preparing us for a change in style in line 78, which moves with great skill from dialogue to parlando as it speaks of crossing a bridge. The key musical words are *to wa*. They are followed by the bridge an octave higher.

Lines 80–83

The most obvious word and action related music occurs as the maid opens the sliding windows during line 80. This is followed by the most musically dense passages of the piece so far, representing the anxious needs of the heroine. The important, melodic, conventional ending of this section and the opening passage of the next illustrate the deliberate use of common contours in the movement from one side of the river to the other. The singer is lower than the shamisen in line 82 to support the change from a female to a male role.

Lines 84–85

The B flat to A movement presents a completely new tonality at the moment the hero imagines the goddess of mercy taking his face in her hands. The use of this modulation often appears in other shamisen genre to support unusual moments in the text. The wonder of spiritual help is further complicated in this case since the words "taking in her hands" is part of the other *tayū's* next line and thus refers to Hinadori rather than Kannon sama.

Lines 86–93

The tonality for line 86 changes since we have crossed the river. The second half of line 86 is declaimed with shamisen background to form an effective transfer from song to speech (an *iro-dome*). The fluid change from declaimed to sung styles is well illustrated in this section. Lines 87 and 88 are spoken by Hinadori, but in her concern about Koganosuke's health the convulsion (*oshaku*) is sung and the last of the line spoken with shamisen cadence. This leads to *kotoba* until the word *to*, marking the end of the quote, is skillfully turned into parlando singing accompanied by a very active shamisen line. The shamisen reflects the reference to sounds of the swollen river (*minagiru oto ni*) with a low dotted rhythm. The transition to *kotoba* by the maid is accomplished by having the shamisen end on a half cadence on the lower leading tone of B (A).

Lines 94–97

After a vain attempt to call across the river, the wild motions of the maids are depicted with a fast shamisen line. The gestures with the word *tsukizukin* tonally prepare one for a cadence on E but remain tense by constant motion between A and F, the lower leading tone of B, and upper lead tone of E. The E tonality flows into the next speech: B is not played before the last E.

Section 3d

Lines 98–104

Hinadori's idea moves to music by line 100, Nanbudayū using his convention of emphasizing the word "love" in that line. He uses the same device for the word "feelings" (*nen*). Musically this section is denser in texture and tonally uses more whole-step upper leading tones, presenting more of a folklike pentatonic flavor, perhaps because such action is less aristocratic. The message crashes into the stream (*karari to kawa*) with a sharp sound of the shamisen plectrum and stacatto arpeggio. The music slows to a cadence as Hinadori watches her message of love being carried down river.

Section 3e

Lines 105–110

After two lines of *kotoba* the music enters with an emotional high point. Line 107 opens with a shamisen D, E, F, rest, rest, F, F that is typical of the opening phrase in lyrical sections (*kudoki*) of other shamisen genre. Whatever its origin, the use of such a convention conveys a sad, lyrical intention to anyone familiar with the shamisen tradition. The section could be classified as being in the lyrical (*jiai*) *sawari* style for it could be sung separately from the play. Throughout the lines that follow, the shamisen frequently begins a passage with a pause on the half-step upper leading tone and ends on a lower leading tone to keep the music moving forward in time by tonal suspense, the full cadence only occurring at the end of line 110.

Section 4a

Lines 111–118

After a brief parlando passage line 111 ends with a full *iro-dome* cadence; a Koganosuke speech begins. Such speech sections can be appreciated musically in terms of their rhythm and contours. For example, in line 112 the word "tossed" (*uttaru*) is given a tossing break on the double *t*, and the tumbling of the rock downstream is caught in the *tayū*'s slow, careful rendition of *yarazu nagaruru wa* (line 113; compare with the following *ruru* of line 5). At line 118 the shamisen returns. Note that the shamisen enters on the lower leading tone of B. The singer, on the other hand, starts with C sharp and goes to F sharp that leads to B, only to "half cadence" on F sharp on the word *mitsugashiwa*, which leads into the next thoughts.

Lines 119–123

As the text speaks of the sinking of things in the water, the line is sung on the lower F sharp, dropping to an even lower C sharp after the word "sinking" (*shizumeba*). The hopes are then dashed (*kanawazu*) to the lowest pitch, B, only to return with a high sliding pitch that ends on a C sharp, an octave higher for the word "floating" (*ukamu*). A shamisen shout prepares the *tayū*, and the listener, for a high F sharp for the opening of line 120. The leaves are picked in line 121 with three staccatto notes on the shamisen. The shamisen moves to the water surface, an octave higher than the singer, the other *tayū* overlapping his entry with an *iro-dome* full cadence to take us back across the river and into the maid's speech.

Lines 124–131

Note again the quick transition from the *kotoba* into the *ji* section between lines 127 and 129. The "happiness" (*ureshisa*) of Hinadori is reflected in the quick shamisen passage on that word. In the same manner, the fluttering action of line 130 is heard in the shamisen part.

Her pose, standing among the cherry trees (*sakura*), is noted by a ritard and pause in the music.

Lines 132–136

The call of Hinadori to her lover is made more plaintive by the shamisen use of F natural repeats, the common signal of a sad, lyrical line in all shamisen music. It is intensified by moving up to A and sliding up from F to B before resolving to E. During this dialogue the parts of the two lovers are sung by the two *tayū*, so their sound in performance is actually heard from the two sides of the stage. The two faces (*kao*) of line 134 are sung separately. Note how the movement from *miya* to *wasu* is kept tense as the *tayū* remains on the D even though the shamisen resolves it to E. On the syllable *to*, the *tayū* and shamisen use different leading tones, the latter never resolving it but moving on to a new upper leading tone (F#), with the *tayū* continuing to make half cadences on D on *kokoro* and *bakari ga*[sic]. When the singers are reduced to one syllable each, note how they continue such half cadences even though the shamisen marks resolutions to E. The change to the upper and lower leading tones of B on the *i* of *ai* prepares us for a joining of the two singers in their versions of the melody for the rest of the line. The fact that neither the shamisen nor the vocal part is the same reflects the importance of individual interpretation in the art of *gidayū*.

Section 4b

Lines 137–147

A new pitch a whole step higher is used in the recording for the next section in which *kotoba* follow brief B-E. (The actual pitch in performance is a whole step higher, C#-F#.) In the parlando section that follows, the shamisen is active when the forging of a barrier is mentioned (*nakagaki*). By line 143 we have entered into another lyrical section. The opening of line 145 is a fine use of unresolved upper leading tones in the shamisen. Listening to the performance one can also hear a pathetic slide for each of the first three notes as Hinadori mentions the mountains. The tonality changes as she speaks of the middle of the river, and the pitch level rises toward the climax of this lyrical section on the word "bridge" (*hashi*). Other rhythmic changes relate to puppet movements.

Section 4c

Lines 148–160

Lines 148–150 are a parlando introduction to a long speech by Koganosuke. Parlando returns to lines 158–159, and the speech continues for line 160 and then moves toward the next big musical section. Note how it was approached by alternating styles.

Lines 161–165

Out of the parlando of 161 we come to Koganosuke's *sawari*. The first high pitched lyricism appears on the word "heart" (*kokoro*) and then the rendition of the word "warbler" (*uguisu*, line 162). Note the unusual (nonhuman) sound in the shamisen. This birdlike difference is even more evident when the open sky (*kumoi*) is sought by the caged bird. A clear cadence marks the end of the *sawari*.

Section 4d

Lines 166–176

The major melodic movement in the accompaniment of Hinadori's impassioned speech is an upward sweep in line 171 when the rapids of the river are mentioned (*hayase no nami*). The most noteworthy aspect of this section is the clear use of the shamisen as a marker of units of text as shown below. It is in passages such as this that one seems to see musical roots in the drum accompaniment of Nō drama, though the sound and distribution of accents are different. The density of the shamisen part at the end of line 176 and the stopping on a lower leading tone adds to the quick, smooth transition to the second *tayū*.

Lines 177–185

Koganosuke's admonitions are delivered in quick speech but break into forceful (*haru*) parlando starting high and moving to a very low *naka* sound as he pleads with Hinadori not to do anything rash (line 183). The second *tayū* completes the scene with line 185.

Section 5

Lines 186–193

The final cadence of line 185 is only a few notes as the call of Lord Daihanji's name overlaps with the ending of the last scene; thus, another smooth transition has been accomplished. Note in line 187 the short notes on the shamisen. They relate to Koganosuke jumping with surprise. Hinadori enters into distraught, quick music for line 188, after a moment of feminine delay, and follows that with a lurching shamisen sound for "Please wait" (line 189). The call of Madame Sadaka's return breaks all hope, and the music moves slowly toward a full sectional cadence. The extended passage is on the word *chikara* of line 192 as this is a sectional cadence. The two characters must exit to their homes, and the audience must prepare for a new set of characters and, in this recording, a new *tayū* to appear.

Section 6

Lines 194–197

Tonality changes to a new pitch center a fourth above the last note of line 193. Though the line has a wide range, it is generally low and heavy to match the militant and serious nature of Daihanji. The glissando in the voice of *shite* after the word "sword" (*katana*) and on "scrape" (*kezuru*) strengthen the image of the thoughts that scrape his heart like a sword.

Lines 198–204

The music concentrates on the middle and upper ranges of the shamisen to reflect the move from a warrior to Lady Sadaka. Sadaka says Daihanji's name with an *iro-dome* accompaniment that prepares one for speech in line 202. The *ji haru* section that follows ends with a *fushi* cadence as the dialogue is only just beginning.

Section 7

Lines 205–214

The transitional line begins with a strong, *haru* style of delivery to contrast Daihanji's character, as an *iro* passage leads into his first speech. His scowl of line 214 is clearly depicted by the quick slides of the finger on the shamisen and the forceful rendition of the line. They also relate to the puppet grimaces that occur at this point. It ends with a *fushi* cadence to flow across the river quickly.

Section 8a

Lines 215–221

The transition to Sadaka's next question is done in the standard form of a *ji* followed by an *iro* for line 215.

Lines 222–229

Daihanji's immediate and bravado-filled reply leaves no time for any musical transition into it. The pause between the syllables on the word *tenchi* in line 228 splits it into its two parts "heaven" and "earth" as the puppet moves its head up and down when the *tayū* renders these words.

Lines 230–243

In Sadaka's story of the fate of her daughter note that a pause is made on the word for empress (*okisakisama*) as a proper vocal bow to someone of that rank. The slow, nervous laugh at the end leads to a closing shamisen pattern. However, it is not played completely in order to flow into Daihanji's next question.

Section 8b

Lines 244–274

In this long, unaccompanied, spoken dialogue, variety is accomplished by pauses or changes of contour at dramatic moments such as line 248 and in Daihanji's next three lines. The descending rendition of the end of line 255 forms a very strong cadence. Music returns for a high singing of line 261 around life and death. In this performance the *tayū* places his cruel laugh before the word *sakai* rather than after it. The basic design thereafter is to shorten the time between the entrance of the two characters' words so that at line 271 the *tayū* sing together. Lines 271 through 273 repeat the design on a shorter scale.

Section 9a

Lines 275–279

A fast *okuri* pattern and the last phrase of line 274 are the transition to a new scene as the mother goes to see her child. Lines 275–76 start with a relatively high lyrical confidence and end with a low *naka* cadence, for the mother is worried. The repeat of the word "daughter" (*musume*) is labelled as an *iro* since the first was spoken. The end of line 279 is a *kakari* because it leads back to words. This is mentioned as a reminder that throughout the piece the conventions of moving from one texture to another are always present in one of their many possible forms. The very active shamisen part, as the mother moves to the daughter, also reflects the *fushi* word seen in the *tayū* text.

Section 9b

Lines 280–282

Hinadori's greetings to her mother proceed from *kotoba* to a long *fushi* for line 282, which relates to her formal bowing and the cadence of that unit.

Section 10a

Lines 283–290

Line 283 follows the *ji* to *iro* pattern to return to dialogue as the mother makes her opening general remarks.

Lines 293–297

Since the maid has been asked to do something for her mistress, the accompaniment for line 294 becomes quick and "lower class." It is followed by the fast talk of the maid but returns to *ji haru* because she cannot bring up the important business. The *fushi* full cadence pattern for line 297 may also be active in response to the term dishevelled hair (*motsuregamin ni*).

Section 10b

Lines 298–314

The full cadence makes it possible for the other *tayū* to overlap his entrance of Sadaka's long explanation of her plans to her daughter whom she wants to convert to the plot. The pause in timing as she asks for approval from the maids brings a quick, nervous response in line 311, for they know they must agree though they know it is wrong.

Lines 315–318

Line 315 begins in fast tempo and slows down as a transition from the maid's style to *tayū* commentary. This anxious style is appropriate since the plan had fallen on deaf ears.

Section 10c

Lines 319–327

The slower, maternal pace of Sadaka's words shows why the previous dialogue was given to a maid. This way, there can be a contrast in style and tempo. The steady rendering of the speech is necessary to overcome Hinadori's surprise in line 324. It is only at the end, when Sadaka says one must be grateful for this (*arigatai*), that there is a pause.

Lines 328–329

Hinadori's gasp *e* leads us smoothly out of the dialogue and into her gasp and crying. The word *hatto* is shouted out, thus forming a bridge between the cry and the sung commentary. Though line 327 is in the heavy range it does not come to a cadence as Sadaka must intervene quickly to convert her daughter. In fact it remains on B without coming up to the usual E ending.

Section 10d

Lines 330–336

Sadaka bravely carries on with her inadequate explanation of the logic of marrying her daughter to someone else. The steadily paced dialogue has that quality of trying to sell an idea. Only when she says "What a fortunate daughter" (line 334) is there a break in the pace. The last syllable of "daughter" (*musume*) includes a trembling in the voice that shows the mother really knows how wrong this effort is.

Lines 337–341

The maids do their best to support the mother though Kogiku's first "yes" is almost a sob. The maids get up to leave in line 339 to the jaunty rhythm and pentatonic shamisen line appropriate to their rank. However, the half-step upper leading tone returns for line 340 for the maids are dispirited. The *fushi* cadence is only F, E, F, E, E as we turn to Sadaka's thoughts.

Section 11

Lines 342–370

Lines 342 and 343 illustrate the typical manner in which transitional commentaries can be structured, remembering always that each transition may have its own special musical features. The cadencing notes of the previous line emphasize the freshness of the F sharp after the F naturals of the previous cadence. Note that the two syllables of "*iro iro*" are done on different pitches to give them contrast. The reciting tone of line 343 is the upper leading tone C, and a *haru* intensity is given to the last word, "branch" (*eda*). The C is resolved by the shamisen while the *tayū* declaims an *iro*-style passage that will lead to speech. The shamisen cadences with motion from the upper and the lower leading tones to B. Note that all this occurs on B rather than E to give the passage a "higher" female quality.

The generally steady flow of this long speech is carefully broken at set points or terms. For example, line 348 at *yaburya* ("break"), line 349 before "duty" (*arisō*), and before Sadaka starts her analogy at line 351. A climax occurs at line 355 with the word *adabana* ("ill-fated flowers"). A stop also occurs between Koganosuke's name (line 358) and the thought of suicide, which is said very slowly to drive the point home to Hinadori. In this skillful manner the speech moves on to a call for a decision in line 370.

Lines 371–372

The intensifying rhythm of the series of *sa* in line 370 leads into a dramatic (*ji iro haru*) rendition of line 371. Line 372 carries on with a high *kami* singing of the term "duty" (*giri*), and the rest of the line seems as tense and entrapped as the lovers. Quickly repeated notes on the shamisen build the tension further as through the tears Hinadori calls out "Mother" (marked as *iro* in the text). The term *kikiwakemashita* ("I perceive") is on the highest pitch. The singer gives a tense (*haru*) rendition of "words" (*kotoba*) before declaiming in *iro* style "I shan't thwart your wishes."

Lines 373–382

A short, sharp shamisen cadence leads to Sadaka's words. At line 376 there is a break before the second *dekashatta* as Sadaka shows her remorse that she seems to have accomplished this sad act. The shamisen starts line 377 with a pizzicato on a new pitch, C sharp, as the mother tries to talk about future court life. An E begins line 379, which is a *kakari*-style transition into a single lyrical line 380 that returns to speech as Sadaka prepares to arrange Hinadori's hair.

Lines 383–386

The style of lines 383 and 384 is sometimes called a long *ji* (*nagaji*). Musically this length can be heard in the extensive use of leading tones that do not resolve until *kushi no.* The shamisen phrase leading to line 385 introduces a low F sharp (the term *u gin* is found in the *maruhon* at that point). The whole passage has a denser shamisen line. A new pitch occurs as Hinadori's hair is done in court rather than marriage style. The F natural returns as the reciting tone when the second *tayū* enters with comments on Hinadori's agony.

Section 12a

Lines 387–394

After a *haru* to *iro* transitional line, Koganosuke's speech begins. The *tayū*'s description of Daihanji in line 392 is given a strong *haru* interpretation, and the *fushi* of the cadence is greatly extended to support tearful head movements of an old warrior and a father.

Section 12b

Lines 395–410

Like Sadaka's earlier speech, Daihanji's monologue remains at a fairly regular tempo with stops on important words like "harboring" (*hitsujō*) in line 400. The parlando (*ji iro*) style returns at line 408. The warrior nature of the words is reinforced by sharp plectrum strokes on the shamisen line markers. The term translated as "behavior" (*dekashi*, line 410) is particularly strong in both voice and shamisen, and the *fushi* that ends the unit is equally strong and ends with a full cadence.

Section 12c

Lines 411–426

Line 414 is a *kakari* out of speech toward song. It is sung at an unusually high pitch, perhaps because of the dramatic period in the play. The rhythmic markers of the shamisen for line 415 are shown below. Though the line is not in strict poetry form, note the tendency toward three-beat divisions, with beat six of special importance.

```
1 2 3 4 5 6 7  1 2 3  4 5 6 1  2 3  4 5 6 7
semekorosaruru kurushimiyori seppuku sasureba
B  BB     B              B    E        G#E


12 3  4  5  67 1  2    3 4   5 678
uneme no sengi no ne o    tatsu taikō
   E        F#      F#E F#   E B
```

The "creeping weed" (*mugura*, line 418) creeps from very low in the *tayū*'s range to high, while the shamisen remains poised on an unresolved half-step upper leading tone. The shamisen time markers of line 419 continue the three-unit tendency. Note that the pronunciation of *itteki* tends to merge beats of two syllables into beat five so the note B also falls into the general time scheme. The half-cadencing A is never resolved as the *tayū* slowly and powerfully declaims the word for "warrior's code."

```
1 2 3 4  5 6 7  1 2 34  56 7  1  23 4567 1 2 3 4   5
hikinuku yori mo sasai na koto to. Nanda itteki kobosanu wa
   F     E      F   F   AF     A     B
1 2   3  45 6
bushi no, omote
```

The unstable pitch F is repeated twice to open line 420. A dramatic pause is made after the word "child" (*ko*) with the unresolved A returning only to come to a release on E after an intense declaiming of the word "love" (*kawayū*). The high point comes in line 426 as Daihanji speaks of fifty years (*gojūnen*), followed by violent plectrum double strokes for the rest of that line.

Lines 427–432

Line 427 starts with quick shamisen repetitions of F that leads into conventional shamisen syllable markers as seen in line 428:

```
12  3   45 6  7 12 3 4 5  6 7
oya no jihishin arigatananda [123 123 12345]
     F    E    D  E       x   x   x x
```

This steady pace comes to a dramatic close down in line 430 and with a declamation of the term "regret" (*zannen*) of line 431. The intense sadness of line 432 is reinforced by repetitions of single notes on the shamisen and, eventually, the entrance of both singers as the father and son weep together over their fate.

Section 13a

Lines 433–439

Line 433 is a contrasting, quiet transition into Sadaka's continued attempt to seem pleased about the proposed marriage. Its *fushi* cadence maintains this spirit.

Section 13b

Lines 440–445

The transitional passage for Hinadori's speech begins on the half-step upper leading tone for the word "anger" (*urameshige*), reflecting her inward tense feelings that have not yet burst to the surface. The first lines of her speech are sung in general style (*u*) until she asks how she could possibly be happy as an empress (line 443), which is in *kotoba* style, preluded by an unresolved lower leading tone.

Lines 446–451

Lines 446–448 are sung quickly against shamisen time markers as Hinadori breaks the doll. Line 449 is reinforced by quickly repeated notes on the shamisen, which are conventional preparations for the singing of an important word at a high pitch. More shamisen repeated notes with an upward set of eighth notes to a lower leading tone occur for the word "tears" (*namida*). The pitch is unresolved, forming a half cadence into the dialogue between mother and child that sets Hinadori's death as certain.

Lines 452–461

Line 454 is declaimed with a wide, intense contour as Sadaka says she must hand over her daughter's head. The exclamation of Hinadori as she expresses joy and thanks in lines 457–458 is half joy and half tears and is held to give more power to the words that follow. Line 460 is spoken against shamisen time markers. It is followed by short lyricism on the words *musume no kokoro* in line 461. The end of that line is an *iro* but is accompanied by a crying pattern on the shamisen that creates a half cadence to overlap with the *kotoba* that follow.

Lines 462–471

As Sadaka explains her motives, the *tayū* breaks the rhythmic pattern of the speech for the "at least one person" term at the beginning of line 467.

Lines 472–475

The shamisen enters with one note before the dramatic "cut your head off" term of line 472 and follows it with the repeating pattern conventional for a high lyrical passage. Lines 473–475 begin marked as a *ji kami* and are sung in a flexible rhythmic pattern climaxed with the word "mother" (*haha*) and then "happy" (*ureshikaro*), which is an *iro*-style declamation done to a shamisen crying pattern that overlaps into the next speech section.

Lines 476–481

The ever nearer call and response of the mother and child in lines 479–481 is again supported by the emotion-laden shamisen signal of a single note repeated ever closer. It leads into another crying pattern with a half cadence.

Lines 482–487

The overlapped shamisen cadence moves on to mark each text unit of Sadaka's speech in line 483 and ends with another signal of a high lyrical passage that occurs at line 484. An unusual pitch area is used by the shamisen when Hinadori embraces her mother. The word "tears" (*namida*) in line 486 is accompanied by repeated, crying-pattern sounds on the shamisen. The two *tayū* perform the last line together.

Section 14

Lines 488–498

The move across the river to Koganosuke's suicide preparations is first marked by a lower shamisen pitch, signaling a male dialogue. Its choice of an unusual B flat-A opening reflects the menacing emotion of the moment, while the short but frequent shamisen syllable markers against the fast tempo declamation of lines 488–492 enhance the drama of the scene. The tempo is broken only at the word "stomach" (*hara*) in line 492 as Koganosuke starts the final act. In lines 490–492 the three-beat pulse of the shamisen helps to drive this section forward to the key word. Note how the normal pitch center (B) is barely touched and an unusual chromatic ascent is used to arrive at the C sharp. The final brief E-C sharp also contributes to the flow of this text into the words that follow. In lines 493–498 Daihanji's words are spoken in a similar fast, steady rhythm that builds to an intense stuttering of the syllable *na* of *naze* ("why," line 498).

Lines 499–514

After a crying out of line 499, a single A on the shamisen marks the beginning of Koganosuke's words and a fast tempo until the word "my" (*watakushi*) of "When she hears of my death." Line 503 is given ample parlando lyricism with a low to high on -*shi aihate*- to a high, slow melisma on *kika*-, to a very low note on -*ba*. Line 504 continues low, as marked in the *maruhon* (a *ji naka*). The *haru* mark for the opening of line 505 is rendered strongly in the recording, and the calling out of *mōsubeshi* is a normal *iro* convention leading back to words, as is the half cadence in the shamisen (C sharp?). The words are spoken steadily and quickly except for the word "abide" (submit, *kōsan*, line 509) and the last words of line 512, which lead us back to parlando style. Lines 513–514 follow a typical parlando pattern from a middle pitch to a higher level that leads to the next speech. Note the convention of a three-note repeat (E, EEE) after the first word, *fugi*, then B and, at end of line, E B for cadence.

Lines 515–519

Daihanji's first line is a declaimed *iro* that leads to his spoken version of line 516. Line 517 begins the building of another dramatic unit with low parlando style, the word *giri* being given the *haru* strength indicated in the *maruhon*. Line 518 moves to a middle pitch, and 519 somewhat higher, so that the concern for her family (*ie*) forms a climactic *iro* declamation returning the music to the father's words. Because of the great seriousness of the moment, both the *tayū*'s interpretation of the word and the shamisen's two-note cadence are deliberately performed slowly and intensely (with *ma*).

Lines 520–526

Daihanji's pledge to his dying son leads to the most dramatic music for this character so far. His heart is torn in line 523, which is depicted with a leap from a very low to a very high pitch and then sharp "tearing" sounds from the shamisen. The *i* vowel of the last syllable begins to turn into weeping in both the vocal and shamisen part. The fast-repeating upper leading tone accompaniment is followed by an equally fast line 525 with syllable markers, a lyrical climax occurring on the "tears of blood" (*chi no namida*). The word "fall" is declaimed, and line 525 is filled with intense sobbing renditions of words and shamisen sounds.

Section 15a

Lines 527–538

Line 527 is the conventional *ji haru* to *iro* transition to a new set of words by Hinadori. These turn into a parlando section in line 530. The "thousand years" (*mannen*) is emphasized by its own long melisma. The shamisen uses two- and three-note units rather than single ones to mark the beats since the tempo is slower, the character feminine, and the puppet gestures more supple. A sliding shamisen passage upward to a lower leading tone leads one from the *iro* unit into further speech. At line 538 Hinadori's call to her mother to cut her throat leads logically to a *haru*-style rendition.

Lines 539–544

Sadaka's determination to kill her daughter begins with a low pitch and rises as she struggles to unsheathe the sword. The words *ima kirikorosu* of line 543 are given a dramatic pause, and after quick action the section ends where it began, at a lower pitch level as the false message floats down the river.

Section 15b

Lines 545–556

The first monologue is Koganosuke's relief at seeing the message, and the next is Hinadori calling for her demise. The alternation between *tayū* also begins to occur at shorter and shorter intervals. The words literally ride (*kotoba-nori*) on shamisen markers. While this is done with higher pitches for Hinadori, the lines by the *tayū* representing her mother and Koganosuke's father are lower. The last alternate lines (555–556) are marked and performed in strong *haru*-style.

Lines 557–561

After Sadaka's words of hope for her daughter in heaven, her Buddhist prayer is done quickly against a shamisen time marker so that it can pause dramatically before the word *kittaru* ("strike off") in line 561. The shamisen conventional prelude to calling out (*oyobi dasu,* [marked *iri*] B A BB) is followed by the mother's cry and sharp blows of the plectrum as the cry echoes through the hills.

Lines 562–568

Daihanji in *haru*-style makes a quick transition to his question of Sadaka. The timing of the whole interchange of disbelief that both lovers are dead has to be quick, for it leads to both characters crying out together in line 566. The same calling-out pattern (B A BBB) precedes Daihanji's "What have we done!" and a *suete* extension of line 567 is in keeping with the intensity of the moment. Line 568 has convulsive shamisen sounds as the parents react to the horrible deeds.

Section 16

Lines 569–584

The moment in the drama obviously calls for a musical highlight. After a transitional *ji haru-iro* in line 569, Sadaka speaks line 570 but uses 571 as a *kakari* passage to turn to a slow, lyrical depiction of Daihanji descending to the river bank to talk with her. Similar music brings Sadaka to the river with the head of her daughter. Thus, the two units form one of the clearest joint performance (*jiai*) sections in the piece. The *maruhon* had returned lines 578–580 to words, but an

extended lyrical section is more appropriate to present-day performance needs. A change of pitch center and a pause help to emphasize
the phrase "A fate too cruel" (*aenaiarisama*, line 579). The shamisen
repeats one high note, a convention that usually relates to sobbing or
similar sad emotions. It also leads into a variant of the standard *yotsuma* pattern (D, E, FFE) that comes at this point in most *gidayū* arias
(*kudoki* or *sawari*). Note that the word aria is a poor Western equivalent
because of the many changes of tempo and texture and the smooth
flow out of the unit to dialogue through an *iro* passage ending line
584.

Lines 585–594

The grief-stricken parents come to peace with each other in a dialogue that is filled with careful pauses and continuing intensity.

Lines 595–605

The comment of line 595 serves as a transition to three lines of
words that return to a musical style as Sadaka thinks of the dolls she
has given Hinadori. The shamisen accompaniment of line 601 is noteworthy for its mournful sliding entrances or ornamentations on its
pitches. The *ji haru* to *u* to *iro* structure leads to Sadaka's spoken
orders to float the dolls as a memorial offering.

Section 17

Lines 606–615

A short set of shamisen double strokes brings us to a new point in
the drama. The following *ji* section includes the sound of a koto as the
dolls will be set on Hinadori's koto for their trip across the river. With
this combination of instruments the music starts with some rubato but
assumes the steady, slow beat of *gidayū* dance music as the memorial
goods are prepared. Lines 608 and 609 use a conventional shamisen
tataki pattern, though only line 609 is so marked in the *maruhon*. The
tone system of this section is pentatonic, with a resulting "brighter"
sound. Half-step passages (C B) mix with the whole step E F sharps in
the interlude between lines 610 and 611 and become dominant. A
change to a very slow tempo before line 612 supports the procession of
wedding gifts that are to be for a funeral. Each phrase stops on a half
cadence that is not resolved until the end of line 613. The full cadence

of the section occurs with line 614. The *fushi* of line 615 is a conventional, wide-ranged cadence melody accompanied by the shamisen only.

Section 18

Lines 616–620

The koto returns and a *naka tataki* is listed. The instruments conform to the standard use of an upper half step leading tone repetition of *tataki* patterns, but it is more melodic as it still has the dance quality necessary for this point in the drama design. The *tayū* sings rather simply as his sound is covered by both the instruments and the action. The interlude after line 618 is a remembrance of the koto tradition to which the text refers. It is followed by a very dense instrumental accompaniment to support puppet action; thus, the *tayū* line remains relatively simple. The only vocalization is on the possessive case sign *no* in line 620. It is used primarily to allow the *tayū* to join the instruments in their melody.

Lines 621–622

The transition to the other side of the river is quite brutal, with a solo shamisen coming in on a different, *in* scale tone system. The shamisen *fushi* for line 622 uses an unusual triplet rhythm.

Section 19a

Lines 623–638

Though Daihanji is the character of this section, the shamisen accompaniment is high since Daihanji is gazing at the head of Hinadori as a sad parent, not as a fierce warrior. The first words of line 625 are spoken like a Buddhist chant. An upper leading tone sung from lower to upper octave moves from the Buddhist text to the words "wedding gift" (*chihako no*). The shamisen markers follow the general pattern C B C B E C B, a lower pattern being used for *to iunaraba* (line 628) and a higher one for "happy" (*yorokoban*), though the singer remains in the middle range since there is no happiness now. Line 633 uses a brief DEF A phrase to prepare for a pause on two people (*futari*) whose misfortune (*fuun*) is rendered low with a half cadence that leads to speech.

Lines 639–644

Shamisen markers accompany Daihanji's parlando section, which is more speech than song.

Section 19b

Lines 645–656

The shamisen prelude to Sadaka's reply is from the conventional *yotsuma* pattern found before the last section of a *kudoki*. The first line is spoken against this background, but line 646 is a restrained musical style done against shamisen markers much in the manner of Daihanji's last speech. The tempo is steady and fairly fast. Only at line 650 is the tempo broken for the word *towaiinagara* ("And now"). The shamisen responds to the remark about cutting down in line 652 with a sudden "slash" with the left hand on the upper string. In lines 653–656 an upward line of the shamisen to an incomplete cadence leads smoothly into Daihanji's reply. It is done unaccompanied, with dramatic emphasis being put on *menboku-* ("face") in line 656.

Lines 657–667

Sadaka's lines return to the fast-tempo static style with shamisen markers in the upper, "female," range. In line 661 an upward line to an incomplete cadence returns us to Daihanji's single line delivered tensely without accompaniment. In line 662 a *yotsuma* pattern precedes a return to the style of Sadaka's earlier lines, but this time it is followed by Daihanji's line, accompanied and sung. Line 664 is then sung by both *tayū* moving back and forth between the pitches A F sharp so that the line does not seem to resolve. The new pitch area arrives at the high note of line 666 when the Yoshino River is mentioned. A long melisma leads to an eventual cadence on low E. This is reinforced in line 667 by a *haru* style, with forceful strokes on the shamisen as the tears flow.

Section 20

Lines 668–675

The closing (*dangiri*) section begins with lines declaimed at a quick tempo with stacatto shamisen markers as Daihanji speaks to his son while he is still alive. (As in Western opera, main characters can die very slowly if need be.) The tempo only stops before the word "rebirth" (*rinne*, line 670) and before line 673, where the victory of enemies is accompanied by a burst of shamisen sounds and intense *tayū ago* (jaw) enunciations such as one would hear in other plays during a battle description.

Lines 676–695

The music pauses briefly for a lyrical rendition of the phrase "this young pair" in line 676 but then moves quickly on as they approach the gates of death. The name of the lord of death (Enma) is declaimed slowly, and then fierce shamisen strokes accompany the fast-moving text. At line 680 the phrase "quickly passing day" is held briefly. The rest of line 680 and line 681 is accompanied by a three-beat pattern on the shamisen that is a conventional prelude to a high note in an active scene. The last word *kirigakure* is shouted out and followed by a shamisen *yotsuma* prelude. However, the shamisen does not mark texts but continues to fill every beat for lines 680–694 until the last word, which is declaimed unaccompanied in line 695. This dense shamisen part is appropriate to a finale section of a play. It also helps support final dramatic posturing on the part of the puppets. The *tayū* move from line exchanges (lines 683–684) to word exchanges (lines 687–689), eventually singing line 691 together. A similar system of exchanges completes the play, a standard last phrase being sung by both *tayū*.

Glossary

ago o tsukau	顎を使う	Chanting technique of moving jaw back and forth for severe effect.
ai no yama	相ノ山	Notation: melodic pattern from folk song.
ai no yama okuri	相ノ山ヲクリ	Type of *okuri.*
aisō-zukashi	愛想づかし	Severing ties to lover.
amido	網戸	Notation: melodic pattern from old Jōruri.
amido okuri	網戸ヲクリ	Type of *okuri.*
ato	跡	Extra scene that follows *kiri-ba.*
banzuke	番付	Playbill listing title and performers.
biwa hōshi	琵琶法師	Blind lute-playing minstrel; storytellers in medieval Japan.
bungo-jōruri	豊後浄瑠璃	Type of Jōruri.

257

bunjin	文人	"Literati," scholars, painters, poets, etc. Important term in 18th-century Japanese culture.
bunraku	文楽	A term now used for *ningyō jōruri* (Jōruri puppet theater). Uemura Bunrakuken (1750–1810) founded a Jōruri theater in the last decade of the 18th century. In 1811 after his death a theater called Bunraku was founded by his successor. This theater flourished in the Meiji period and today is the only professional Jōruri puppet theater organization.
bun'ya	文弥	Notation: sad melodic pattern from old Jōruri.
chari	チャリ	Comedy.
chikara	チカラ	Notation: melodic pattern.
chikuzen	筑前	Melodic pattern.
chūshin	注進	Return from battle and relate events.
dan	段	Act. Also refers to portion of play one chanter performs that is better termed a "scene."
dangiri	段切り	Finale of scene.
dannashū	旦那衆	Patrons of art.

dōgu-gaeshi	道具返シ	Notation: musical pattern (cadence or prelude) used to begin or end a scene when there has been a change of scenery.
dōguya	道具屋	Notation: melodic pattern from old Jōruri.
edo	江戸	Notation: martial-like melodic pattern from old Jōruri.
enkiri	縁切り	Severing ties to a lover
fū	風	Style.
funa-uta	舟歌	Notation: melodic pattern from folk song.
fushi	フシ	Notation: cadence pattern. Also general term for melody.
fushigoto	節事	Song portion of play (*michiyuki*, etc.); contrasts with *jigoto* parts.
fushi kakari	フシカカリ	Notation: type of *fushi-ochi*.
fushi-ochi (fushi-otoshi)	フシ落チ フシ落シ	Notation: (written *fushi* in text) cadence pattern. Signaling musical paragraphs (primary unit).
fushi okuri	フシヲクリ	Type of *okuri*.
fushi-otoshi	フシ落シ	See *fushi-ochi*.
fushi tataki	フシタタキ	Type of *fushi*.

geiki	外記	Notation: martial-like melodic pattern from old Jōruri.
gidayū	義太夫	One tradition of Jōruri music founded by the chanter Takemoto Gidayū (1651–1714).
gin	キン	Notation: pitch above *kami*.
gin okuri	キンヲクリ	Type of *okuri*.
gomashō	胡麻章	Notation: marks inserted alongside text to indicate variation in melody.
gyōgi (fushi) (kioi)	行義 （フシ）（キヲイ）	Type of *fushi-ochi*.
ha	破	See *jo ha kyū*.
haba	端場	Introductory scene of act (*dan* or *maki*).
hanchū	半中	Notation: melodic pattern from Jōruri other than *gidayū*.
handayū	半太夫	Notation: melodic pattern from Jōruri other than *gidayū*.
haneru	ハネル	Melodic pattern.
harima	ハリマ	Melodic pattern used to express sadness.
harima-ji	播磨地	Name of melodic pattern.
haru	ハル	Notation: high pitch; voice is taut.

haru fushi	ハルフシ	Notation: melodic pattern.
haru gin	ハルキン	Notation: high pitch.
harutayū-fū	春太夫風	Style of Harutayū.
haru u	ハルウ	Notation: pitch above *haru*.
hatsumi	ハツミ	Notation: melodic pattern.
hayari-uta	流行り歌	Notation: melodic pattern from popular song.
heike	平家	Notation: style of delivery in Heike chanting manner.
higashi-fū	東風	Style of music originating in Toyotake Theater. Echizen no shojō (Toyotake Wakatayū, 1681–1764) was founder of this tradition. More "flowery" style than more "solemn" *nishi-fū*.
hiki-dashi	弾き出シ	Notation: melodic pattern used to begin or end scene.
hikitori sanjū	引き取り三重	Type of *sanjū*.
hinagata-bushi	雛形フシ	Type of *fushi-ochi*.
hina okuri	雛ヲクリ	Type of *okuri*.
hiroi	ヒロイ	Notation: melodic pattern. Refers to rhythm of shamisen.
hitotsu yuri (fushi)	一ツユリ（フシ）	Type of *fushi-ochi*.
honbushi	本フシ	Notation: melodic pattern.
hon-chōshi	本調子	Shamisen's "normal" tuning.

hyōgu	表具	Notation: melodic pattern from old Jōruri.
iken	意見	Advice.
inbon	院本	See *maruhon*.
iro	色	Notation: chanting style in between speech and song. Often used as transition between *ji* (or *ji-iro*) and *kotoba*.
iro-dome	色ドメ	Shamisen musical pattern used to "close" or end *iro* line.
iro okuri	色ヲクリ	Type of *okuri* used as melodic pattern.
iru	入	Notation: voice technique used at emotional moments.
itoayatsuri-uta	糸操歌	Notation: melodic pattern from folk song.
ji	地	Notation: melodic delivery style accompanied by shamisen. "Third person" narrative section as opposed to "first person" *kotoba*. Also called *ji ai*.
ji ai	地合	See *ji*.
jidaimono	時代物	History or period play.
jigoto	地事	Dramatic parts of play (in contrast to *fushigoto* song portions).
ji-iro	地色	Notation: rhythmical delivery style (parlando); less melodic than *ji*.

jikken	実検	Verification of authenticity.
ji naka	地中	Notation: melodic *ji* line with low or falling pitch. Sometimes similar to *iro* in being cadencelike and transitional.
ji-uta	地唄	Notation: melodic pattern from *ji-uta* shamisen tradition.
jizōkyō	地蔵経	Notation: melodic pattern from Buddhistic song.
jo	序	See *jo ha kyū*.
jo ha kyū	序破急	Concept of musical structure: introduction, intensification, rapid conclusion. Usually divided into five part: *jo, ha₁, ha₂, ha₃, kyū*.
jo no kotoba	序詞	Notation: formal delivery style used at beginning of *jidaimono* play.
jōruri	浄瑠璃	Style of singing in puppet theater that developed from 1600; a general term for the puppet theater. General term for various styles of singing.
junrei-uta	巡礼歌	Notation: melodic pattern from Buddhistic popular song.
kaeshi	返シ	Practice of repeating part of final line of previous scene when a chanter begins his performance.

kaishin	改心	Change of heart from bad to good.
kakari	カカリ	Notation: melodic pattern used as transition from *kotoba* to *ji*.
kakutayū	角太夫	Notation: sad melodic pattern from old Jōruri.
kami (kan)	上	Notation: high pitch used at emotional points.
kami-mori	上モリ	Notation: melodic pattern.
kami sanjū	上三重	Type of *sanjū*.
kami u	上ウ	Notation: highest pitch.
kan	上	See *kami*.
kandō	勘当	Disinheritance.
kasane bushi	重フシ	Type of *fushi-ochi*. Melodic pattern.
kasumi	霞	Melodic pattern.
kawachi-ji	河内地	Name of melodic pattern.
kei	ケイ	Notation: melodic pattern.
keiko-bon	稽古本	Woodblock text of individual scene containing chanter's notation. Used as practice text.
kengyō	検校	Blind musician of *heikyoku* or *ji-uta sōkyoku*.
kioi sanjū	キオイ三重	Type of *sanjū*.

kiri-ba (kiri)	キり場　（切り）	Climax scene of an act (*dan* or *maki*).
kiyari ondo	木遣り音頭	Notation: melodic pattern from folk song.
kodama	谺	Melodic pattern.
ko-jōruri	古浄瑠璃	Jōruri before 1684.
komatayū okuri	駒太夫ヲクリ	Type of *okuri*.
komori-uta	子守歌	Notation: melodic pattern from folk song.
komurobushi	小室節	Notation: melodic pattern from folk song.
ko okuri	小ヲクリ	Type of *okuri*.
koroshi	殺し	Murder.
kotoba	詞	Musical notation. line delivered without musical accompaniment. Also "first person" portion of text.
kotoba-nori	詞ノリ	Notation: rhythmical delivery style with shamisen accompaniment. Usually used near climactic point in scene.
kowari	コハリ	Notation: pitch above *haru u*.
kuchi	口	Introductory scene.
kudoki	クドキ	Notation: melodic pattern expressing sadness. Refers also to arialike miniscene when (usually) a woman expresses love for husband or child.

kujira	鯨	Melodic pattern.
kuriage	クリ上ゲ	Notation: melodic pattern.
kuru	クル	Notation: melodic pattern used to end *kudoki*. Refers to shamisen rhythm.
kuruma bushi	車フシ	Type of *fushi-ochi*. Melodic pattern.
kyōran	狂乱	Madness.
kyū	急	See *jo ha kyū*.
ma	間	Pause in temporal or spacial sequence.
mago-uta	馬子歌	Melodic pattern from folk song.
mai	舞	Notation: style of chanting in Kōwaka-mai ballad manner.
maki	巻	Term used to denote divisions of *sewamono* plays, which usually have three *maki*. The five *jidaimono* "acts" are called *dan*. The *maki* is often translated as "act," but in Chikamatsu's time three *maki* equaled one *dan*.
makura	マクラ　（枕）	Prelude.
maruhon	丸本	Jōruri woodblock text of complete play published with chanter's notation. See also *inbon, shōhon*.
meriyasu	メリヤス	Shamisen background music.

mi-arawashi	見現シ	Revealing of true identity after time in disguise.
michiyuki	道行	Journey; usually a pair travel from one place to another. *Fushigoto* (song) scene in play.
mi-gawari	身代り	Sacrifice in place of another.
mitsu yuri (fushi)	三ツユリ （フシ）	Type of *fushi-ochi*.
miyato okuri	宮戸ヲクリ	Type of *okuri*.
miyazono	宮園	Notation: melodic pattern from Jōruri other than *gidayū*.
monogatari	物語	Long monologue, relating a story.
monshita	紋下	Head of theatrical troupe.
musha okuri	武者ヲクリ	Type of *okuri*.
mushū-oki	無終翁	Posthumous name for Tsuruzawa Bunzō. "Never-ending."
nagaji	長地	Notation: melodic pattern.
nagauta	長唄	Style of shamisen music.
naka	中	Introductory (middle) scene. Notation: low or falling pitch.
naka u	中ウ	Notation: pitch above *naka*.
naka fushi	中フシ	Type of *fushi-ochi*.

nanatsu-yuri fushi	七ツユリフシ	Type of *fushi-ochi*.
naosu	ナオス	Notation: return chanting or shamisen to "normal" *gidayū*.
narabi	ナラビ	Melodic pattern.
nenbutsu sanjū	念仏三重	Type of *sanjū*.
netori	音取	Gagaku *makura*.
ni agari	二上り	Tuning of second string of shamisen is raised a whole step.
nishi-fū	西風	Style of music originating in Takemoto Theater. Takemoto Gidayū (1651–1714) and Harima no shōjō (Takemoto Masatayū, 1691–1744) are the founders of this tradition. More "solemn" than the more "flowery" *higashi-fū*.
nishiki	ニシキ	Name of melodic pattern.
noru	ノル	Notation: style of "riding" lively rhythm of shamisen.
okazaki	岡崎	Notation: melodic pattern from folk song.
oki-jōruri	置き浄瑠璃	*Makura* of Bungo-jōruri.
oki-uta	置き唄	Nagauta *makura*.
okuri	ヲクリ	Notation: melodic pattern (cadence or prelude) used to begin or end scene when there has been no change of scenery.

ō-otoshi	大落シ	Notation: major cadence in a scene that usually follows dramatic climax.
orinobashi	ヲリ延シ	Melodic pattern.
oroshi	ヲロシ	Notation: cadence signaling end of formal preface at beginning of *makura* in *jidaimono*.
ōsanjū	大三重	Type of *sanjū*.
otoshi	ヲトシ	Cadence pattern.
rakugo	落語	Comic storytelling.
reizen	冷泉	Notation: elegant melodic pattern from old Jōruri.
renbo	恋慕	Love.
rinsei	林清	Notation: melodic pattern from popular song.
rinsei okuri	林清ヲクリ	Type of *okuri*.
roppō	六法	Melodic pattern used at end of dramatic scene.
saguri sanjū	サグリ三重	Type of *sanjū*.
saimon	祭文	Notation: melodic pattern from popular or folk song.
sanjū	三重	Notation: melodic pattern (cadence or prelude) used to begin or end a scene when there has been a change of scenery.

san sagari	三下り	Tuning of third string of shamisen is lowered a whole step.
sawari	サハリ	Used to mean the insertion of a non-*gidayū* melody into the play. Also used to mean *kudoki*.
sekai	世界	"World" or time setting of play. Used in relation to *shukō* (theme innovation). Playwright puts play in *sekai* but introduces new elements to traditional story.
sekkyō	説経	Notation: style of chanting in *sekkyō-jōruri* manner. *Sekkyō* were religious plays.
seme	責め	Torture.
sengi	詮議	Investigation.
senritsukei	旋律型	Melodic pattern.
seppuku	切腹	Suicide.
sewamono	世話物	Contemporary-life play.
sharebon	酒落本	18th-century "witty" fiction mainly about the Edo Yoshiwara pleasure quarter.
shibagaki	柴垣	Notation: melodic pattern.
shidai	次第	Nō *makura*.
shigetayū	繁太夫	Notation: melodic pattern from Jōruri other than *gidayū*.

shika-odori	鹿踊り	Notation: melodic pattern from popular song.
shikoro sanjū	シコロ三重	Type of *sanjū*.
shimo	下	See *shita*. Notation: lowest pitch.
shimo-mori	下モリ	Notation: melodic pattern.
shimo sanjū	下三重	Type of *sanjū*.
shirimochi	尻持	Melodic pattern.
shita kowari	下コハリ	Notation: pitch level below *kowari*.
shōden	正伝	Melodic pattern from Jōruri other than *gidayū*.
shōhon	正本	See *maruhon*.
shōmyō	声明	Traditional Buddhist *sūtra* chanting.
shukō	趣向	Innovation in plot or theme. See *sekai*.
shura	修羅	Marital-like mood.
sōga	早歌	Medieval "fast" songs.
sometayū	染太夫	Melodic pattern or style.
sonae	ソナエ	Musical prelude used at beginning of a scene.
sue	スエ	Notation: abbreviated *suete*.
sue kakari	スエカカリ	Notation: abbreviated *suete*.
sue naka	スエ中	Notation: type of *suete*.

suete	スエテ	Notation: melodic pattern used to express sad or extreme emotion, usually concluding with a cadence.
suri-age	スリ上ゲ	Shamisen player's technique of sliding hand up neck of instrument for effect.
suri-sage	スリ下ゲ	Shamisen player's technique of sliding hand down neck of instrument for effect.
tataki	タタキ	Notation: melodic pattern from song other than *gidayū*, used to express extreme sadness.
tayū	太（大）夫	Suffix for performers. Bunraku chanter.
tennō okuri	天王ヲクリ	Type of *okuri*.
toru	トル	Notation: refers to rhythm of shamisen.
tosa	土佐	Notation: melodic pattern from old Jōruri.
tsunagi	ツナギ	Notation: melodic pattern used at transitional points in play between scenes.
u (uku)	ウ	Notation: pitch level above *naka*.
u fushi	ウフシ	Type of *fushi-ochi*.
u gin	ウキン	Notation: pitch above *naka u*.
uki	ウキ	Pitch in Nō drama.
uku	浮く	To float.

u okuri	ウヲクリ	Type of *okuri* used as melodic pattern rather than as cadence.
ura-roppō	裏六法	Melodic pattern used at end of dramatic scene.
urei	ウレイ	Notation: pitch level.
urei sanjū	ウレイ三重	Type of *sanjū*.
utai	ウタイ	Notation: solemn style of chanting in Nō manner.
utazaimon	歌祭文	Notation: melodic pattern from popular ballads.
ya	矢	Notation: pitch above *gin*.
yagurashita	櫓下	See *monshita*.
yamato ji	大和地	Name of melodic pattern.
yanagi (fushi)	柳（フシ）	Type of *fushi-ochi*. Melodic pattern.
yobidashi	ヨビダシ	Melodic pattern.
yotsuma	四ツ間	Shamisen melodic pattern.
yotsu-ori	四ツヲリ	Melodic pattern.
yowagin	弱吟	Basic scale in Nō music.
yukahon	床本	Chanter's handwritten text of one scene used in performance.
yuri	ユリ	Notation: chanter's technique of varying intonation during emotional passages. Melodic pattern.
yuri nagashi	ユリ流シ	Melodic pattern (cadence).

Bibliography

Note On Sources

For any aspect of Edo-period drama, see an excellent recent publication, *Kinsei engeki kenkyū bunken mokuroku* (Bibliography of research on Edo-period drama), edited by Chikamatsu no kai (Tokyo: Yagi Shoten, 1984), which lists works published in Japan from 1951 to 1982.

For research on Chikamatsu Hanji, see the article by Matsui Kesako, "Chikamatsu Hanji chosaku nenpu to kenkyū no tebiki" (A guide to research on and a chronology of Chikamatsu Hanji's plays), in *Geinōshi kenkyū* 58 (1977). This article has been reprinted in *Jōruri sakuhin yōsetsu (3): Chikamatsu Hanji-hen* (Essential reference for Jōruri texts (3): The works of Chikamatsu Hanji), edited by Kokuritsu gekijo geinō chōsashitsu (National theater section on research into the performing arts) (Tokyo: Kokuritsu Gekijo, 1984).

Imoseyama onna teikin Texts Consulted

Bunraku jōrurishū (A collection of Bunraku plays). Ed. Yūda Yoshio (Nihon koten bungaku taikei 99). Tokyo: Iwanami Shoten, 1965.

Chikamatsu Hanji shū (Collection of Chikamatsu Hanji's plays). Ed. Shuzui Kenji. Tokyo: Asahi Shimbunsha, 1949. (The notation is neither complete nor entirely accurate.)

Imoseyama onna teikin (Mt. Imo and Mt. Se: An exemplary tale of womanly virtue). Osaka: Yamamoto Kyūemon, 1771 woodblock.

Kichibei V (1841–1911). Ōsaka Ichiritsu Chūō Toshokan (Osaka City Library). *Nozawa bunko*, no. 1366.

Mameushi. Text dating to around 1800 in Matazō-style notation.

Nagakodayū (Yadayū V, 1837–1906). Dated 1853.

Nagatodayū (1800–1864). Ōsaka Ichiritsu Chūō Toshokan (Osaka City Library). *Yadayū bunko*, no. 799. Dated 1863.

Seihachi II (1879–1970). Ōsaka Ongaku Daigaku Collection, no. 2073. Dated 1931.

Seiroku III (1868–1922). Ōsaka Ichiritsu Chūō Toshokan (Osaka City Library). *Seiroku bunko*, no. 445.

Shinzaemon II (1867–1943). Waseda Theater Museum Library. *Toyozawa Shinzaemon bunko*, nos. 11–531, 11–647, 11–663.

Yadayū V (1837–1906). Ōsaka Ichiritsu Chūō Toshokan (Osaka City Library). *Yadayū bunko*, no. 800.

References

Aoe Shunjirō. "Chikamatsu Hanji shōkō: *Ōshū Adachigahara o tegakari to shite*" (An essay on Chikamatsu Hanji's *Ōshū Adachigahara*). *Geinō* (June 1973): 22–26.

Ayatsuri awase kendai (1757) (Puppet theater—east and west). In *Nihon shomin bunka shiryō shūsei*, vol. 7.

Bandō Mitsugorō and Takechi Tetsuji. *Geijūya* (Ten nights of art). Kyoto: Shinshindō, 1972.

Beth, Monica, and Brazel, Karen. *Nō as Performance*. East Asia Program Papers 16. Ithaca, NY: China-Japan Program, Cornell University, 1978.

Bunraku kōgyō kiroku (Record of Bunraku productions in the Shōwa period). Ed. Takaki Hiroshi. 1980.

Chikamatsu no kenkyū (Research on Chikamatsu). Ed. Tsubouchi Shōyō et al. Tokyo: Shun'yōdō, 1900.

Chikamatsu Hanji. *Hitori sabaki* (One man's judgment, 1787). Reprinted in Yoshinaga Takao, "Chikamatsu Hanji 'Hitori sabaki' no honkoku ni attate" (On printing Chikamatsu Hanji's "One Man's Judgment"). *Hagoromogakuen tanki daigaku kiyō* 8 (January 1972). Also reprinted in *Jōruri sakuin yōsetsu (3): Chikamatsu Hanji-hen*. (See below.)

Chikuhō koji (1756) (A history of the Takemoto and Toyotake theaters). In *Nihon shomin bunka shiryō shūsei*, vol. 7.

Fukumatsu Tōsuke. *Naniwa nikkikō* (1780) (Diary of a journey to Naniwa). In *Gobun*, March 1953; March 1954.

Gerstle, C. Andrew. *Circles of Fantasy: Convention in the Plays of Chikamatsu*. Cambridge, MA: Harvard University Press, 1986.

————. "Tsuruzawa Bunzō to Chikamatsu Hanji no jōruri" (Tsuruzawa Bunzō and the plays of Chikamatsu Hanji). *Engekigaku* 27 (1986).

Gidayū nenpyō—kinsei-hen. (Chronology of Edo-period *gidayū*). Ed. Gidayū nenpyō kinsei-hen kankōkai. Tokyo: Yagi Shoten, 1979.

Gidayū nenpyō—Meiji-hen (Chronology of Meiji-period *gidayū*). Ed. Gidayū nenpyō kankōkai. Osaka: Gidayū Nenpyō Kankōkai, 1956.

Gidayū nenpyō—Taishō-hen (Chronology of Taishō-period *gidayū*). Ed. Bunraku Kyōkai. Osaka: Gidayū Nenpyō Kankōkai, 1970.

Gidayū shūshin roku (1819) (A record of devoted *gidayū* artists). In *Nihon shomin bunka shiryō shūsei*, vol. 7.

Hanakenuki (1797) (Outwitting the fool). In *Nihon shomin bunka shiryō shūsei*, vol. 7.

Hanawarai (1803) (Sneering). In *Ongyoku sōsho.*

Hirano Kenji. "Gidayū-bushi keiko tebikisho to gomashō" (*Gomashō* and writings on *gidayū* practice texts). *Dōkyō daigaku kyōyōshogaku kenkyū* 5 (1971), pp. 67–84.

Hosokawa Kagemasa. *Tōryū jōruri shamisen no hitobito* (Jōruri shamisen players). Tokyo, 1953.

Hyōban hana-zumo (1763) (Critique of flowers). In *Nihon shomin bunka shiryō shūsei*, vol. 7.

Hyōban sangokushi (1766) (Critique of puppet theaters: The three great cities). In *Nihon shomin bunka shiryō shūsei*, vol. 7.

Hyōban tori awase (1765) (Critique of Jōruri). In *Nihon shomin bunka shiryō shūsei*, vol. 7.

Hyōban tsuno-gumu awase (1764) (Critique of Jōruri). In *Nihon shomin bunka shiryō shūsei*, vol. 7.

Inobe Kiyoshi. "Jōruri no 'fū' ni kansuru ni-san no mondai" (Jōruri *fū*: Two or three questions). *Dentō engeki* 17 (September 1965).

————. "Gidayū-bushi ni okeru ishukei no shamisen shushō" (Alternate traditions of shamisen notation in *gidayū* music). *Ōsaka ongaku daigaku kenkyū kiyō* 7 (1968).

————. "'Katari-mono' ongaku ni okeru katari to bansō" (Narrative and accompaniment in narrative music). In *Nihon tōyō ongaku ronkō* (Essays on Japanese and Asian music). Ed. Tōyō ongaku kai. Tokyo: Ongaku no Tomosha, 1969.

————. "Shamisen to kyokusetsu" (Shamisen and Jōruri music). In *Jōruri* (Jōruri). *Nihon no koten geinō* (Traditional Japanese performing arts 7). Ed. Geinōshi kenkyūkai. Tokyo: Heibonsha, 1970.

———. "Okuri kenkyū joron" (Preliminary research on *okuri*). *Ōsaka ongaku daigaku kiyō* 10 (1971).

———. "Matsuya Seishichi no shushō" (The shamisen notation of Matsuya Seishichi). In *Nihon ongaku to sono shūhen* (On Japanese music). Ed. Koizumi Fumio et al. Tokyo: Ongaku no Tomosha, 1973.

———. "Jōruri ni okeru 'daijo'—sono seiritsu to hōkai" (Jōruri's *daijo*: Its development and demise). *Ōsaka ongaku daigaku kiyō* 16 (1978).

———. "Kudoki no seiritsu to keishiki" (The development and form of *kudoki*). *Ōsaka ongaku daigaku kenkyū kiyō* 21 (1982).

Inobe Kiyoshi and Yokomichi Mario et al. *Gidayū-bushi no yōshiki tenkai* (The development of *gidayū* music). Tokyo: Akademia Myujikku, 1986.

Jōkyō yonen gidayū danmonoshū (1687) (The 1687 *gidayū* collection of Jōruri scenes). In *Nihon shomin bunka shiryō shūsei*, vol. 7.

Jones, Stanleigh. "*Moritsuma's Camp*: An Eighteenth-Century Play from Japan's Puppet Theatre." *Asian Theatre Journal* 2 (Fall 1985).

———, trans. *Sugawara and the Secrets of Calligraphy*. New York: Columbia University Press, 1985.

Jōruri-fu (1801) (Chronology of Jōruri). In *Chikamatsu sewa jōrurishū* (Collection of Chikamatsu's domestic Jōruri). Ed. Shuzui Kenji. Tokyo: Hakubunkan, 1928.

Jōruri hottan (1825) (The origin of Jōruri). In *Nihon shomin bunka shiryō shūsei*, vol. 7.

Jōruri, kabuki (Jōruri, Kabuki). Ed. Toita Yasuji (*Kanshō Nihon koten bungaku* 30). Tokyo: Kadokawa, 1977.

Jōruri sakuhin yōsetsu (3): Chikamatsu Hanji-hen (Essential reference for Jōruri texts (3): The works of Chikamatsu Hanji). Ed. Kokuritsu gekijo geinō chōsashitsu (National Theater section on research into the performing arts). Tokyo: Kokuritsu Gekijo, 1984.

Jōruri shamisen hitori keiko (1757) (Do it yourself shamisen lessons). In *Nihon shomin bunka shiryō shūsei*, vol. 7.

Kamakura Keiko. "Hōgaku no gihō 'Jūshukō' no dan yori" (Techniques in Japanese music: The "Jūshukō" scene). *Rikkyō daigaku Nihon bungaku* 29 (1972).

Keene, Donald. *Bunraku: The Art of the Japanese Puppet Theatre*. Tokyo: Kodansha International, 1965.

———. *World Within Walls: Japanese Literature of the Pre-modern Era, 1600–1867*. New York: Holt, Rinehart and Winston, 1976.

Kinsei engeki kenkyū bunken mokuroku (Bibliography of research on Edo-period drama). Ed. Chikamatsu no kai. Tokyo: Yagi Shoten, 1984.

Kurata Yoshihiro. Notes to *Hasse Takemoto Tsunatayū daizenshū* (Complete works of Takemoto Tsunatayū). King Record, Tokyo, 1981.

Malm, William P. "A Musical Approach to the Study of Japanese Jōruri." In *Chūshingura: Studies in Kabuki and the Puppet Theater.* Ed. James Brandon. Honolulu: University of Hawaii Press, 1982.

———. "The Four Seasons of the Old Mountain Women." *Journal of the American Musicological Society* 31.1 (1978).

———. *Six Hidden Views of Japanese Music.* Berkeley: University of California Press, 1986.

Matsui Kesako. "Chikamatsu Hanji shōron" (A short article on Chikamatsu Hanji). *Engekigaku* 18 (1977).

Matsuoka, Seigow, ed. *Ma Space and Time in Japan.* New York: Cooper-Hewitt Museum, 1981.

Nami no uneri kanae-uwasa (1748?) (Undulating waves and balancing rumors). In *Nihon shomin bunka shiryō shūsei,* vol. 7.

Naniwa ima hakkei (1773) (Eight contemporary views of Naniwa). In *Sharebon taisei* (Great collection of sharebon), vol. 6. Tokyo: Chūō Kōronsha, 1979.

Naniwa kidan (1835) (Strange tales from Naniwa). Manuscript in Tenri University Library.

Naniwa sono sueba (1747) (Leaves of Naniwa). In *Naniwa Sōsho,* vol. 15.

Naniwa sōsho (Collection of sources on Naniwa), 15 vols. Osaka: Naniwa Sōsho Kankōkai, 1926–1930.

Nihon shomin bunka shiryō shūsei (Collection of sources on Japanese popular culture), vol. 6. *Kabuki.* Ed. Geinōshi kenkyūkai. Tokyo: San'ichi Shobō, 1973.

———, vol. 7. *Ningyō jōruri* (Jōruri puppet theater). Tokyo: San'ichi Shobō, 1975.

Nozawa Kizaemon. *Nozawa no omokage* (The shadow cast by Nozawa performers, 1934). In *Nidai Nozawa Kizaemon* (Nozawa Kizaemon II). Tokyo: Seiabō, 1976.

Ongyoku saru-gutsuwa (1746) (Music of gagged monkeys). In *Nihon shomin bunka shiryō shūsei,* vol. 7.

Ongyoku sōsho (Collection of works on music), 3 vols. Ed. Engei chinsho kankōkai. Tokyo: Gannandō, 1973 (reprint).

Onna daimyō tōzai hyōrin (1758) (Women daimyo, criticism east-west). In *Naniwa sōsho,* vol. 15.

Ōsaka kichin domari (1780–1781) (Collection of strange happenings in Osaka). *Ōsaka furitsu naka no shima toshokan kiyō* 11 (1975).

Setsuyō kikan (1833) (The wonders of Setsuyō). In *Naniwa sōsho,* vol. 5.

Shichiku shoshinshū (1664) (Shamisen songs for beginners). *Nihon kayō shūsei* (Collection of Japanese songs), vol. 6. Ed. Takano Tatsuyuki. Tokyo: Tōkyōdō, 1942.

Shin-hyōban kawazu no uta (1761) (New critique of frog songs). In *Nihon shomin bunka shiryō shūsei*, vol. 7.

Shiroto jōruri hyōbanki (1786) (Critique of amateur Jōruri performers). In *Nihon shomin bunka shiryō shūsei*, vol. 7.

Sōkyoku Naniwa no ashi (1751) (Reeds of Naniwa). In *Nihon shomin bunka shiryō shūsei*, vol. 7.

Sometayū ichidaiki (1851) (Autobiography of Sometayū). Ed. Inobe Kiyoshi et al. Tokyo: Seiabō, 1973.

Sugiyama Sonohian. *Jōruri shiroto kōshaku* (Amateur interpretations of Jōruri). Tokyo: Hōshuppan, 1975 (1926).

Suwa Haruo. *Kinsei gikyoku josetsu* (A survey of Edo-period plays). Tokyo: Hakusuisha, 1986.

Takechi Tetsuji. "*Fū no rinri*" (The ethics of style). In *Kabuki no reimei* (The dawn of Kabuki). Tokyo: Seizensha, 1955.

Take no haru (1761) (Spring bamboo). In *Nihon shomin bunka shiryō shūsei*, vol. 7.

Takenokoshū (1678) (A collection of bamboo shoots). In *Nihon shomin bunka shiryō shūsei*, vol. 7.

Tōkanzasshi (1759) (Writings on Jōruri puppet theater). In *Nihon shomin bunka shiryō shūsei*, vol. 7.

Tōsei shibai katagi (1777) (Characteristics of modern theater). Printed in *Nihon shomin bunka shiryō shūsei*, vol. 6.

Tsubouchi Shōyō. *Shōyō senshū* (Collection of Shōyō's works). Tokyo: Shun'yōdō, 1926.

Tsunoda Ichirō. "Jōruri ayatsuri sannindō no sōshi to fukyū ni tsuite" (On the origin and spread of three-man puppets in Jōruri). *Kokugakuin zasshi* 85.11 (1984).

Uchiyama Mikiko. "'Chikamatsu Hanji shōkō' ni tsuite" (On the article "Chikamatsu Hanji shōkō"). *Geinō* (August 1973), pp. 28–33.

Uchiyama Mikiko and Matsui Kesako. "*Honchō nijū shi kōron: sandanme o chūshin ni*" (Analysis of "Japan: Twenty-four cases of filial piety": The third act), *Geinōshi kenkyū* 58 (1977).

Yami no tsubute (1781) (Stones in the dark). In *Nihon shomin bunka shiryō shūsei*, vol. 7.

Yokoyama Tadashi. "Jōruri sakusha Chikamatsu Hanji: Jōruri-kabuki no setten ni okeru" (Chikamatsu Hanji as a Jōruri playwright: On his work's relationship to Kabuki). *Geinōshi kenkyū* 58 (1977).

Zōho jōruri ōkeizu (1885) (The great genealogy of Jōruri performers, expanded version). In *Ongyoku shōsho*.

Index

Act. *See Dan*
Ai no yama okuri, 46
Amateur theater, 6
Amido okuri, 46
Ana saguri (Hunting for holes), 112,
113

Banzuke (playbills), 107
Battles of Coxinga, The, 12
Blindness (blind minstrel tradition),
108, 109, 112, 115
Bunraku drama. *See* Jōruri puppet
theater
Bunzaburō. *See* Yoshida Bunzaburō
Bunzō. *See* Tsuruzawa Bunzō

Cadences
"Mountains Scene" examples,
47–49
"Mountains Scene" structure,
20–24, 67, 75–76
as punctuation, 35
to scene, 46
stereotypical for historical personages, 42
Chanters
cadences, 35, 47–49
emergence of senior, 5
flexibility in text interpretation, 84
fluid style changes, 83–88
fushigoto singing, 35
Hanji's complaints about, 114

higashi-fū or *nishi-fū* traditions,
30–33
interpretation, 6
notation, 4, 39–63, 97–99
pitch changes, 37, 66
prominence of, 107
puppeteers and, 2–3, 6, 108
senior, 5, 8n.7
shamisen and, 29–30, 31, 101,
109–10, 115, 116
styles in "Mountain Scene," 19, 28
text setting by, 70–71
voice technique and pitch, 53–57
voice variations, 34–35
women as, 6
see also Chūshingura incident
Characters
chanters' techniques to distinguish, 41–42
musical notations for, 56–57
musical styles for individuals and
types, 28–29
pitch changes for, 37, 66
Chikamatsu Hanji, 1, 3, 5, 6, 7,
8n.2, 103–7, 110, 111,113, 114,
117n.1
*see also Mt. Imo and Mt. Se: An
Exemplary Tale of Womanly
Virtue*
Chikamatsu Monzaemon, 1, 5, 12,
104, 105, 106, 107, 113, 114, 117n.1
Chikuzen no shōjō. *See* Takemoto
Konotayū
Chūshingura incident, 3, 29, 32, 108

A NOTE ABOUT THE AUTHORS

C. Andrew Gerstle is Professor of Japanese at the Australian National University. His numerous works on Japanese theater and music include, most recently, *Circles of Fantasy: Convention in the Plays of Chikamatsu* (Harvard, 1986) and *Eighteenth Century Japan: Culture and Society* (ed.) (Allen and Unwin, 1989). Kiyoshi Inobe is a scholar and researcher of Bunraku music. He is currently Professor of Musicology and Director of the Museum of Musical Instruments, Osaka College of Music. William P. Malm is Professor of Music and Ethnomusicology and Director of the Stearns Collection of musical instruments at the University of Michigan. His publications include *Studies in Kabuki* (with James Brandon and Donald Shively, Hawaii, 1977) and *Six Hidden Views of Japanese Music* (California, 1986).